THE SANTEE CANAL

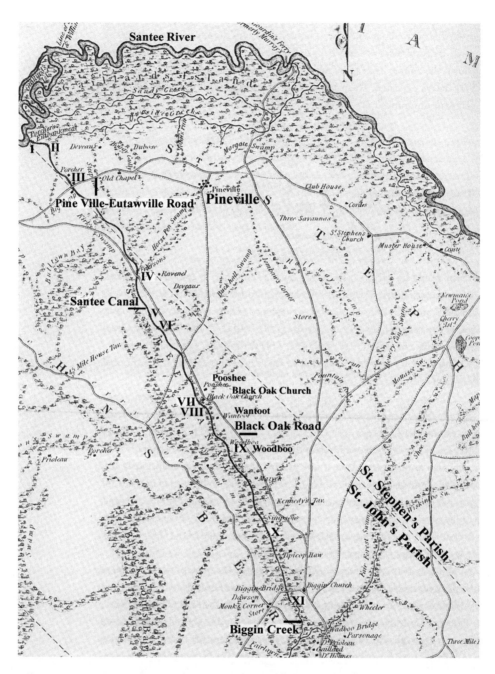

The Santee Canal on Robert Mills' "Charleston District, South Carolina, Surveyed by Charles Vignoles and Henry Ravenel, 1820, Improved for Robert Mills' Atlas, 1825." Authors added Santee Canal, Santee River, Pineville, Black Oak Road, Pine Ville-Eutawville Road, Biggin Creek, Santee Canal Locks I–XI, parishes, Pooshee, Wantoot, Woodboo, and Black Oak Church.

The Santee Canal

SOUTH CAROLINA'S FIRST COMMERCIAL HIGHWAY

ELIZABETH CONNOR,
RICHARD DWIGHT PORCHER JR.,
and WILLIAM ROBERT JUDD

© 2024 University of South Carolina

Published by the University of South Carolina Press
Columbia, South Carolina 29208

uscpress.com

Printed in the United States of America

Library of Congress Cataloging-in-Publication Data
can be found at https://lccn.loc.gov/2023057921

ISBN: 978-1-64336-471-1 (hardcover)
ISBN: 978-1-64336-472-8 (ebook)

MAP INSERT: Senf's "General Plan of the Santee Canal and Environs," 1800, South Carolina Historical Society.

In loving memory of
Anne Sinkler Whaley LeClercq
(1942–2014)

CONTENTS

ACKNOWLEDGMENTS   ix
SANTEE CANAL CHRONOLOGY   xi

        Introduction   1

ONE   Transportation in Early South Carolina   7

TWO   Formation of the Santee Canal Company   12

THREE   Johann Christian Senf   20

FOUR   Choosing the Santee Canal Route and Land Acquisition   42

FIVE   Construction of the Santee Canal: The Wedding of Two Rivers   60

SIX   Grand Opening of the Santee Canal, Buford's Inaugural Passage, and Life along the Canal   115

SEVEN   Attempts to Solve the Water Deficiency of the Santee Canal   136

EIGHT   End of Commercial Operation of the Santee Canal   155

NINE   Field Survey of the Santee Canal and Environs, 2019–21   165

        Epilogue   189

SOURCE NOTES   203
NOTES   207
BIBLIOGRAPHY   235
ABOUT THE AUTHORS   251
INDEX   253

ACKNOWLEDGMENTS

The authors would like to thank the many people who contributed to our understanding of the Santee Canal and assisted us with the production of this work. We are indebted to the fine staff at The Citadel's Daniel Library, College of Charleston Libraries (Special Collections and South Carolina Historical Society collections), Charleston Museum, Gibbes Museum of Art, Charleston Library Society, University of South Carolina Libraries, Chester County (South Carolina) Historical Society, Charleston Public Library, Georgetown Public Library, Berkeley County GIS Office, and Santee Cooper. A debt of gratitude goes to Mrs. Patricia Simon of Russellville for sharing her proud Glindkamp heritage. T. Keith Gourdin, Drew Ruddy, Norman Sinkler Walsh, and the Dwight family are among the many who shared their extensive knowledge and unpublished documents with us. John B. Whitten of Multimedia Services at The Citadel was most helpful. Cecelia Naomi Dailey and Shannon Marie Donohue edited and labeled many of the images. The authors acknowledge the financial support for this book from William Cain III, MD; Richard (Rick) LeNoble Wilson and David Charles Trachtenberg; Elizabeth McLeod Britton; Arthur Ravenel III in honor of his father Arthur Ravenel Jr.; and The St. John's Hunting Club. We honor the memories of Santee Canal country descendants, especially from the Glindkamp and Artope families, many of whom still live in Pineville and Russellville.

SANTEE CANAL CHRONOLOGY

1681. Canal du Midi in France was completed.

1773, January 18. James Cook proposed a canal between the Santee and Cooper Rivers and published "A Map of the Province of South Carolina...."

1775. Henry Mouzon Jr. published a map showing five possible routes for a canal between Santee and Cooper Rivers.

1777. As a Hessian muster clerk, Johann Christian Senf drew a map of the Sorel River near Quebec. By summer 1777 Senf was captured, probably after the Battle of Walloomsac; on October 20, 1777, Senf was named captain in Continental Army.

1778, November. Senf was appointed Continental Army engineer at the rank of captain.

1779. Senf was appointed chief engineer of the South Carolina Militia.

1780. Senf was promoted to lieutenant colonel.

1781. Virginia governor Thomas Jefferson expressed interest in engaging Colonel Senf as an engineer.

1783. Senf's father, Lukas Senf, was discharged from Prinz Ludwig's Dragoon regiment, probably in Canada.

1785, October 7. Thomas Jefferson issued a two-month passport to Senf and his Native American servant.

1785, November 10. Meeting was held in Charleston to discuss plans for a canal between the Santee and Cooper Rivers.

1786, February. Several South Carolinians presented to the South Carolina Senate a petition to charter a company to build a canal between the Cooper and Santee Rivers.

1786, March 22. South Carolina Legislature passed "An Act to Establish a Company for the Inland Navigation from Santee to Cooper River." 1786. Gov. William Moultrie wrote to George Washington inquiring about hiring James Brinley [Brindley] to supervise the Santee Canal construction Senf began his reconnaissance of the area of the proposed Santee Canal. 1786, June. Senf visited George Washington and examined Great Falls (Potomac River).

1787, April 2.   Senf wrote to the canal directors proposing his three reservoirs.

1788, August 23.   Senf's half-brother, Dr. George Vack (Johann Georg Vach), died at Rocky Mount, South Carolina.

1792.   On May 31, 1792, in New York, Senf married Geertruid (Gertrude) Jacoba van Berckel, daughter of the first Dutch ambassador and sister of the second Dutch ambassador to the United States. On July 24, 1792, Senf wrote to the president of the Canal Company stating that he understood the original subscribers intended for the canal to begin at or near Greenland Swamp. By Summer 1792 Senf was announced as being in charge of the Santee Canal project. On August 2, 1792, Nathaniel Russell advertised in the *City Gazette* for two hundred Black laborers to work on the Santee Canal.

1793.   General William Moultrie planted the first Santee long-staple cotton at Northampton. In May 1793, actual construction began on the Santee Canal with ten laborers.

1794.   Stone marker noting Senf as colonel of engineers and director in chief of the Santee Canal was placed at an unknown point on the canal.

1795.   On May 5, 1795, in his diary, Charles Drayton sketched a perspective drawing of the Santee Canal showing "its proportions as at a transverse section of the bridge." On July 2, 1795, the *City Gazette* announced 195 laborers were employed on the Santee Canal. In September 1795 some fossils found at Biggin Canal were shown to members of the Santee Canal Company board.

1796, January.   A great flood swept away much of the Santee Canal infrastructure.

1797.   Botanist Henrietta Marchant Liston visited Colonel and Mrs. Senf at Big Camp.

1798–1800.   Undeclared war with French Republic drew Colonel Senf away from Santee Canal work to focus on military fortifications.

1799, May.   Senf took a boat through the double lock near Biggin Basin. On June 29, 1799, Lukas Senf died at Rocky Mount, South Carolina.

1800.   Senf's "General Plan" (see foldout map) of the Santee Canal was dated. In March 1800 the Santee Canal was declared completed. On May 19, 1800, Senf told Santee Canal Company directors that the canal was ready to receive boats. On May 28, 1800, the *Times* of Charleston reported William Buford passed through the Santee Canal. On December 17, 1800, Gertrude Senf's father, former Dutch ambassador Pieter van Berckel, died in New York.

1802. Charles Drayton's *A View of South Carolina* was published.

1803. Charles Fraser painted *A Bason and Storehouse Belonging to the Santee Canal.*

1804. George B. Artope (1768–1818) was named canal superintendent.

1805. Santee Canal Company bought Ray's (Flint's). On September 6, 1805, Colonel Francis Mentges died at Rocky Mount, South Carolina, not long after being sent to assist Senf with work at Great Falls (South Carolina).

1806, August 24. Senf died at his home at Rocky Mount, South Carolina.

1807. "Report of the Secretary of the Treasury on the Subject of Public Roads and Canals" published.

1809. Gertrude Senf married Christian Friedrich Breithaupt and moved to Edgefield, South Carolina.

1816. Santee Canal closed because of drought.

1818. On January 15, 1818, George B. Artope died at his home on the Santee Canal; Sims LeQueux was named canal superintendent.

1818–19. Santee Canal closed because of drought.

1819. Two steam engines were installed to pump water into the Santee Canal. Bull Town Drain was constructed.

1820. Henry Glindkamp was named canal superintendent.

1822, January. Black Oak Lock closed due to damage from a vessel and an extraordinary accumulation of water in the lock. Henry Ravenel produced plat of White Oak. *Southern Patriot* reported on steamboat service between Granby and Charleston.

1823, May 7. Abram Blanding published "Report of the Inspection of the Santee Canal."

1824. Henry Glindkamp died. Benjamin LeQueux was named canal superintendent. On May 17, 1824, Samuel Saylor's boat exploded in the Santee Canal.

1825. Henry Ravenel published plat showing land acquisition by Canal Company: "Plan Exhibiting the Shape, Size and Situation of 12 Tracts of Land Owned by the Canal Company containing 5,684 1/2 Acres."

1827, December 13. The South Carolina Canal and Rail Road Company was chartered.

1830. The South Carolina Canal and Rail Road Company opened a six-mile track west from Charleston.

1833. The South Carolina Canal and Rail Road Company ran steam service from Charleston to Hamburg.

1835. On December 4, 1835, Christian Breithaupt died at Mount Vintage, Edgefield, South Carolina. On December 15, 1835, Gertrude Senf Breithaupt died at Mount Vintage, Edgefield, South Carolina.

1836. Pine Ville was abandoned because of malaria.

1839. South Carolina Railroad Company was formed from a merger of the Louisville, Cincinnati and Charleston Railroad and the South Carolina Canal and Rail Road Company.

1840. Peter Layton was named canal superintendent.

1842. Branchville to Columbia railroad line in operation.

1843. Maxcy Gregg made his three-day trip down the Santee Canal.

1844. Peter Layton died.

1845. R. Press Smith was named canal superintendent.

1846. Columbia to Camden railroad in operation.

1848. South Carolina Railroad Company constructed rail line from Kingsville near Columbia to Camden.

1849. Santee Canal Company tried to quell rumors about abandoning the canal.

1852. "How to Kill Three Birds with One Stone" was published in the *Charleston Daily Courier.* Andrew Gibbes sketched "A Cotton Box at Black Oak Lock." Local planters signed a petition requesting that the Santee Canal not be abandoned.

1853. Santee Canal Company petitioned the state legislature to allow it to surrender its charter. Local planters presented a counter memorial to the legislature to keep the canal open.

1854, March. The Santee Canal Company board of directors met and decided to sell bonds to pay the stockholders. On June 9, 1854, the Santee Canal Company paid a dividend of one dollar per share. On June 10, 1854, the Santee Canal Company closed the canal for the summer season.

1855. On February 3 the Santee Canal Company announced a two-hundred-dollar toll. On March 2 the Santee Canal Company announced they had rescinded the toll.

1875. Frederick A. Porcher prepared *The History of the Santee Canal,* dedicating it to the South Carolina Historical Society.

1881, January 26. US Army Corps of Engineers Office published "Survey for the Reopening of the Santee Canal, South Carolina."

1902. State legislator Benjamin Elliott resurrected the idea of connecting the Santee and Cooper Rivers for water traffic.

1903. The South Carolina Historical Society published Porcher's *History of the Santee Canal.*

1927. Mabel Webber published "Col. Senf's Account of the Santee Canal" in two issues of the *South Carolina Historical and Genealogical Magazine.*

1935. President Roosevelt's Works Progress Administration was created. Francis Marion Kirk Sr. published in the *News and Courier* a series of articles on the plantations to be flooded by the Santee Cooper lakes.

1938. On May 23, 1938, the US Fourth Circuit of Appeals denied a suit filed by three utilities to stop the Santee Cooper Project. David Kohn and Bess Glenn published *Internal Improvement in South Carolina, 1817–1828* (Washington, DC).

1939, May. The South Carolina Assembly passed the Eminent Domain Act, giving the power to take private property and convert it into public use through condemnation.

1942. Lakes Marion and Moultrie were fully flooded.

1950. Santee Cooper published a reprint of Porcher's *History of the Santee Canal.*

1981. George D. Terry wrote "'Champaign Country': A Social History of an Eighteenth-Century-Lowcountry Parish in South Carolina, St. John's Berkeley County," PhD dissertation, University of South Carolina.

1989, September. Mark M. Newell and Joe J. Simmons III published "The Santee Canal Sanctuary Part II: Preliminary Archaeological Investigation of a Portion of the Old Santee Canal and Biggin Creek, Berkeley County, South Carolina" as part of the Underwater Antiquities Management Program, South Carolina Institute of Archaeology and Anthropology, University of South Carolina.

1990. Robert B. Bennett Jr. and Katherine H. Richardson of Heritage Preservations Associates, Inc., published *History of the Santee Canal, 1775–1939.*

2005. Richard D. Porcher Jr. and Sarah Fick published *The Story of Sea Island Cotton.*

2007–08. Lake Moultrie level dropped low enough to reveal Frierson's Lock.

2010. University of South Carolina Press published Robert J. Kapsch's *Historic Canals and Waterways of South Carolina.*

2019–21. Richard Porcher and friends surveyed the extant sections of the Santee Canal.

2020–21. Richard Porcher and friends surveyed Bull Town Drain and first suggested it was used to provide water for the Summit Canal.

Introduction

This story begins in the earliest days of the province of South Carolina. Our founding fathers, some living in Carolina, were fascinated with inland navigation to overcome geographic barriers, reduce the distances between settlements, and connect civilization with the wilderness. As early as 1770, Carolina statesmen imagined a safer, less circuitous route for taking raw materials from the Midcountry, Backcountry, and Upcountry forests and plantations to coastal markets for sale and export.[1] As physician and historian David Ramsay (1749–1815), an early investor in the Santee Canal and son-in-law of Henry Laurens (1724–92), noted, "Nature has made such ample provision for feeding the inhabitants of South Carolina, that little room was left for art. The sea, rivers, and ponds, abound with fish; the banks of salt-rivers, with oysters, prawns, shrimps, and crabs; the woods with game.... A fertile soil repays with large increase what is planted in it."[2]

Completed in 1800, the Santee Canal provided the first inland navigation route connecting the Santee, Congaree, and Wateree Rivers and their tributaries with the Cooper River, allowing planters to improve their livelihoods following the economic devastation and property destruction experienced during the Revolutionary War. As Samuel DuBose observed, "The war terminated this state of prosperity. On the return of peace every planter was deeply in debt. For the period of ten years following no income was realized on account of freshets; in many cases not even provisions. Prime gangs of Negroes were publicly sold at an average of less than two hundred dollars. Rice and indigo and naval stores became of little value, because of the loss of the bounty formally allowed under the colonial system."[3] The largely untold story of this groundbreaking canal's genesis includes founders, framers, signers, statesmen, and planters such as Henry Laurens, George Washington, Thomas Jefferson, Alexander Hamilton, John Rutledge, Thomas Sumter, William Moultrie, Edward Rutledge, Nathaniel Russell, Ralph Izard, Charles Pinckney, Charles Drayton, Aaron Loocock, Pierce Butler, John Lewis Gervais, Samuel Porcher, and Daniel Ravenel. Other works published about the Santee Canal have not emphasized the viewpoints of the planters. The lesser-known narrative also involves the experiences and perspectives of the laborers (free, indentured, and enslaved) who made this engineering marvel possible and, in the process, reversed the economic fortunes of planters living in St. John's and St. Stephen's Parishes. Many descendants of these talented individuals still live in Berkeley County and surrounding areas.[4]

The authors argue that the story of South Carolina's first commercial highway has been told before but not completely and not through the lenses of planters and free and enslaved laborers. The decline of indigo and rice cultivation and the rise of cotton had differing but profound effects on labor availability for canal construction, and we examine this issue from the frames of reference of the Santee River and St. John's planters and residents whose former home sites lay submerged under Lakes Moultrie and Marion long after the canal was constructed.

Who would imagine that a mercenary soldier captured in 1777 would later design and build the first summit-level canal in the United States? Henry Laurens recognized the talents, brio, and zeal of prisoner of war Johann Christian Senf.[5] On April 10, 1778, Brig. Gen. William Moultrie (1730–1805) of the Continental Army wrote to Maj. Gen. Robert Howe (1732–86): "Captain Senf, engineer, is lately arrived from the northward for this department; if you should have any occasion for him, I will send him off with the detachment you have ordered."[6] Senf was appointed engineer for the Continental Army in 1778, and in 1779 he was named chief engineer for the South Carolina Militia. By 1792 Colonel Senf was tapped by the Santee Canal Company to plan and build the Santee Canal, but he had been involved in the planning as early as 1786 as part of his role as state engineer for South Carolina.

The authors contend that while many historians and laypersons interested in early American history have known Senf's name, much of what has been written about him has been sketchy and formulaic, repeating many of the same inaccuracies and assumptions. This work delves into Senf's background and enigmatic personality, including his strategic marriage to Geertruid Jacoba van Berckel, daughter and sister of the first ambassadors to the United States from the Netherlands; his relationships with his half-brother, Johann Georg Vach, who served as a surgeon in Klock's Second Regiment, and his father, Lukas (Lucas) Senf, who was discharged from Prinz Ludwig's Dragoon regiment in 1783; his European travels with a Native American manservant; his career successes and failures; and the tumultuous final months of his life in Rocky Mount, South Carolina, where his half-brother, father, and an assistant, Lt. Col. Francis Mentges, also died.

Senf had a profound and enduring influence on South Carolina's transportation infrastructure by improving the system of roads, canals, and dams. Such improvements allowed Santee River and St. John's settlers and Charleston area merchants to recover from economic losses related to frequent flooding and the Revolutionary War's destruction and set the stage for future prosperity.

This book focuses on the Santee Canal project from start to finish, including plans and maps not yet published. We provide the first comprehensive biography of Johann Senf, describe his canal superintendent successors, and include extensive details about the families associated with plantations affected by the canal. We dispute the myth of the canal's starting point. Senf knew better than cartographer/surveyor Henry Mouzon where the canal needed to start. Senf could read the land and knew what to do. Time was on his side for understanding the physical environment. Natural water courses would have filled the locks with silt. We take issue with most writers, who side with Frederick A. Porcher's viewpoint that Mouzon's ideas were superior to Senf's and that Senf's overbearing personality prevented him from accepting Mouzon's ideas.[7] But no matter the route, even natural waterways would have been dry during times of extended drought, as was the case in 1816–19.

Other unique features of this book are the diagrams of locks specially drawn by William Robert Judd. (Judd drew the diagrams published in the work he coauthored with Richard Porcher and in Robert B. Bennett's master's thesis on the Santee Canal.[8]) His drawings for this work elucidate numerous aspects of the lock construction in addition to detailing how the locks operated and other mechanical aspects of the canal system. The book includes other pertinent Judd illustrations that have appeared in technical reports but never have been published in books or articles readily available to the public. Underwater archaeology expeditions by Judd and Drew Ruddy that took place in 2019–20 revealed more details about how the locks were constructed and offered theories as to why they were designed differently from one another. Over the years Richard Porcher has photographed the Santee Canal environs, and some additional photographs were taken of structures that are still visible at the site.

The authors had access to an eight-mile stretch of the canal near Pineville, South Carolina, that was not flooded by the Santee-Cooper hydroelectric project. This privately owned property is not accessible to many others. At that site the brickwork at White Oak Lock is in good condition, although the wooden structures are long gone.

We argue that some of the past historians did not search the archival records for plats, did not conduct adequate field research (even today there is much to learn from field work in extant parts of the canal), and did not search and use numerous records pertaining to the canal's construction and operation, especially Senf's water control system. Without his water control system, the canal would never have been successful. Consequently, the technical aspects of the canal have not been adequately explained.

Our research took us deep into the lives of the Santee River community, native and émigré, enslaved and free, elite and laborers, Black and white and Red. The histories of these rich cultures and personalities enhance our understanding of early American life and ingenuity. The Santee Canal transformed the lives of South Carolinians by connecting distant settlements, reversing the fortunes of planters, altering slave-master relationships through slave hiring,[9] and proving the value of military engineers in the design of internal improvements such as inland navigation.

This book is organized into nine chapters and an epilogue, beginning with chapter 1, devoted to transportation in early South Carolina. In the early days of Carolina, ocean travel was perilous. It took months for goods and produce to move by overland routes from the Midlands and upper parts of the state to the coast and beyond.

In chapter 2 we explain how imaginative statesmen saw the need to connect existing rivers with man-made canals and capitalized on European ingenuity to make it possible. The Santee Canal Company received its charter from the South Carolina General Assembly in 1786. These dreams were delayed by the prolonged Revolutionary War and other factors. The Canal Company's board of directors included notable merchants, planters, and statesmen such as William Moultrie, John Rutledge, Francis Marion, Henry Laurens, Thomas Sumter, and many others. The Santee Canal Company, a private enterprise, used shareholders to finance the protracted planning, design, and construction project.

Chapter 3 provides a comprehensive biography of Johann Christian Senf, the German mercenary who parlayed his role as muster roll clerk in the Brunswick troops commanded by Col. Friedrich von Riedesel into serving as a colonel in the Continental Army and chief engineer for the South Carolina Militia responsible for designing various fortifications and, eventually, canal projects in several southern states.

Chapter 4 details the controversies surrounding the canal routes and the properties that were acquired to make these choices possible.

Chapter 5 focuses on how Colonel Senf may have been influenced by manmade waterways in Holland and France that he observed during his extended European travels prior to the start of canal construction; describes why the construction process took as long as it did; and explains the labor challenges, slave hiring practices, design issues, construction materials, and other factors. During the excavations, fossils of mammoths and other prehistoric creatures were unearthed, and this contributed to wide interest in geology and paleontology in the state. Anticipated economic gains may have been overestimated because of forces beyond the ken of the canal's planners, but early utilization benefited the region and the state and inspired other canal projects elsewhere in the country.

Chapter 6 describes the opening of the canal and the 1801 journey from Pinckney's Courthouse, South Carolina, through the Pacolet and Broad Rivers to the canal and then Charleston with a commercial crop of cotton. After more than eight years of work and extensive cost overruns, the Canal Company and the press celebrated this trip made by a Backcountry planter.

Chapter 7 describes how the various locks functioned and who may have influenced Senf in his choice of materials. What has been learned from examining and making diagrams of the two locks that remain standing? This chapter also includes photographs and information gathered from recent diving explorations conducted in this region. These underwater expeditions revealed some new information about the locks that had not been understood or photographed previously.

Chapter 8 covers some of the unforeseen challenges that beset the canal, including disease, drought, frequent repairs, and narrow profit margins. The development of railroads and steamboats signaled the doom of South Carolina's first superhighway.

Chapter 9 describes treks taken in Santee Canal country during that time period. These field trips replicated by foot and canoe parts of William Buford's inaugural journey through the canal, described how the canal looks today, and explained aspects of the canal's construction revealed in the extant parts of the structure. Church ruins, old paths and roads, evidence of old settlements, lack of evidence for the existence of a ferry canal or Izardtown, missing fossils, old pipes and drains, and various grave markers combine to paint a complex picture of Santee Canal country.

The epilogue, written by Richard Porcher, imagines the experiences of landowner descendants as they faced the intentional flooding of their lands to create manmade lakes. Charleston mayor John P. Grace was keen on building a hydroelectric plant that would transform the economic future of the state by providing power and improving navigation. These plans resulted in considerable fear, loss, and upheaval experienced by the Black and white populations displaced by this project. Just as some Santee River planters opposed the Old Santee Canal, many plantation families and other residents were against the Santee Cooper Project. The opposition centered on eminent domain and the buildings, properties, and cemeteries that were displaced or lost to the flooding needed to create Lakes Marion and Moultrie.

In much the same way that in 1875 Frederick Adolphus Porcher documented the influence of English, Scottish, and Huguenot planters on the cultural and economic history of the state,[10] this book describes and analyzes the culture of patriots, planters, and free and enslaved workers involved with imagining and executing inland navigation improvements that started with the Santee Canal. The canal served as the first commercial highway in South Carolina, connecting the state's Upcountry (Backcountry) with the Midland and coastal regions. This monumental achievement increased the fortunes of many associated with the canal's design, development, and operation and brought prosperity to many more agriculturalists who wished to bring their goods to market in Charleston.

Our research showed direct genealogical connections from the canal designers to the African American community in St. Stephen's Parish; these relationships are key to understanding the Santee River communities and their history. Join us as we unfold and connect the fascinating stories of this extraordinary generation of planters, engineers, merchants, botanists, agriculturalists, politicians, and laborers.

ONE

Transportation in Early South Carolina

To understand the Santee Canal's significance as a transportation route to the state's economic development and prosperity, it is worth examining factors such as internal improvements, including inland navigation projects imagined by the founding fathers and other leaders;[1] the push for inland navigation in the early days of the republic; and the state's terrain and topography, including its old-growth forests and treacherous sea coast, which prompted canal developments as solutions to regional transportation challenges.

Charles Town during the colonial period was the primary port available for Upcountry Carolina planters and farmers to ship goods overseas. Getting goods to Charles Town was difficult and impractical, and often impossible, by land routes. Roads were treacherous to traverse in wet weather, and wagon time from the Upcountry to Charles Town was considerable and expensive. The main river route was the Santee, but this was not a reliable route. The circuitous Upcountry rivers that fed the Santee River passed through rock-strewn rapids and were often blocked by downed trees that tested the fortitude of those who dared make the passage. The course of the Santee from the Upcountry was so sinuous that it flowed two hundred twisting miles to reach the ocean only a hundred miles distant. Near its mouth the river followed a course through swampy lowlands. Construction of tidal rice fields had not yet begun in the Santee Delta before the Santee Canal was built.

Once vessels reached the mouth of the Santee, treacherous sandbars impeded their passage to the open ocean. River sandbars were impressive and must have inspired awe and trepidation for captains of sailing vessels in the

1700s coming down from the Upcountry via the Santee to reach Charles Town. Surveyor General John Lawson noted the sandbars on his expedition into the Santee River in 1700: "Yet the Mouth is barr'd, affording not above four feet or five Foot Water at the Entrance."[2] Just as intimidating was the fifty-mile offshore trip along the coast from the Santee to Charles Town Harbor, where an inclement tempest often took its toll on ships. The shallow-draft vessels required for passage downriver loaded with goods were not suited for ocean traffic, and there was no convenient site at the mouth of the Santee River to transfer goods to oceangoing vessels. In addition, there was no safe passage from the Santee River to Charles Town for commercial traffic because the string of barrier islands was broken at several places, allowing surges of the sea to penetrate to what otherwise might have been a safe route.

But the produce and goods had to move, and there was no other viable choice for colonists in the Upcountry to get their goods to Charles Town Harbor. The Cooper and Ashley Rivers, which formed the deep Charles Town Harbor, are coastal rivers that do not reach the Upcountry. The explosion of upland cotton (the state's main cash crop at the time) after the Revolution created an urgent need for a safer and more direct route to Charleston. Eli Whitney's new saw gin for ginning upland cotton, invented in 1793, increased the urgency to bypass the ocean route along the coast. There was no other option—or so it appeared until the construction of a canal to link the Santee and Cooper Rivers was completed. The Santee Canal would meet a long-desired need to shorten the circuitous river route from the Backcountry to the port of Charleston.

A letter from David Humphreys to George Washington, dated July 25, 1785, conveyed the national interest in such internal improvements:

> My attention is more immediately engaged in a project, which I think big with great political, as well as commercial consequences to the States, especially the middle ones; it is by removing the obstructions and extending the inland navigation of our rivers, to bring the States on the Atlantic in close connexion with those forming to the westward, by a short and easy transportation. Without this, I can easily conceive they will have different views, separate interests, and other connexions. I may be singular in my ideas, but they are these; that, to open a door to, and make easy the way for, those settlers to the westward (who ought to advance regularly and compactly) before we make any stir about the navigation of the Mississippi, and before our settlements are far advanced towards that river, would be our true line of policy.[3]

In an April 7, 1786, letter written to Washington, William Moultrie stated:

> Convinced of your wish & desire to promote every public benefit that may possibly present itself to you, in which any part of the United States may be concerned: I presume to take the liberty of addressing you in a matter relative to this State, & without further apology for the freedom I now use, shall proceed to the point. A number of Gentlemen of this State have entered into an association which is sanctioned by the legislature to open an Inland Navigation, by a communication from the Santee to the Cooper River, the distance across being about twenty miles; we intend it to be done by Locks & Canals, & will be a means of shortening the present Navigation at least 150 Miles.[4]

Washington answered Moultrie, showing support for the project: "I should be very happy if I could render any service to the company which are engaged in the laudable and important design of opening a cut between the rivers Cooper and Santee."[5]

Another early account gives a sense of typical journeys long before the Santee Canal and railroads transformed local and regional travel. When William Drayton toured wilderness areas of South Carolina in 1784, he averaged just nineteen miles per day over four weeks, noting his travels near the High Hills: "At 15 miles we pass'd Jack's Creek, an ugly step, much broken by Waggons, tho' the Water is not very deep. From hence it is 11 or 12 miles to Nelson's Ferry, the last 3 of which were exceedingly bad through the low Land near the River. It had been overflow'd by the late Freshes, and the Road was considerably out of Repair before."[6]

Balthasar Henry Meyer and Caroline Elizabeth MacGill pointed out that prior to the American Revolution, South Carolina's transportation issues were perceived as local problems; after independence the connection of Charleston Harbor to the rest of the state became paramount.[7] Completed in 1800, the Santee Canal provided the first inland navigation route connecting the Santee, Congaree, and Wateree Rivers with the Cooper River, allowing planters to improve their livelihoods following the economic devastation and property destruction experienced during the Revolutionary War. As Samuel DuBose observed:

> When peace was restored every planter was in debt; no market crops had been made for years; and where the river swamp was their sole dependence,

even provisions had not been made. It was not a season therefore merely of embarrassment; ruin stared many in the face. Besides, with the exception of rice the country had no staple crop; for since the bounty, which as colonists they had enjoyed on the export of indigo and naval stores, had been discontinued, these products ceased to have any value, and [slaves] fell in price.[8]

Kenneth E. Lewis stated that "South Carolina's decision to improve its waterways to facilitate the transport of bulk agricultural commodities from its interior followed a larger trend of canal construction in the United States that began during the closing decades of the eighteenth century. Plans involved opening navigation on the Saluda-Broad-Congaree-Catawba-Wateree-Santee River system as well as the Pee Dee and its tributaries to the north."[9] The Santee Canal did not provide public transportation, as its sole purpose was for commercial traffic. Residents still had to travel via wagon or carriage (later railroad) down wretched dirt paths or along muddy roadways until they arrived at Stony Landing, where they could travel by steamer to Charleston. One wonders why some sort of public transportation was not made available on the Santee Canal. An unintended consequence of canal transport was the relative decline of several cities in the state. According to Lewis, "Rivers now dominated the flow of commerce in the state, and the growing reliance on water transport promoted the growth of inland towns like Camden, Granby, and Augusta at the expense of Orangeburg, Williamsburg, and others that had occupied central locations in the state's road network."[10] As Frederick Porcher claimed in 1875, "More than half the State may use the waters of this noble river as their commercial highway."[11] Porcher also emphasized South Carolina's spirit of enterprise that led to many internal improvements including inland navigation, exemplified by the Santee Canal. Commercial waterways made for cheaper, faster, and safer transport of goods to market. The canal brought considerable wealth and prosperity to the state and its landowners and heralded future internal improvements within the state and the nation.

THE SANTEE CANAL was the most prominent man-made feature of Middle St. John's in the first half of the 1800s.[12] Its path affected every aspect of life for planters, Native Americans, and laborers, free and enslaved. The canal created an avenue for planters to recover financially after the disruption of the American Revolution because of the more reliable market route to Charleston. This financial recovery led to the purchase of additional enslaved Africans to work cotton fields. The Santee Canal linked the Upstate, St. Stephen's, and Middle St. John's with the markets of the world, allowing Upcountry goods to go to Charleston for export. Imagine the excitement when a report such as the following was made: "There is a notice this year of a boat constructed by 'Mr. Chesnut of Camden, on a plan directed by Colonel Senf' for passing through the Santee Canal, 'at half the expense and in half the time of those that go round by mouth of the Santee.' This boat would carry nine hundred barrels of flour, or thirty-five hogsheads of tobacco. Seven boats were built in Camden in 1800 for this inland navigation."[13] The environmental landscape changed as natural wetlands were converted to reservoirs for the canal and more land was cleared for cotton fields. The sites of support facilities to operate the canal became social and economic centers, bringing people together more often to socialize, always a positive factor in community development. One center, Black Oak, became a prominent political, economic, and social meeting site. One might argue that the creation of the Santee Canal showed how a central government could positively affect the daily lives of a community (the Santee Canal was chartered by the state). Journals and letters of the planters and families seemed to support the construction of the canal. In retrospect it is hard to find serious negative consequences from the Santee Canal construction. It is interesting to contemplate what social, cultural, and economic paths these parishes and Charleston would have evolved toward without the Santee Canal. Fortunately for the planters, the canal did not bring a shift to industrialization to St. Stephen's and St. John's, and they were able to maintain their coveted plantation lifestyle yet stay connected to Charleston and the world.

TWO

Formation of the Santee Canal Company

The idea of a Santee Canal was not new by the time the Company for Opening the Inland Navigation Between the Santee and Cooper Rivers (better known as the Santee Canal Company) was formed. According to Arthur P. Wade, "As early as 1770 a committee of the Commons House of Assembly had reported favorably a plan for a canal to connect the Santee to the upper reaches of the Cooper."[1] The Revolution intervened and delayed such lofty plans. The decision by Santee planters to form a private enterprise to realize the founding fathers' national and regional dreams of improved inland navigation is indicative of the pioneering and innovative spirit of South Carolinians. According to James W. Ely Jr., "After the Revolution many [state] . . . legislatures chartered private corporations for [the] purpose [of improving river navigation] and granted these corporations the power of eminent domain."[2] The company met for the first time in November 1785 at the State House in Charleston, the state capital at the time.[3] The general public was informed of the upcoming meeting:

> We are happy to inform our readers and the public in general, that a meeting will be held in the Assembly-room at the Statehouse, on Thursday the 10th of November ensuing, at 10 o'clock in the forenoon, to take into consideration a plan for opening communication by a *Canal,* from *Santee* to *Cooper* Rivers.—On this occasion, it is hoped and requested, that all persons who are willing to contribute to this laudable undertaking, will give their attendance.[4]

South Carolina lawmakers passed legislation in March 1786 to establish an inland navigation company expressly to connect the Santee and Cooper Rivers after an august group of merchants and statesmen petitioned the General Assembly of South Carolina to do so.[5] Several of the petitioners were legislators.[6] This petition stated that a number of shareholders had already subscribed. This legislation set the stage for the continued planning that would follow, including the selection of a board of directors.[7] In April 1786 Gov. William Moultrie explained the situation to George Washington:

> A number of Gentlemen of this State have entered into an association which is sanctioned by the Legislature to open Inland Navigation, by a communication from the Santee to the Cooper River, the distance across being about twenty miles; we intend it to be done by Locks & Canals, and will be a means of shortening the present Navigation at least 150 miles. Many of the Gentlemen who compose the Board of Directors for carrying the plan into execution, having the honor of being personally acquainted with you were induced to recommend that, endeavour be made to obtain Mr. Brinley to superintend it, if in your Opinion, you judged him capable of the undertaking.[8]

John L. Conger provided a perspective of early public works in South Carolina:

> In its prosperous days, South Carolina had entered eagerly upon a program of comprehensive public works, even before many of the northern states had made a move. Nearly half a generation before Gallatin drew up for President Jefferson his famous report, the old Palmetto state had chartered its Santee canal company. This company spent vast sums on a system designed to render navigable the five principal rivers of the state. Of the twenty-two districts of the state, this system of public development would have covered fourteen completely, and five more partially.[9]

Our current understanding of these circuitous and protracted planning processes is hampered by the dearth of remaining records related to the company itself.[10] As best as can be reconstructed from various newspaper reports and correspondence, the company formed and reorganized itself leading up to actual excavation and construction. By 1786, the year when the Santee Canal Company was incorporated, Johann Christian Senf was involved with the planning of this monumental project.[11] From 1786 until 1793, the only on-site work that was conducted related to the Santee Canal was surveying. Despite the lack of extant corporation records, one can surmise that Senf benefited mightily by this extended passage of time. During that period he corresponded with influential politicians, visited other sites in the United States and abroad, married the politically and socially connected Geertruid Van Berckel, and built support for his groundbreaking ideas before being formally named in charge of the project in 1792.

According to Washington's diary, Senf visited him at Mount Vernon starting on June 11, 1786.[12] A few days later Washington and Senf took a trip: "After an early breakfast Judge Harrison left this for his own house and in Company with Colo. Senf, I set out for our Works at the great falls; where we arrived about 11 Oclock and after viewing them set out on our return & reached Colo. Gilpins where we lodged."[13] In April 1788 Antoine Terrasson wrote to Thomas Jefferson in Paris that Terrasson was a Santee Canal Company stockholder and had been elected to the company's board of directors.[14] In his response to Terrasson a few days later, Jefferson did not sound fully supportive of the plans that were underway:

> I have read with attention the papers on the subject of the canal of the Santee and Cooper rivers, and shall be glad to do any thing I can to promote it. But I confess I have small expectations for the following reason. Genl. Washington sent me a copy of the Virginia act for opening the Patowmac. As that canal was to unite the commerce of the whole Western country almost, with the Eastern, it presented a great view. The general detailed the advantages of it, and it had the weight of his name, and was known to be under his immediate direction. It was pushed here among the monied men to obtain subscriptions but not a single one could be obtained. The stockjobbing in this city offered greater advantages than to buy shares in the canal. I tried whether they would lend money on the security of the canal, but they answered they could get as good an interest by lending to their own government, with a douceur in the outset, and would have their money under their own eye, more at their command and more sure as to the paiment of interest. However if you find any opening and can point out to me how I may be useful in promoting it I shall do it with infinite pleasure.[15]

In 1792 Santee Canal Company outlined a set of rules.[16] These rules were agreed upon by the stockholders at a meeting held on January 10, 1792. An earlier report of a stockholder meeting was published in December 1791.[17] In April 1792, before actual excavation work for the canal was underway, Thomas Pinckney (1750–1828) added a postscript to a letter written from Philadelphia to his good friend Edward (Ned) Rutledge (1749–1800): "If I am in time to increase my shares in the Santee Canal company as far as three or four I wish to do it."[18] In May 1792 David Ramsay, as president of the Canal Company, wrote to Thomas Pinckney in the latter's role as minister plenipotentiary at the Court of London:

> The company for opening the inland navigation between Santee and Cooper Rivers have unanimously adopted the inclosed resolution which I with great pleasure forward to you[.]
>
> You are left to your own discretion as to the number of persons to be employed and also as to the place from which they are to be procured; it is the wish of the Company to have such Engineers and subordinate Artists at all events as will insure the success of the work—
>
> Your known attachment to this Country precludes any necessity of apologizing for the trouble the execution of the wishes of the Company must necessarily give you.[19]

On July 14, 1792, Charles Cotesworth Pinckney (1746–1825) wrote to his brother Thomas that he "believe[d] the Canal Company will employ Senf."[20] On the same day, Ramsay informed Thomas Pinckney of the same news:

> Your very obliging letter of June 16th has been received and laid before the Board of Directors of the Santee Canal Company. I have the pleasure to inform you, that your representations in favor Colo. Senf have been so well received that the Board, after conversing and corresponding with him have unanimously agreed to employ him as director in chief of the proposed Canal.—I have it therefore in charge, to request that you suspend any further measures for procuring Artists for the use of the Company, as they are determined to trust the execution of the business to Colonel Senf.[21]

In July 1793 Ramsay in Charleston wrote to Thomas Pinckney in London, asking for assistance with purchasing a machine that could speed up the canal excavation work and mentioning the canal progress to date:

> The inclosed paragraph respecting a machine for shortening the labor of cutting canals, which was cut . . . out of the Star, a London newspaper dated March 26th 1793:[22] was, this day read & commented on, before a meeting of the Stockholders in the Santee Canal Company. At the request of the directors of that Company I am desired to beg the favor of you to enquire into the matter, & if in your opinion the machine would be of essential service in expediting the views of the company, that you procure one & send it out by the first opportunity together, with any workmen that . . . may be necessary for working it. The whole matter is left to your discretion & any contracts you may enter into, or any draughts you may make on the company in consequence of complying with their wishes will be sanctioned & paid.
>
> I have the pleasure to inform you that there are 195 laborers employed on the Canal and that four hundred yards of it are completed and the whole going on, as well as can be expected.[23]

In July 1793 Charles Pinckney leveled this mild, technical criticism of Senf in a letter written to brother Thomas:

> I now enclose you the last letter I have had from your plantation; I wish it was more particular, but I am informed your prospects are not bad. Ours at Charleywood are very flattering, but at the Congaree the freshes have destroyed both Corn & Indigo, we have already planted three times & at this late Season are attempting a fourth time—If we do not succeed, we shall bring down our hands to Tippecutlaw & cut up the wood which Senf has there fallen for the Canal; he is going on very well, but does not understand "puddling" at least as Marshall describes it. If you have seen any thing of the operation pray inform me how it is done.[24]

Santee Canal Company leadership published regular progress reports in the local newspapers. Year after year high hopes were expressed for the rapid completion of the long-anticipated canal, even as early as 1795:

> A committee of the directors of the Santee Canal Company, consisting of the late Governor, Mr. Laurens, Mr. Gilchrist, and Mr. John Rutledge, jun. have, within the last five days, examined the canal from one end to the other, and found every department conducting with regularity and economy; that the work was advancing as fast as the well-directed exertions of

700 labourers could forward it; and that there was, on the whole, a fair prospect of speedy and complete success in the great undertakings.[25]

One can imagine that with the passage of time between when the company was formed and when excavation/construction work commenced, there were other projects that caught the interest of various statesmen. Senf took the opportunity to study and consult, to read the terrain, and to pay attention to the planters who served on the company's board of directors. In addition he was involved in other military preparation projects related to regional and national maritime concerns about America's undeclared war with the French republic.[26] Charles Pinckney explained Senf's involvement in a few of these efforts in an April 1799 letter to James McHenry (1753–1816), then serving as secretary of war:

> It is difficult to obtain from meer description, an accurate knowledge of a country, particularly, when it is intersected by water & that water is at various depths.—Col. Senf has promised to give me when I return to Charleston, an accurate plan of the harbor, with the soundings mark'd thereon, which after having taken a Copy, I will transmit to you. The most accurate <u>printed</u> plan, of Port Royal Harbor is in the Map published by Mouzon & others, but there are errors in that, which will be corrected in the one I shall transmit.—Col Senf proceeded no farther with [us] than in reconnoitring this harbor, as he was obliged to return to complete the Santee canal.[27]

In July 1799 Ramsay made this prediction to Jedidiah Morse (1761–1826):

> Our Santee Canal will be in operation in two months. It was to have been done in three years and to have cost £55,000. It has been in hand above 6 years and has already cost above £400,000 sterling. I unfortunately became a large stockholder, and actually paid £6,000 sterling towards it, which was double the sum I expected when I entered so largely into the business. The completion of the work will I trust amply repay us all, but it had hitherto been a source of great derangement to all who are deeply engaged in.[28]

Other chapters cover the completion of the canal, various climatological challenges, and its functioning after the rocky and uncertain years that resulted in the company's charter, incorporation, and blustery promises of imminent canal completion.[29] As early as 1849, though, the Santee Canal Company tried to quash rumors of its demise by publishing this announcement:

> SANTEE CANAL. THE Directors of this Canal having learnt that many rumors are circulated to the effect that the Canal is to be abandoned before next Winter, take this opportunity of informing the public that such rumors are without the shadow of foundation, and that they are now enlarging their Reserves beyond what they have ever been, and expect to have a supply of water, except in times of extraordinary drought. HARRIS SIMONS, Sec'ry. and Treas'r, Santee Canal Co.[30]

In 1853 the following notice appeared in the local newspaper: "OFFICE SANTEE CANAL COMPANY, May 25, 1853.—Notice is hereby given that the COMPANY FOR INLAND NAVIGATION FROM SANTEE TO COOPER RIVER, (commonly known as the Santee Canal Company,) will apply to the Legislature at its next session, for leave to surrender its charter and close its affairs. HARRIS SIMONS, Sec'r and Treas'r."[31] By the time the Santee Canal Company sought to surrender its charter, its financial situation was grim. In an 1853 petition to the South Carolina General Assembly, the board of directors made this plea: "Your memorialists further show to your Honorable Body, that the business of the Company is entirely superseded by the Rail Roads and Steam Boats, which penetrate all that region of the State from which the custom of the Company has hitherto been drawn."[32] Area planters, on the other hand, stepped forward to protest the charter surrender.[33] In many ways the Santee Canal Company had served "as a neighbor to the planters of the parish. They functioned as an agricultural and social unit, as did the other plantations in the area."[34] The canal had afforded the planters "a new channel of communication, transportation, and commerce. Some re-oriented their buildings and houses towards the canal."[35]

The possibility that Santee Canal Company assets might be distributed among the stockholders also concerned the planter memorialists: "Your memorialists further submit that if the Company be allowed to surrender their charter and close up business, they be required to make a free transfer of the 210 feet of land on which the canal is located to respective plantations through which it passes . . . as the sale of such land in small tracts must prove injurious to those plantations and to the property of the neighborhood generally."[36] Weighing the concerns expressed by the various sides of the situation, the state's

Committee on Incorporations responded: "That after a full consideration of the facts addressed before them . . . they were satisfied that the said company was annually exhausting the little property left and in discharging the duties imposed on it by its charter and recommend that the prayer of the said company be granted upon certain terms and under terms set forth in a Bill to authorize the sale or Surrender of the Charter of the Company."[37] A few years later, the achievements of the Santee Canal Company were considered more broadly:

> The Santee Canal, in this State, was the first enterprise of any extent of this kind undertaken and executed, and was for many years the largest in extent. The other lines of our canal system along the Broad and Catawba Rivers were designed as parts of a general chain, looking ultimately towards the solution of the great problem, a connection with the Northwest or with the Ohio valley. Much time, labor and money were spent on this project in canals before the era of railroads—perhaps we may now say foolishly and extravagantly spent. The time may soon come when we shall be called on calmly to consider whether all this outlay shall or need be lost, and whether we have not erred as much in neglecting and abandoning inland resources of water communication as our fathers erred in premature and excessive expenditures for them. What is the present state and condition of our canal works? It may be worth while for citizens locally interested and having opportunities of information to consider the question.[38]

As late as 1886, the formation of the Santee Canal Company was viewed in a sanguine light: "[The Santee Canal] was the grandest work of internal improvement that had been attempted in all America (although it was soon afterwards surpassed by similar schemes in other States), and nothing can show more conclusively the devolution and resolute spirit of its promoters than the fact that after the charter was obtained six years were consumed in making up the company."[39] As emphasized by DuBose, every planter was in debt after the Revolutionary War.[40] In a way, by the 1850s every Carolinian was in debt to the Santee Canal Company for the years of prosperity and technical ingenuity that improved inland navigation, allowed commerce to flourish, and increased interstate communication despite the droughts and other logistical issues that brought this state's first superhighway to an inglorious end.

THREE

Johann Christian Senf

More than 250 years after his birth, Johann Christian Senf remains an enigma. To get a more complete picture of the man, it is worth examining the myths and realities surrounding his ethnic origins, temperament, early life and immediate family, military service in the Brunswick Dragoons and Continental Army, marriage and influential in-laws, travels abroad, and final years. All of these elements combine to make up a portrait of a complex, brilliant, and sometimes misunderstood person who transformed South Carolina with his groundbreaking and forward-thinking projects.

Many sources repeat the same incomplete and often inaccurate details about this fascinating figure's origins, military career, motivations, and achievements. Several late nineteenth-century accounts claimed that Senf was Swedish, while others surmised he was French, Dutch, or Danish. Statements of Swedish origins and differing birth dates were repeated and perpetuated in works published in the twentieth century and beyond. Prior to widespread assumptions that Senf was a Swede, his contemporaries understood and appreciated his true origins, and some acquaintances remarked on his ethnicity.

Henry Laurens's March 11, 1778 letter to statesman John Lewis Gervais (1741–98) stated that Senf was "a Saxon who speaks a tongue you have no aversion to."[1] In a January 30, 1784, letter to South Carolina governor Benjamin Guerard (1740–88), Senf mentioned his native land as a way of explaining his desire to take a leave of absence: "Having always felt a Desire, that if I should outlive the late War, and as soon as Business would admit, to pay a Visit to Saxony, as my Native Country [to] see my Relatives, and endeavour to qualifie myself more for the Office I have the Honor to be entrusted with."[2] As botanist Henrietta Marchant Liston (1751–1828) noted in a travel journal entry dated 1797:

We proceeded to Colonel Sinfs, for whom we had a letter. He is a native of Germany: the superintendent of a Canal, the most considerable work of that kind yet attempted, in America, it is intended to join the Santee river to the Coopers river. Before we reached Col. Sinfs, indeed, a few miles from our last stage Woodbine, on the side of the road, one of the servants pointed out to us a small inclosure, at the edge of a Wood, with a board on it, commemorating the Death of Major Majoribanks who had behaved gallantly at the Battle of the Eutaw [September 8, 1781] & died a few days after at a Plantation opposite this Wood, in consequence of the heat & fatigue he suffered during this engagement. At the Banks of the Canal, we found Col. Sinf & his Wife living on a pretty little spot, created & beautified by themselves, it was laid out with peculiar neatness & taste, after experiencing their hospitality we proceeded to Pinckneys Ferry over the Santee river, & passing the Euclas Creek, over a Bridge, slept at a Tavern three miles on.[3]

In a letter dated January 20, 1811, to Thomas Moore (1760–1822), US Navy chief engineer and inventor Benjamin Henry Latrobe (1764–1820) stated that the "Santee canal is the work of a German, Colonel Senf." As cited in Talbot Hamlin's biography of Latrobe, the name Senf was mistranscribed from Latrobe's letter as Leuf.[4] Senf was born in 1752 in Wasungen, a town in the Schmalkalden-Meiningen district of the central German state of Thuringia, the son of Lucas Senf (1721–99) and Eulalia Mahler. Eulalia was born in Uttershausen, Schwalm-Eder-Kreis, Hesse, making her a Hessian. In publications Senf's name has been spelled or transcribed variously as *Leuf, Senf, Senff, Senaf, Sempf, Semph, Sinf, Sinff, Snelf, Cinf,* and *Zinf*.[5] Phonetic spellings of surnames were common during this time period. In German *Senf* means mustard. Perhaps the simplified spelling suited Senf, as he and his father appear as Sempf in some Hessian military records. His first name has been misconstrued as Charles or Christopher because of his tendency to abbreviate his middle name, Christian, as *Ch*. Contemporaries of his did not make this error, but subsequent generations of researchers sometimes misinterpreted his use of the abbreviation in written correspondence.

Aside from speculations about his ethnic origins, Senf's brilliance, ingenuity, and volatile personality traits continued to intrigue and fascinate. Surgeon Julius Frederick Wasmus of Braunschweig, Germany, provided a firsthand account of working with Senf. Wasmus was captured at Bennington, Vermont, in 1777 and spent four years as a prisoner until he was exchanged from Rutland, Massachusetts, in summer 1781 after a truce was declared at Halifax.[6] According to Helga Doblin, the translator of Wasmus's account, "the Braunschweig prisoners were popular dinner guests in Brimfield [Massachusetts] and were often invited to local celebrations."[7] Long after Senf changed allegiance, he remained a subject of conversation, as shown in a January 1778 entry Wasmus's diary: "He also told us a great deal about the talents of our former Master Clerk Senf, and that he was captain of engineers in their army. I was pleased about that because he [Senf] is a good and righteous man who was, however, too harshly treated by us in spite of his work and ability."[8]

Regarding Senf, then-governor of Virginia Thomas Jefferson (1743–1826) stated the following in a letter dated May 10, 1781, to Virginia's Speaker of the House of Delegates, Benjamin Harrison (1726–91):

> I think it is necessary to inform the General Assembly that the State is at present without an Engineer. Lt Colo Warneck, who formerly acted in that Capacity, was made prisoner by the enemy at Westham, and should he be exchanged, it will remain questionable whether he shall resume the office. We have it in our power at present to engage Colo Senf, a gentleman eminent for his skill as an Engineer, his zeal and activity. But holding the Rank, Command and emoluments of a Colo in another State, with an assurance that the office will not be discontinued with the War, and it is not expected that he will relinquish these but on an offer of equal Terms from this State, which under the Act of assembly of October 1776, the Executive are not authorized to engage. I cannot but add that I think he will be a valuable Acquisition and such a one as if lost will not be easily replaced.[9]

Contemporaneous observations of Senf reveal a great deal more than what was printed decades later. A letter from Henry Young to William Davies, dated May 21, 1778, mentions Senf and a British deserter named Beesly Edgar Joel: "A little fellow by name Joell, and a deserter from the British with a full stock of impudence and with some little knowledge in drawing like Coll. Senf has procured himself the command of the first Troop in Brents Corps. I dont know what they call them, perhaps waisters of the public stores. This Joell will have the rank of Majr. I think the time will shortly come when it will be disgraceful to rank above a Captain."[10] Another eyewitness, James Fergus, observed about Senf in April 1778, during Senf's time in the American Continental Army:

> As soon as I got clothed for the summer campaign, I volunteered again with a few others and followed on to Orangeburg and fell in with our

regiment under Colonel Neal there. Colonels Wynn and Brown and some others were there with their men, all under the command of Colonel Senf, a foreign officer who it was said was sent out to discipline our southern men. While we lay here, Colonel Senf laid off the ground for a fort and employed our men in cutting turf and working on it until we heard that the British had crossed Savannah River and got to Purysburg. I now, for the first time, began to keep a small journal in a memorandum book, which I continued until I was taken with the fever and carried into Charleston.[11]

In a letter written to Secretary of War James McHenry (1753–1816), dated May 13, 1799, George Washington counted Senf as among the best military engineers:

And this conjecture, leads me to the consideration of another matter, of very serious importance. It is well known that the great advantage which the Armies of France have over those they contend with, lyes in the Superiority with which their Artillery is served, and in the skill of their Engineers. Let me entreat, therefore, that the most prompt & pointed attention be given to the procuring—and instructing—men in these Sciences. Lamentable indeed must be our case, if we shall have to acquire the knowledge of these arts in the face of an enemy, when *that* enemy ought to experience our Skill in the exercise of them. I do not mean to *recommend* characters as instructors in these branches; but I will mention the names of some who have passed through my mind, & have been recalled to it. Du Portail, Lamoy, Senf, Rivardi, and Latrobe. The last of whom I know nothing of, but have been told that he has knowledge *in,* & professes to be well acquainted with, the *principles* of Engineering. I notice these as persons within your reach, in case nothing better can be done—It is necessary to be provident. Let us not have things to prepare, when they should be in use.[12]

In his *History of the Santee Canal,* Frederick Porcher describes Senf as vain, jealous, and having "infirmities of temper."[13] Porcher's account does not elaborate on the sources of his information, but one can surmise that he gleaned his insights from Santee River planters who were his friends and relatives. Porcher was born just a few years after Senf's death, and Senf's actions and personality traits would have been important elements of local lore and frequent topics of conversation.

In a story related by Porcher, Senf was displeased that his knowledgeable German servant upstaged him in his reveal of the functioning canal to esteemed guests. Out of jealous spite, Senf banished the servant to work at General Moultrie's house at Northampton, not far away.[14] Although Porcher does not mention him by name, the servant was Henry Glindkamp (1768–1824), who later served as canal superintendent.[15]

Gaining an understanding of Senf involves learning more about his blood relatives. Senf's father, Lucas, was born in Thierbach, Anspach, Bavaria. Technically this birth location does not make him a Hessian, but German troops from various territories commonly were referred to by this name.[16] According to Stephan Huck, there was an investigation into the circumstances surrounding eight dragoons who deserted under the elder Senf's leadership in 1779.[17] An index of Braunschweig troops in North America listed an individual named Lucas Sempf who was released from Hessian service in America in 1783 and settled in Canada afterward.[18] The 1790 census shows a Lucas Senaf living in Montgomery, Palatine, New York, with six other household members.[19] In 1789 Delia Gerster Vache (1739–1814), widow of Johann Georg Vach, granted land in Montgomery to Lucas Senf.[20] It is not clear when Senf then moved to South Carolina to join his son. Christian Senf's half-brother, Johann Georg Vach (1753–88), was presumably the son of Eulalia Mahler and Johannes Vach. Georg Vach served as a surgeon from 1776 to 1780 in the Second Regiment (Colonel Jacob Klock's Regiment) stationed at Tryon, New York.[21] Records show that Vach requested reimbursement of £390 from New York governor George Clinton for various wounds dressed over a period of several months from April to October 1779.[22] Vach's five children were baptized at the Reformed Dutch Church in Stone Arabia, New York. For at least one of these baptisms, Senf served as a sponsor.[23] In an act passed by the New York legislature on May 4, 1784, John George Vach was made a naturalized citizen.[24]

In a letter to George Washington dated February 24, 1790, Senf emphasized his own educational background, service as a mercenary, American citizenship, financial concerns, and responsibilities toward his father and his brother's widow and orphaned children:

> In the last War, it was my Disappointment, that, besides the Disadvantage, under which I entered the American Service, I never could have the Satisfaction to serve under your immediate Orders, to give You Proofs, that I was the Man in reality, what I professed myself—I did not recieve my Military Education in a Royal Corps; But I have had very able Instructors and

many opportunities, as to give me both Theorie and practice. It was often painful to me, when Brethern officers of our Corps assumed a Superiority of Knowledge, which was not founded on any thing else, but a National Prejudice, and mixed with too much Envy and Jealousy.

On a nice Examination there is an Impropriety in the Manner, I entered the American Service; but, it can not be called dishonest. It is now above twelve Years—At that time a very young Man—A Prisoner of War—Compelled, through Necessity, to enter into a Service of Mercenaries, which I heartily despised—Not bound by the one; and left at Liberty to act, as I pleased by the other—Anxious for Promotion in a Military Life—The Capacity, in which I served, being well known to the generous Conqueror—He made me such kind offers and flattering Promises, which overcame all Scruples, which arose in my young Breast—I could no longer look on Him as my Enemy, but as my friend—I resigned my Mercenary Employment—Left the Rest to Generous Minds to forgive me for it—And became One in Support of Freedom; without acting against the Country, where I was born and educated. During these twelve Years, I may mention, I believe, I have done my Duty as a Citizen and as a Soldier. In the year 1779 the State of So. Carolina honored me with a generous appointment, as Engineer of the State, for Life. Ever since that time I did not draw any Emoluments from the United States; although I allways served under the immediate orders of the Continental Generals with the army....

The Emolument of So. Carolina I found fully sufficient for my Support. Concieving it inconsistent to recieve two Emoluments. The funds were different—The Service was but one—After the War I never have asked for those Benefits Native and foreign officers are intitled to by the different Resolves of Congress. I had no Intention to demand them; as this State had provided for me for Life. But, after my Return from Europe, the Civil List of this State seemed very burthensome to the People; almost every where I heard Complaints of; Being one of the Number, whose Emoluments amounted to near five hundred pounds Sterling pr year, tired of the Complaints; and not wishing to be considered so soon as a Pensioner, I thought, I acted becoming a Citizan to retain my Commission, but resign my Emoluments, untill the State should want my Services: Having at the same time several flattering Views in the Inland Navigation Business to make a suitable Provision.

Since that, my only (but half) Brother, who followed me through brotherly affection, served as a Surgeon for Six Years in the American

Army, and settled since the War on Mohak River, paid me a Visit the Summer before last on the Catawba River, where he took sick and died—He has left me now to my sole Care an aged Parent, a Widow and four very young Orphans, without any Property. I have used my utmost Endeavour to raise the Means for their Support; But, such is the Scarcity of Money and Distress in this State, that I can scarce obtain as much to carry on the Works of this Navigation in a very languid Manner, much less to obtain any thing for myself nor for my poor family.

I am sure, you feel for the poor Orphans—you feel for the aged Parent—A compassionate Heart like yours will readily protect me to obtain to what I may be intitled to as an officer of the United States. I make so free, to enclose three Papers. They may be of Service—I have requested two of my friends at New York (one of them will have the Honor to hand this Letter to you), to recieve, what ever I may obtain from the United States like other officers, and apply it for the best Purposes for my poor family—Till I may be able to add to it by my Industry. I have wrote to the Secretary of the War Office on the same Business, and enclosed the like Papers—I hope, I have not forfeited my Right by not demanding it sooner—I pray to God for Success for the Sake of the poor orphans—For my Part, I shal always think myself happy, to be honored with your good opinion; and of your Confidence, whenever my Country should intrust me with its Commands. I have the Honor to be with the highest Respect Sir, Your very humble and faithful Servant, Ch. Senf.[25]

Beyond what was revealed by Senf in various letters, very little is known about his early life and education. Accounts of his talents and interests, however, indicate a man of letters who traveled and who read widely in a variety of fields and in several languages. His probated will's inventory attests to his reading interests and language fluencies.[26]

According to several accounts, Senf and his father were members of the Brunswick Dragoons. The Prinz Ludwig Dragoons was an elite regiment in the Braunschweiger Jaeger. Long before Senf was referred to as an engineer, his name appeared in records as a Musterschreiber, or muster roll clerk, a role that involved serving as a scribe for the attendance rolls.[27] Later accounts refer to him as a draftsman. Douglas A. Irwin and Richard Sylla refer to Senf and Pierre L'Enfant (1754–1825) as "artsy architects" rather than engineers.[28] During this time period, America relied on European-trained engineers as their supply of engineers was limited.

Hessian records list a Wilh. Sempf, muster roll clerk, from Hesse, age thirty, deserting from a prisoner of war camp in 1778, and his father, Lucas Sempf, born in Thierbach, age fifty-five, discharged from Canada in 1783.[29] According to the *German Canadian Yearbook,* Lucas Sempf, dragoon, deserted on June 28, 1783.[30] These records contradict the date recorded for Senf's commission as a captain in the Continental Army, October 20, 1777.[31] Perhaps this commissioning date was the source of confusion for several researchers who assumed that Senf was captured at Saratoga in October 1777 rather than earlier that year.

In a letter written to Jacob Christopher Zahn, dated March 10, 1778, Laurens referred to the date of Senf's capture, perpetuating some possibly erroneous information:

> This [letter] will be delivered to you by Capt[n] John Christian Senf, lately a Lieut[t] & Engineer in General Reidesel's Hessian Troops this Gentleman was made prisoner in the Action of 19th October near Saratoga—Gen. Gates countenanced him & from reflection upon the Cruelty of his late Master in compelling him to engage in the present War he determined to change Counties & breath in the Air of Liberty.[32]

In a letter dated the following day, Laurens explained more about Senf to John Lewis Gervais:

> Gen. Gates Commissioned him to be a Captain of Engineers but here are so many foreigners, the pay allowed by the public so small & every article of subsistence so extravagantly Dear I have after receiving a very warm recommendation of him from the General advised him to try his fortune in a more Southern Latitude . . . he is an ingenious sensible Man . . . & may be made very useful in public life as an Engineer or in the service of Individuals as a Surveyor you will soon discover his abilities & so far patronize him as to direct him how to apply them to the best purposes, I am sure he will be found of great benefit in directing & superintending any of our public Works.[33]

Senf wrote a letter dated August 5, 1778 to Laurens, explaining his knowledge of the missing German regimental colors from Saratoga, stating "by wich [*sic*] I was already taken prisoner."[34] If Senf had been taken prisoner by the summer of 1777, as believed, it is not possible for him to have been captured at the battles of Bemis Heights near Saratoga in September and October 1777 or to have had firsthand knowledge of Gen. John Burgoyne's capitulation that same month, which provoked the issue of where the colors were stored.

Given the estimated time of Senf's imprisonment, it is more likely that he was captured during the Battle of Bennington, which was actually fought in nearby Walloomsac, New York, on August 16, 1777;[35] was kept prisoner until his talents attracted the attention of Laurens and Gen. Horatio Gates; and was exchanged. Gates succeeded Gen. Philip Schuyler in August 1777. Senf's commanding officer, Lieutenant Colonel Baum, died during the battle.

For the expedition into Vermont, Burgoyne assigned Baum to lead a regiment that was composed of 434 German dragoons and infantry in addition to about 400 other troops.[36] It is likely that Senf was part of this regiment, because of the sheer number of captives and his claim that he was captured in summer 1777. The battle that took place in Walloomsac on August 16 resulted in 700 troops under Baum's command, including 30 officers, being captured.[37] Soldiers captured during "the Battles of Bennington and Saratoga [October 1777] would arrive in Massachusetts later in the year."[38] It is understandable that historians assumed that Senf had been captured in October 1777, but because of the letter he wrote to Laurens, it is clear that he was captured earlier in the summer. The Battle of Bennington is considered part of the Saratoga Campaign, and the American victory was considered a turning point in the campaign that culminated with the surrender at Saratoga.

Regardless of the confusion over where and when Senf was captured, his abilities were recognized by many other high-ranking individuals.[39] On January 16, 1779, Moultrie wrote to Charles C. Pinckney: "I wish the [state] assembly would allow Capt. Senf, an additional pay, to enable him to live amongst us, he is a very useful man, and allowed on all hands, to be such a one as we want; he is an extraordinary field engineer; pray keep him if you can."[40] On September 27, 1780, Gates wrote about Senf in a letter to Jefferson: "I send him to your Excellency to be employed upon the service mentioned in my last Letter. His Abilities are great, in the Engineer's Department, and a better draughtsman I never saw. His integrity I am satisfied is unquestionable, but for the satisfaction of the Executive I think Genl. Nelson, or some person of the First Consideration in the State might be requested to go with Colonel Senf, to see, and report, His plans and observations."[41] In a May 17, 1781, letter to Friedrich von Steuben, the Marquis de Lafayette related that "Senfes is Going up to Albermale [sic] County. His Activity and zeal Have Induced me to give Him this Commission."[42]

After Senf left the Brunswick Dragoons to serve in the Continental Army, a rumor circulated that he had courted the daughter of an influential general. A diary entry written by J. F. Wasmus in April 1781 stated:

> While I was visiting patients in Brookfield [Massachusetts] today, I had the opportunity of being in the company of an American colonel. He assured me that our former Chief Clerk Senf from the Dragoon Regiment had been appointed colonel and commander of an American engineer corps and invested with a commission and that either he had already married the only daughter of General [Nathanael] Greene or would shortly do so. After Gen. Washington, this Gen. Greene is the second-in-command and has large estates in Virginia and Pennsylvania. Thus, Senf will be sole heir there.[43]

This contemporaneous account suggested that Senf's future father-in-law was Gen. Nathanael Greene (1742–86), but Greene's first child was not born until 1776. It is possible that the statement was made in jest or that the imprecise story referred to Daniel Morgan (1735/36–1802), who owned considerable properties and had two daughters of marriageable age.[44] According to Higginbotham, Morgan used prisoners of war in 1780–81 to build his mansion Saratoga, located eleven miles from Winchester, Virginia.[45] Another possible candidate, however unlikely, was Philip Schuyler, Washington's second in command during the time of Senf's capture, but Schuyler's properties were near Albany, New York. In any event, there is no evidence that Senf married until 1792, when he wed the daughter of the first diplomatic minister to America from the Dutch Republic. This marriage was strategic in terms of vital connections to Holland and access to his wife's political friendships.

It is not known how or when Senf met Geertruid "Gertrude" Jacoba van Berckel (1761–1835).[46] One can imagine that within the rarefied New York social circles in which Senf and Gertrude moved, a chance meeting would have been likely. Gertrude frequently entertained the likes of John Adams's daughter Abigail Adams Smith; John Quincy Adams; Martha Washington; Ralph Izard and his wife, Alice DeLancey Izard; Catherine Schuyler; and John and Sarah Jay. Or perhaps they met when Senf traveled to Holland to inspect the Hedraulique Works, as mentioned in his September 27, 1784, letter written from The Hague to Thomas Jefferson:

> It gives me real Pleasures to hear of Your Excellency's safe Arrival at Paris and being in good Health. I hope Miss Jefferson is the same, And sincerely wish You so to continue.

Colo. Humphrey will have Your Excellency informed that I was a Brother Passenger of His. But on my Way from Brest to Paris, I thought best to hasten to this Country to make Use of the favourable Season to examine the Hedraulique Works before the Weather would be too severe, and postponed to see Paris till next Spring on my Return to America. I make here all necessary Inquiries and hope I shall well informed return to America to the Satisfaction of my friends. Finding it necessary to remain longer at this Country than I at first thought, I shall be under the Necessity to draw on South Carolina or my friends at Charleston for a hundred Guineas to enable me to reach Saxony, as I fall short in my Calculations. I am well furnished with Letters of Introduction to the first People for almost every capitol Place in Holland, and where I pass I am recieved and treated with the greatest Attention, yet I canot think with any Propriety to apply to them to advance me Cash on my Bill of Exchange alone on my first Acquaintance. Your Excellency Know my Situation in America, and having allways had the Kind Assurance to look on You as a real Friend of mine I hope I may assume to ask the favour of You to procure me that Credit for the mentioned Sum in Amsterdam, and to inform me in a few Lines as soon as it may be convenient, on whom I may address myself to draw in favour of, on Governor Guerard, Comodore Gillon or any of my friends in Charleston, where it may be thought most Suitable. And I give you my Promise that my Order will punctually be answer'd as soon as it shall arrive.

If I can serve Your Excellency with any Information from this Part of the Country, I wait Your Commands. Mr. Dumas, to whom I have given my Direction, will be so good to forward Your Letter to me. You should please to honor me with. I have the Honor to be with perfect Respect Your Excellency's most obedt. and most humble Servant,

CH. SENF
Colo. Engineer So. Carolina[47]

According to a letter that diplomat Charles W. F. Dumas sent to the president of Congress, Thomas Mifflin (1744–1800), from The Hague on October 8, 1784,

Colonel Senf, Chief Engineer of South Carolina, has honored me with a visit. I have shown him the fine cannon foundry here; and Mr. De Roo, of the Executive Council of Holland, honored us by taking us to Delft in his carriage, for the purpose of showing the superb arsenals and workshops of that Province, which were opened by his influence, a favor seldom granted, either to the inhabitants or to strangers. The Colonel then went on his journey, by way of Rotterdam, to Bergenopzoom, and perhaps to Zealand, where he will see General Dumoulin; and from thence will go, by way of Amsterdam, to Saxony, for the purpose of visiting his family. He intends to be here again in the spring, in order that he may be in Charleston at the expiration of his furlough. The pleasure which he experienced form the sight of those objects, the knowledge of which he intends to turn to the advantage of the United States, can only be equalled by mine in procuring it for him. Foreign officers passing through this place, generally request to be presented to the Prince of Orange, as Captain General. But the measures which the Colonel had taken to see the arsenals at Delft, have, in addition to want of time, caused him to prefer what was more important. He can, however, be presented, if he pleases, on his return.[48]

As mentioned, Senf's travels may have placed him in contact with Gertrude, her close relatives, or her extended family. Gertrude's father was Pieter Embert Johan Van Berckel (1725–1800), who was named first minister plenipotentiary to the United States from Holland. Pieter arrived in October 1783 after a lengthy and difficult sea voyage, escorted by four ships. One of the four ships wrecked; Van Berckel's first cousin once removed, Gijsbert Karel Van Hogendorp, survived the shipwreck and joined his cousin in New Jersey, where Van Berckel met and formed friendships with Jefferson and others.[49] Previously Van Berckel had served as *burgomaster* (mayor) of Rotterdam. For the most part, Gertrude served as her father's hostess while he served as minister. Because she played such a prominent role in her father's social life in New York and Newark, New Jersey, some contemporaneous accounts inaccurately stated that Gertrude's mother, Geertruid Margaretha du Bois (1736–1803), was deceased.[50] During Van Berckel's diplomatic service, his wife remained in Rotterdam.[51] In a March 18, 1785, letter to John Adams, translated from the original French, Dumas mentioned Mrs. van Berckel, who reportedly never joined her husband in America:

> Mrs. Van Berckel, whose elder daughter is leaving to go to her father, asked me if she risked anything from the Barbaries in an American vessel, one of which is ready to depart from Amsterdam, taking the northern route. My opinion, which I let her know, is that there is nothing to fear

along that route in this season. If I am mistaken, a prompt warning from your excellency would enable me to recant and to save Miss Van Berckel from the misfortune of being captured. Our respects to the Adams ladies. Your excellency's very humble and very obedient servant

Cwf Dumas.[52]

John Adams responded in part to Dumas's query about Gertrude's safety in a letter dated March 30, 1785:

> I think that Miss Van Berckel, will be in no danger from the Barbaresques, in the Way She is going, and I believe [sic] there is much less danger in any other route than is represented in the English Papers—which abound with Lies frabricated [sic] by Scheming Insurers, whose Robberies are not less detestable than those of the Affricans, for Fraud is even more wicked than violence—. we have no Information of any American Vessels taken, excepting one, by the Emperor of Morocco who has promised that no more Shall be taken untill Congress can send him a Consul which he desires.[53]

John Quincy Adams had met Gertrude's father in 1783, a few months before Van Berckel sailed to Philadelphia to become the first Dutch ambassador. In a July 1785 letter to his sister Abigail, Adams explained Gertrude's forthcoming arrival:

> Mr. van Berkel, with whom I dined to day, begins to expect his Daughter: he has certain information that she sail'd, from Amsterdam, the 2d. of May, in a *Dutch vessel*. She has now been nearly 12 weeks out, and consequently it is almost time for her to arrive. It is observed that there is here now a Dutch vessel, that sailed from Amsterdam 3 days before the ship that returned lately from China, sailed from Canton, and arrived here three days after her.[54]

Gertrude was a frequent topic of conversation in letters exchanged between Adams and his sister. He mentioned Gertrude in a July 27, 1785, letter: "At length after a passage of a little more than 12 weeks, Miss van Berkel, arrived two days ago at Philadelphia. Her father is gone to meet her. The young Ladies here are all very impatient to see her, and I dare say, that when she comes, remarks, and reflections, will not be spared on either side. The Beauties of this place, will triumph, but I hope with moderation."[55] In an August 1 letter to Abigail, Adams reported:

> I was at a party at tea this afternoon, and Miss van Berkel was present. There were only two or three persons in Company that could speak to her, so, I was obliged to converse with her, near two hours together. And here I must tell you, that I believe more and more firmly, that what a certain Friend of mine said of her, is a most infamous falsehood. She behaves as well, as any young lady I know of, and I believe if her brother knew what that coxcomb said of her, he would make him repent it heartily. She complains of not understanding the language, as bitterly, as you did when you first arrived in France. She says she had no idea, how awkward one appears in a large company, where one can neither hear what is said nor speak one's self. You have had sufficient proofs of the truth of this observation: tho' you was not often subjected to the inconvenience.[56]

In his diary entry dated August 4, 1785, Adams noted: "Young Mr. van Berkel said his Sister had arrived, somewhat sooner than he expected she would. The minister is gone to Philadelphia, to meet her, and she is expected here tomorrow or the next day."[57] Gertrude was mentioned again in an August 7 entry:

> I was introduced to Miss van Berkel whom I had formerly seen in Holland. She cannot be called handsome but has that affability which is to me much more agreeable in a Lady than Beauty alone. She complains much of her misfortune in not speaking the Language, and is fearful that she appears awkward and ill bred, because she does not speak: and really, no person can, have an idea, how disagreeable it is to be in a Country, and not speak the Language; without having been himself in that predicament. Here it is worse than anywhere else, because there are fewer persons who speak any foreign Language: and the few Ladies, that can speak a little french, are so bashful, that there is no persuading them to talk.[58]

In a September 5, 1785, letter from Abigail to her brother, Gertrude again was a topic: "Miss Van Berkel, must have had a disagreeable time I think. The Ladies, make remarks, and perhaps triumph, if there is opportunity. They had better appear conspicuoes for their Candour, for their is not a more amiable . . . trait in the Character of a Lady, and, prove themselvs superior, by their behavour towards her, than a greater degree of beauty could render them."[59] Another letter from Abigail to Adams, dated October 9, 1785, stated this about Gertrude: "Mr. Duker secretary of Legation to the Baron de Lynden dined with us en famile. He has been in America as secretary to Mr. Van Berkell and speaks English very well. I asked him about Miss Van Berkel who is in America. He [hears] She speaks French and is a very worthy agreeable young Lady—this to confute the assertion of a certain Gentleman."[60]

Gertrude's father was recalled in 1788, and his former position was reduced to a resident ministry, to which Gertrude's brother, Franco Petrus van Berckel (1760–1836), was appointed in May 1789. The younger Van Berckel served until September 1795, when the post was restored to its original rank. In a September 12, 1795, letter written by John Quincy Adams to his father, John Adams, the plans to unseat Franco were explained:

> They have determined here to recall Mr: Van Berkel, who is to be directed to take leave in the most friendly manner, [with] giving the express assurance that his recall is owing solely to the intention of their High Mightinesses to send another person in his stead. That other person is a Mr: Van Polanen, a Zeeland Patriot, who is already in America, having some years ago, found a refuge there from public oppression and private misfortune. I have seen his Lady here; who is much esteemed; he is also as well spoken of as the virulence of parties will admit.
>
> Mr: Van Berkel's recall I understand is owing to his having dismissed or suspended a Dutch consul, for rejoycing at the emancipation of this.[61]

According to Dutch Reformed Church records, Senf and Gertrude were married in New York City on May 31, 1792, witnessed by Ger. van Polanen and Marg. Kunze.[62] Several newspapers published notices of the marriage.[63] Intriguingly, Gertrude's uncle Engelbert Francois van Berckel (1726–96) was directly responsible for the events that resulted in Henry Laurens's being imprisoned in 1780 in the Tower of London. Laurens remained imprisoned until General Lord Cornwallis was released in exchange.[64] Uncle Engelbert, first pensionary of Amsterdam, sponsored the ill-fated Lee–de Neufville Treaty of 1778. After Holland chose not to punish him, the Fourth Anglo-Dutch War broke out between Great Britain and Holland.[65]

On October 7, 1785, Jefferson issued two-month passports for Senf and "his domestic Oneida."[66] Records from the Camden Court House include this 1797 entry composed by Senf:

> I do herewith certify that the bearer Onaeh Kampae Oneyda is one of the Northern Indians of the Oneyda Nation—that he with consent of his parents and friends, and with permission of the Governor of the State of New York, went in the year 1784 with me to Europe as a servant, that in the year 1786 he returned with me to Albany again, where he saw his Mother and Relations—But not wishing to remain with his people he came with me, with their consent, to South Carolina, where he has ever since continued.
>
> Santee Canal, in the State of South Carolina, the Sixth of February 1797
> To all it may concern
>
> Ch. Senf (LS)[67]

By all accounts, Senf did not leave behind offspring.[68] His relationship with Oneyda, albeit as a servant, might be construed as a rather close bond. After Senf passed away, Gertrude struggled financially and sent some plaintive letters to various influential friends and acquaintances of her late husband, explaining her dire situation, including this September 3, 1806, letter to Jefferson:

> You will before the receit of this have heard of my Great, and irreparable Loss by the Death of your Old friend, my dear Husband Colo. Ch. Senf but the cause of it will be unknown to You till the perusal of the inclosed Lettre with Speaking the feelings of my Sorrowfull, and wounded heart, and that of a Republican, where they think to have a right, and to Lett it be know'd were their friend's or theirself are infected in their feelings of honor, and integrity excuse to the Wife of your friend, and the Widow of an honest Veteran whom You have know'd, as a Friend, and particular attached to this Country, if She has gone beyond the bound's in Speaking her feeling's—Since the Year Seventy Seven when You were Governeur of the State of Verginien, He faught and bled, for the Good cause of this Country, and He has never Since made himself unworthy in any respect of Your friend Ship, trust, and confidence—
>
> With every wish for Your honor, peace and Contentment, I am with Sentiments of Esteem Sir Your Humble Servant
>
> GERTRUDE JOAN SENF[69]

Just over a week later, on September 11, 1806, Gertrude wrote another letter to Jefferson that provided additional insights into the challenges her husband faced near the end of his life:

Sir,

    Excused if trouble You with an other Letter, but I feel to Sensible my Great loss, than that I can remain quired against them who has occasioned all my unhappiness; Last year a party work begun here against my Husband with Colo. Mentges* who was Send by the Gen as an Aid, or to be Arsenal keeper, he was in correspondence with the Clerk's, of Your Minister's, of the different Department's, a Lettre what a Mr. Shaffer, wrote to his friend, from Philadelphie, Since his dead, and what my Husband openend in hope's, as he thought it would inform him how he would gett reembourse again, of the money what he had advt. Colo. Mentges, (and what never he gott back for all the War office Own'd him for Six Month's Servis to Mentges). but how astonish was my Dear Husband, to See the duble face, and Caracter, what Gen. Dearborn is, in the way that, that Gentleman explained about Some business himself to his friend of Some Demand's, what Colo. Mentges hadt against the War office—Lett the Gen Show You that Same Letter, Dear Sir, in what my Husband rapt up Some other papers of the Deceased, and Send it, to make him aware that his Duplicity was knowed, and I don't doubt or it will explain many things what will be of Service—lett the Gen produce the accts with the expences, and Lettre's, of my Husband, what will explain what work was done, what people he had there, and at what date they were there, untill the Gentlemen tradesmen was come, what the General hadt Send from Philadelphie, Some of them, only direct in his Line the work, other's do Some, and are there at the extravagant rate of three Dols a day, and what is call'd Journemen at two dol. the Secret correspondance was kept up against my Husband by the Gen with the Carpenter at the work's a Mr. Jackson, who was inform'd by the above mentioned in the latter end of the Year, or the beginning of this, that my Husband would Soon be Succeeded by an other Officer, what was an Capt and what was one of their Own or a Northern Man. the New's Soon Spread abroad, but it was kept a profound Secret for Us, untill Capt MaComb's arrival, whose father you have knowe'd in New York, and he entirely young for Such important buseness, in respect to my Husband, where is the Man of feeling's, and honor, Dear Sir, who can Serve, Submit, and give Satisfaction, where Such Mean proceeding's is going on against him when he has Served his Country faithfully for thirty Year's has enrished by his talents and is Grown poor by his enthusiasme and with having to do with Speculators, the last money what my husband received from the War office, was 5000 dols the ten of June 1805 he was oblige'd instantly to pay the half away. by the latter end of the Year the Gentlemen Tradesmen, took a Large Sum of money for Wages, boarding, and other extravagant expences, what hitherto had been unknowe'd to my husband as accounts will Show, and what was not allowed without order's.

My husband Sold Some of Our bank Stok (the proprety what my Parent's has left me) to have allway's some private money to dispose of in case of necessity, he adv for the publick nearly two thousand dols. Till this day his accts are not yet Settled, not withstanding they have been Send three different time's by my husband acg to order's. during his Sickness he has been in want of the necessary's to make his last moment's a little confetable, had no Doc to attend him, all for the want of money, being oblige to Send thirty mylles distances for an able physician As Sick as my dear Husband was, and was oblige to keep his bedt the people came to insult him, So that in Self defence he was oblige to gett up, and take his pistol's. them Same people a few day's after that took a bail writ and would have carried him to Goal was it not for the Gentleman behaviour of the Sheriff—untill it please's the Gen. to Settle the accts of my Dear Husband, I have not a Shilling, and may be well be in want of bread in that time, Lett he reflect what his Animosity, and party has done, this is the poor unhappy Situation of the Widow of Senf, this is the distresfull circumstances of the daughter of Your old friend, both of them have Sacrifice their happiness for the welfare of this Country.

I have promessed Sacredly upon the Dead bedt of my dear Husband, that as far as my abilities, with the Langues, and pen would permit me, I would do my endavours to acquant you with the above mentioned thing's, in hope's, Dear Sir that you as his friend, and father to this Country, will See Justice done to his Memory, and his honest feeling's, what has made him fall a Victim, Favor me, as much, as to Send an impartial Gentleman [No] Whitney, or a federal to enquire unto the conduct of my dear Husband, conserning the work's. with Order's of you, Sir, I will furnish him, with every receipt, Lettre, and paper, conserning that work, from the time it was begun, untill the order's for my Husband to quit it, and in the own handwriting of the deceased if necessary copies can be take, but I cannot part with the origenals.

> Lett my present unhappy Situation, by my great loss, be an excuse in what I could have explained myself to freely With every Sincere wish what can contribute to your Contentment,
>
> I am with greatest Esteem Sir Your Humble Servant
>
> G:J: Senf
>
> * a strong ennemy to this present Government, as Judge Grimke who was with the Gen in correspondance, and a great ennemy to Senf [70]

In December 1806 Gertrude petitioned the South Carolina legislature, "praying that a sum of money due to her deceased husband, late engineer of this state, may be paid to her."[71] Throughout his life Senf sought payment for his work on various engineering projects. Because he was not paid promptly, he incurred debts to many other individuals. This was evident in a letter dated August 17, 1790, from Pierce Butler (1744–1822) to Edward Rutledge (1749–1800): "Is it not hard my dear Sir, that I can not get in any of the money owing to me by Colcock, Senf, or Taylor? I request You will take the most decided measures against Senf and Atkinson. Senf's place on the Mount where he lives, may be sold."[72]

By 1809 Gertrude had married Christian Friedrich Breithaupt (1781–1835), an Edgefield, South Carolina, planter and businessman originally from Thuringia, who had purchased some items from the Senf estate.[73] This marriage took place in Williamsburg County, South Carolina. It is possible that Gertrude met Breithaupt through that estate transaction or that they were introduced earlier through associate Joel Poinsett (1779–1851). On the surface Breithaupt seemed similar to Gertrude's first husband. He emigrated from Baden, Germany, through Philadelphia on the *Juno* in October 1802, but it seems likely he settled in America earlier, considering his meteoric success as a businessman.[74] A poem composed in 1822 by J. G. M'Whorter and republished in 1853 addressed Breithaupt:

> Late from Thuringia came this shepherd god,
> And here, with freedom fix'd his last abode.
> A Priest and Priestess, from a foreign land,
> With cheerful gladness at his altar stand.
> ....
> Why, Breighthaupt, art thou blind to nature's smiles,
> And seek'st thy joys in intrigue's legal wilds?

Breithaupt built a cotton mill called Vaucluse, in Horse Creek Valley, considered by many to be an early, ingenious combination of agriculture and manufacturing:

> In its initial manifestation, Vaucluse was the primitive but impressive progeny of OK. a local immigrant-planter by the name of Christian Breithaupt. Like Henry Shultz, Breithaupt was a European native who came to South Carolina in search of fortune. Unlike Shultz, however, Breithaupt chose the South's more traveled road to wealth, becoming a successful planter in Edgefield District and acquiring no fewer than eighty slaves by 1830. Aside from his ability and ambition, we cannot be sure of Breithaupt's motivations for building a cotton factory. Whatever the source of his inspiration, his Vaucluse mill launched the initial stage of the Horse Creek Valley's transformation from a bucolic haven for grist and saw mill into the South's cradle of industrialization.[75]

Senf's working career was punctuated by several leaves of absence. It is not clear whether these leaves were related to exhaustion, illness, or the desire to travel. In addition to serving as the engineer for the state of South Carolina and other states, he was a justice of the quorum for South Carolina, a role he held until his untimely death.[76] Although Senf occupied the director's house near the double lock (Big Camp) near Major Porcher's house while building the Santee Canal, long before that time, and after the canal was completed, he lived at Rocky Mount, south of Great Falls, along the current State Road 22. Senf would have been familiar with this place from his service in the Continental Army. The esteemed architect Robert Mills (1781–1855) described Rocky Mount as Senf's final resting place:

> Rocky Mount, or [Grimkeville], Close by, is one of those commanding situations that interest the naturalist. Here repose the ashes of one whose memory should be cherished by Carolinians, for his devotion to their cause in the Revolution, and his subsequent efforts to serve them in his professional capacity—Col. Senf, the engineer, both of the Catawba company and of the Santee canal. He sleeps, in what was his garden, at Rocky Mount; but no obituary stone records his name. A few trees, (which he planted in a spot that he had cut in the fashion of a falling garden,) shade his grave. Col. Senf was a military engineer of considerable talent.[77]

According to an undated account by L. M. Ford, presumably written in the 1880s or 1890s long before the Rocky Mount railroad depot was built,

> Col. Senf, was the engineer of Both the Catawba Company and of the Santee Canal. He sleeps in what was his garden at Rocky Mount, but no obituary stone records his name. A few trees which he planted in a spot that he cut in the fashion of a hanging garden, shade his grave. Col. Senf was a military engineer of considerable talent. The great works of this German engineer in our State are now little known. The bed of the Santee Canal is dry, and the very ruins of his arsenal and magazine on Rocky Mount have perished. If the proposed Rail road from Camden to Rocky Mount is built, the silence of the hills around his grave will be disturbed by the scream of the engine, a power little dreamed of in his day. Let a stone by placed under those trees to mark the spot where he rest away from home and kindred, the foreigner who helped us in our day of weakness and trials. Co[l]. Senf's grave is somewhere on what is now known as the "Sweat Place" the exact spot is known to few, if any, white persons in this community. (Note by M. Strange in 1934. The mention of Col. Senf's burying place on the last page was a part of the copy of Dr. Carlisle's article which was written many years before Mr. Ford's. Now many more years have slipped away since Mr. Ford's article [was] published and I suspect that Col. Senf's grave is now many feet under waters of the Power Company developed there in this generation.)[78]

How did foreign mercenary Senf gain the trust and confidence of Continental Army officers? It would seem that Americans would be distrustful of soldiers of fortune employed by the British. During the Revolutionary War, Americans also relied on foreign soldiers, some from European countries, but referred to them as "volunteers."[79] How did Senf overcome the barriers of being a foreign combatant? How did he climb through the ranks as a muster clerk to be tapped as an engineer on the other side? According to Eric Spall, "Despite the assertion that mercenaries were the tools of tyrants, Congress eagerly welcomed many of these foreign soldiers [as volunteers] into the Continental Army, and several of them, such as the Marquis de Lafayette of France, Baron Friedrich Wilhelm von Steuben of Prussia, and Count Casimir Pulaski of Poland, became American heroes."[80] If some Americans were dubious of these volunteer officers, how did they come to accept and revere a Hessian mercenary deserter such as Senf? How did Senf overcome any misgivings about his talents, ideologies, allegiances, and trustworthiness? Perhaps his known fluency in several European languages and facility in written English as early as 1780 helped with this. According to Spall, "Contrary to the expectations born of American antimercenary rhetoric, many America leaders based their objections to foreign soldiers on practical, not ideological, concerns. The language barrier posed an obvious problem to the use of foreigners in the Continental Army."[81] In a May 7, 1777, letter to John Adams, Nathanael Greene stated:

> I have no wish to see such a large [proportion] of important Offices in the Military department in the hands of foreigners. I cannot help considering them as so many Spies in our Camp ready to take their measure as their Interest may direct. If foreigners are introduced their command should not be very extensive then the injury cannot be great—but even in this case it is an injury to America, for the multiplying foreign Officers gives us no internal strength. A good Nursery of Officers taught by experience firmly attacht to the interest of the Country is a great security against foreign invaders.[82]

Perhaps a constellation of factors, including his willingness to learn, his innate technical skills, boundless energy, and enthusiasm, also played in Senf's favor. According to Spall, "The necessity of good engineers could trump all objections to the use of foreigners in the Continental Army," as America had produced few engineers of the same caliber as their European counterparts."[83]

Despite his foreign birth, Senf was an original member of the Society of the Cincinnati, the elite hereditary organization formed in May 1783 by Henry Knox, Friedrich von Steuben, George Washington, and others, which drew its membership from Continental Army officers.[84] Gen. William Moultrie formed the South Carolina chapter later that same year, as did many of the other original states. Alexander Moore described this organization as "a force of unity both with [South Carolina] and between the state and nation."[85] In the same way that the Society of the Cincinnati helped unify the country, the Santee Canal helped unify the state of South Carolina and paved the way for other internal improvements that benefited the nascent nation.

FOUR

Choosing the Santee Canal Route and Land Acquisition

The Santee Canal was the most prominent man-made feature of Santee Canal country in the first half of the 1800s. The canal's path affected every aspect of life for both planters and enslaved people. It created an avenue for planters to recover financially after the disruption of the American Revolution because of the more reliable market route to Charleston and caused the enslavement of more Africans to work cotton fields. The Santee Canal linked the Upstate and Santee Canal country's planters with the markets of the world since their goods went to Charleston for export. The environmental landscape changed as natural wetlands were converted to reservoirs for the canal and more land was cleared for cotton fields, requiring additional laborers.

Journals and letters of the planters and families indicated they supported the construction of the canal. In retrospect it is hard to find serious negative attributes to the construction of the Santee Canal at the time (apart from continued enslavement of Africans). It is interesting to contemplate what the social, cultural, and economic path of the land through which the Santee Canal passed would have evolved toward without the canal. Fortunately for the planters, the canal did not bring a shift to industrialization to Santee Canal country, and they were able to maintain their coveted plantation lifestyle while being connected to Charleston and the world.

EARLY HISTORY LEADING TO THE SANTEE CANAL

The origins of the Santee Canal date back to 1770, when surveyor James Cook wrote to Mr. Peter Timothy (1724–82), a local printer, proposing a canal between the Santee and Cooper Rivers: "The opening [of] a communication from *Santee* to *Cooper* river, by a navigable cut, is very practicable to be performed, and will be productive of infinite advantage to the community."[1] Cook's "Map of the Province of South Carolina" (1773) showed that he had a command of the countryside where a canal might be cut between the rivers (fig. 9.4).[2] Cook envisioned that the canal would be of great advantage to the state by carrying agricultural goods from the Upstate to Charles Town, including lumber sawed on numerous mills powered by the Santee and other rivers. "I have reckoned a hundred and twelve millseats on the navigable waters of the *Santee* river, above the cut, all situated next to the best of timber and rich lands." Cook even calculated that the 112 mills would produce in one day "eighty-nine thousand six hundred feet" of lumber, most being sent to Charles Town.[3]

Continuing interest for the connecting canal between the Santee and Cooper Rivers prompted surveyor and mapmaker Henry Mouzon Jr. (1741–1807) to produce in 1775 a map with five possible routes for a canal to connect the two rivers (fig. 4.1).[4] Route 1 on Mouzon's map went from Greenland Swamp through the South Branch of Biggin Swamp to the West Branch of the Cooper River at Stony Landing, twenty-three miles; route 2 went from Greenland Swamp through the North Branch of Biggin Swamp to the West Branch of the Cooper at Stony Landing, twenty-two miles; route 3 went from Mattasee Lake along Fair Forest Swamp (Wadboo or Watboo Creek by most sources) to the West Branch of the Cooper River, sixteen miles; route 4 went from Savannah Creek to Huger Creek, fourteen miles; and route 5 went from Santee Creek through Hell Hole Swamp to Huger Creek, a distance of fifteen miles. Huger Creek joins Quinby Creek to form the East Branch of the Cooper River. The West and East Branches join to form the Cooper River, which flows into Charles Town Harbor. All Mouzon's routes made extensive use of natural watercourses. Mouzon was not an engineer and probably had little knowledge of canal technology. Understandably he would have reasoned that the best routes for a connecting canal between the rivers would have made use of natural waterways—hence he chose the five routes he did. We shall see, however, that as canal technology improved, natural waterways were eschewed for overland routes with reservoirs and chambered locks.

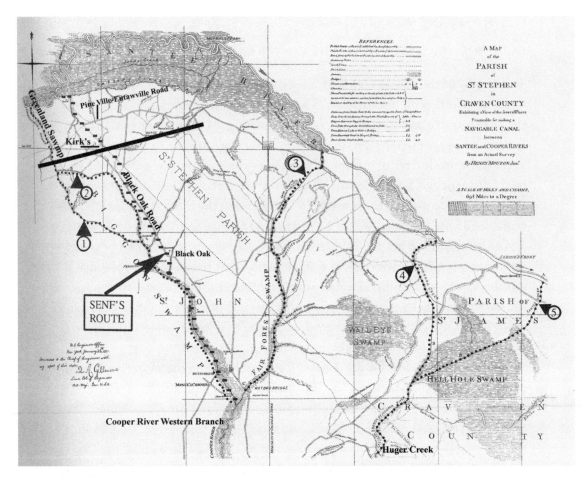

FIGURE 4.1. Henry Mouzon, "A Map of the PARISH of St. Stephen, in CRAVEN COUNTY, Establishing a View of the Several Places Practicable for making a NAVIGABLE CANAL between SANTEE and COOPER RIVERS." June 1771. As adapted by Sarah Prestemon for Kapsch, *Historic Canals and Waterways of South Carolina,* 23. Mouzon's map from US Senate, *Letter from the Secretary of War* (1881), was the basis for Prestemon's adaptation. Prestemon added Mouzon's five routes, labeled 1–5. Authors of this book added Greenland Swamp, Pine Ville–Eutawville Road, Kirk's, Black Oak, Black Oak Road, Huger Creek, Cooper River West Branch, and a black line, which is the approximate location of the ridge between the Santee and Cooper Rivers. Fair Forest Swamp is also known as Wadboo Creek.

All discussion of the connecting canal halted during the Revolution. With the Revolution over, interest in the connecting canal reemerged as one means for the state to recover financially. Charleston became the center from which planters and merchants ruled the state and province. It was like a city-state, the state's center of culture and economy. Growth in transportation and communi-

44 ⌒ THE SANTEE CANAL

cations was changing life in the new republic, and Charleston was at the center of these changes after the Revolution. The city was ideally situated to benefit significantly if only its harbor and citizens could be connected to the rest of the state. The great Santee drained the largest and most productive watersheds in the country. Two major rivers, the Wateree and Congaree, joined to form the Santee. The tributaries of the Wateree drained two-thirds of north central South Carolina and reached well into North Carolina. The tributaries of the Congaree (the Saluda, the Broad, and the Pacolet) reached the northwest section of the state. If the Santee and its tributaries could be joined with Charleston and overseas markets and trade, a statewide economic juggernaut would be created.

A meeting was held in Charleston on November 10, 1785, to discuss plans for a connecting canal. Governor William Moultrie presided over the meeting, which included seventeen other notable citizens. Participants endorsed a plan for opening communications between the Santee and Cooper Rivers by a canal and locks. They agreed to form a company consisting of one thousand shares and planned to issue subscription papers of one hundred shares each, to be filled as soon as possible.[5] A committee was appointed to receive subscriptions and prepare a petition on their behalf to be presented to the General Assembly, with much support for the proposed canal among Charleston business interests.

On February 7, 1786, a second meeting was held, where the participants presented to John Lloyd, president of the South Carolina Senate, and the Senate as a whole, a petition for the state legislature to charter a company to "wed the Santee and Cooper Rivers" with a canal that would join the waters of the state with Charleston. The petitioners assured that the subscriptions would soon be filled if the state would sanction the project.

On March 22, 1786, the South Carolina legislature passed "An Act to Establish a Company for the Inland Navigation from Santee to Cooper River," usually referred to as the Santee Canal Company. The following day the company held its first meeting, electing Moultrie as its president and John Rutledge as vice president.[6]

COLONEL SENF CHOSEN AS CHIEF ENGINEER

The first order of business for the Canal Company was to find a competent canal engineer to oversee the project. There were few engineers in South Carolina or the new republic in 1786. Canal engineering in America was almost unheard of at that time. In April 1786 Moultrie wrote to President Washington for help in finding an engineer.[7] Moultrie and other board members were under the impression that Washington was acquainted with a capable engineer named Brinley, a close relative of another illustrious English engineer, and wanted his help in acquiring Brinley to oversee the project. The "Brinley" Moultrie wrote of was James Brindley, nephew of the celebrated engineer of the same name, who had built the first commercially successful canal in England, the Bridgewater Canal. On May 25, 1786, Washington responded to Moultrie that the nephew Brindley was occupied indefinitely with the Susquehanna Company and would not be available for the Santee Canal. Washington was, however, able to obtain a loan of Brindley to come to South Carolina and advise them on the possibility of opening a canal between the rivers.[8] Moultrie wrote to Brindley on August 7, 1786, to arrange the trip, relating his understanding that "the Susquehanna Company have given you permission to be absent four months in the next winter, and that you have authorized Mr. Hughes to say that you will be in Charleston in December next. The board of directors have requested of me to urge your coming to South Carolina and give your opinion upon the possibility of opening the communication between Santee and Cooper Rivers."[9] By early 1787 Brindley was in South Carolina, apparently to consult on the canal, although there is no record of his meeting with any state or private officials concerning the canal.[10]

The earliest record of Senf's working on the canal is evident in a letter he wrote to the directors on April 2, 1787: "I have examined the Situations in and about Greenland Swamp, and I beg leave to recommend the same Course of the Canal, as I mentioned in my letter of the 16th January last except that on a nearer Survey, I find it necessary to carry the Canal as far as Mazÿck's Spring, before it will be advisable to join the creek in Biggin Swamp."[11] From this letter it appears that Senf was employed by the company before January 1887 if he had already done a survey of the canal's route. Since Brindley was in South Carolina in early 1787, Senf and Brindley could have met and discussed the proposed connecting canal. Brindley left Charleston on March 17, 1787.[12] Since Senf never stated in any of his letters or the Final Report that he met with Brindley and no archival record reports they met, we will never know what, if anything, Brindley contributed to the plan of the Santee Canal. But it is possible they met and discussed technical aspects of the canal's construction. This is all the historical record permits.

With the engineer chosen, the Canal Company turned again to securing financing. Senf's estimate for construction of the canal was £55,600.00

($233,000.00), a significant sum for an economically depressed state following the Revolution. The company met on April 22, 1791, and again on October 17 of the same year. A third meeting was held on January 10, 1792, by which time the company was better organized. The stockholders adapted rules for its operations. The company would issue one thousand shares. To subscribe to one share of the company would cost £5 ($21.45), and the subscriber agreed to pay an additional £5 twice a year until the canal was completed. In addition the president and directors had the authority to access an additional amount up to £5 twice a year if judged necessary. With the original cost of a share and the additional payments through 1800, total capitalization would be around £90,000.00, well in excess of the £55,000.00 estimated by Senf. We will see, however, the cost overruns over the life of the canal well exceeded the initial estimate. The company authorized lotteries and borrowed money to complete the canal but still never made a profit for its subscribers, even though they kept the canal open until 1853.

CHOOSING THE CANAL ROUTE

Construction of the canal was delayed until 1793. Since no records of the Santee Canal Company survive for this period, we have little knowledge of what was happening during these years from 1786 to 1793 besides arranging financing. Senf must have been active continuing his survey for a possible route and determining the levels along the route and where locks would be located. He wrote the canal's directors on April 2, 1787, about carrying the canal to Mazÿck's Spring and his plans for the reservoirs for the Summit Canal: "Kirk's Swamp (A) will serve as the first reservoir, into which the water from the second reservoir (B), at the head of Greenland Swamp, may be drawn, as occasion requires, by a drain (C)."[13]

Senf felt somewhat discouraged during this period, writing Gen. Thomas Sumter on January 3, 1790: "I find my zeal and few Abilities do not meet with that Incouragment [sic] I could, with honest pride, have expected—my too great confidence has exposed me to suffer Indignity—I thank God, that through the Interference of my friends I have been able to pary the Blow on my Reputation till this time."[14]

Despite his discouragement, however, he made progress with surveying the canal's route. Senf cited numerous reasons for not choosing any of Mouzon's five routes. First, he rejected the third, fourth and fifth routes, stating that using them, while opening up the possibility of inland routes connecting to

Georgetown and benefiting the lower Santee planters, would not have benefited planters higher up the Santee. He wrote on July 24, 1792, to the president of the company: "I presume it was not an idea at that time to assist, with this canal, the planting interest on the sea-coast, but to give the inhabitants of the up-country an opportunity to receive a reward for their industry, which would at the same time benefit the metropolis."[15] He stated that those routes involved a tedious and uncertain fifty-mile passage farther down the Santee River and that there was a better supply of water for a Summit Canal "in the upper to those in the lower." Proponents of starting the canal lower on the Santee pointed out that the land near Greenland Swamp was underlain by limestone and sand, which would cause leaking of the canal. Senf, however, pointed out that in Hell Hole Swamp, "limestone and sandy ground is not wanted at that place."[16] The lower route through Hell Hole Swamp had the same problem with a limestone and sand bed as did the routes higher up the Santee near Greenland Swamp, making both routes equal to that extent.[17]

In the July 24 letter, Senf wrote that "the original subscribers to the undertaking determined, and very justly in their subscription paper said, that the intended canal was to begin at or near Greenland Swamp."[18] Since Senf was in their employ, he must have felt some obligation to reject these routes lower down the Santee. The equality of the limestone and sand beds between the lower and upper routes made his decision technically defensible.

Senf wrote further that he wished he could have found a source of water for a summit canal higher up the Santee than Greenland Swamp to start the canal, which would have avoided more of the tedious and uncertain river passage. But there was none, so he started the canal at White Oak Landing, where he could secure water for a summit canal from Kirk's Swamp and later from Greenland Swamp and Bull Town Bay.

Senf appeared to have been a better judge of the canal's route than historians have given him credit for when he rejected Mouzon's route starting at Greenland Swamp. As canal technology improved in the country, the idea of using natural waterways and low swamplands for canal beds was seen as impractical and dismissed by canal builders. The reasons were evident to Senf. Natural waterways tended to flood when rivers that supplied their water reached flood stage, as often happened on the Santee, and they went dry during droughts. Both situations would have rendered Greenland Swamp (as well as routes 3–5) useless. Also storms blew down trees, clogging natural waterways, which required time and money to clear. No inland water route would have remained in operation continuously. Furthermore Mouzon's two routes using the natural watercourse of Greenland Swamp as the beginning of a connecting canal would also have had to contend with an elevated ridge to cross (figs. 4.1 and 5.21).[19] Senf had already determined that Kirk's Swamp was on "the dividing point," the top of the ridge between the Santee and the Cooper.[20] Any route starting on the Santee at or near Greenland Swamp had to cross the ridge, which would have necessitated a series of chambered locks to ascend it and then descend to the Cooper. And any route starting on the Santee in the general area of Greenland Swamp would have needed a reservoir at the summit, for which Senf concluded the terrain was not suitable for. Unlike the route chosen starting at White Oak Landing, a canal started at Greenland Swamp would have been excavated in swamp land, which would have been more costly and difficult. A canal starting at White Oak (fig. 4.2) at the beginning of Outside Creek would not have been as prone to flooding from the Santee as Greenland Swamp because it was five feet higher, and the reservoirs Senf crafted for a summit canal would have been reliable except in extreme droughts.

Senf could also draw upon technology already proven successful from the Canal de Briare and Canal du Midi in France, both summit-level canals (see chapter 5 for discussion of these canals). Senf more than likely knew about Canal de Briare and Canal du Midi; the latter, completed in 1681, was considered at the time one of the greatest construction works of the seventeenth century. Senf had spent time in Paris since he wrote to Thomas Jefferson from The Hague on September 27, 1784, stating that he wanted to examine the "Hedraulique works there" before the weather became too severe, and he wanted to get some credit in Paris as he wished "to draw on Governor Gerard [Guerard], Commodore Gillion, or any other of my friends in Charleston."[21] Although there is nothing evident in the archives that Senf was formally trained as a canal engineer, he must have had the skills, and with his knowledge of summit canal construction (perhaps learned in Europe), he was more than capable of constructing a summit-level canal connecting the two rivers.

Senf was very persuasive in his arguments to the board of directors, backing up his arguments for a summit-level canal starting at White Oak with substantial facts, and subsequently his route was approved. Choosing White Oak as a starting point meant that water for the Summit Canal had to be almost exclusively supplied by rain-fed reservoirs. Unfortunately Senf was without measurements of water flow that would have told him if there would be enough water in the reservoirs in extreme dry years for the canal to operate. The lack of this information would prove disastrous, since severe droughts closed the canal for three years. He depended on his survey levels of the surrounding

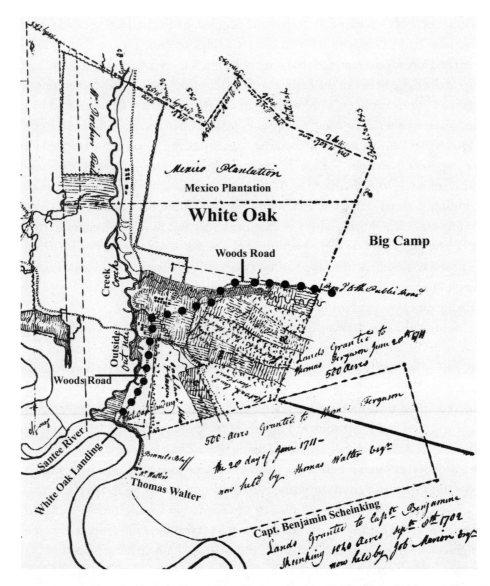

FIGURE 4.2. Plat of White Oak, ca. 1772, by Joseph Purcell. The plat of White Oak is in the Elias Ball Bull Papers, South Carolina Historical Society (call number 0376.00, box 22, 376.02 (H) 01.08.01), and in the Charleston Office of Deeds, McCrady Plats. This plat is very complicated, because the surveyor tried to show over the years how the land changed hands. The date of interest here is 1772, when Ralph Izard came into clear ownership of White Oak. The features of interest on the plat are ones Senf dealt with when he began construction. The plat was cropped to show only these land features. For clarity the authors reworded White Oak Landing, Out Side [Outside] Creek, White Oak, Big Camp, Thomas Walter, the woods road leading from the landing, Santee River, Mexico, and the property of Capt. Benjamin Scheinking, granted in 1702. Senf used the woods road as the path of the canal since it would have been free of trees, reducing the work required to excavate it. The woods road has been enhanced with black dots.

lands and information from locals on water flows in the general area, which proved unreliable during extreme droughts. In retrospect, however, we know reservoirs on any route starting near Greenland Swamp would have been dry during extreme droughts. Whether he would have chosen another starting route with more knowledge we will never know. The authors argue, however, that starting at White Oak was the best route no matter how much additional information Senf could have gathered. Field surveys by the authors and archival records indicate there were no sites besides Kirk's Swamp that could have adequately functioned as a primary reservoir for a route at or near Greenland Swamp.

Choosing White Oak as the starting point for the canal was not without controversy, at least according to one historian. Frederick Porcher suggested that Senf rejected the Greenland Swamp starting point to deny Mouzon credit and to claim it himself for choosing to start the canal at White Oak. Porcher also claimed that a White Oak starting point required a climb over a thirty-five-foot dry bluff through virgin oak-hickory forest, and tree removal would have increased the cost of construction (fig. 4.3). Porcher, writing years later (1875) on the history of the canal without the archival material available to historians today, claimed that if any one of Mouzon's five routes had been selected, the canal would not have dried up during the droughts of 1816 and 1818–19. Porcher, however, was wrong. All of Mouzon's routes, including Greenland Swamp, would have dried up during severe droughts and made a canal unusable. Later, Abram Blanding (see chapter 7) wrote from personal observations that Greenland Swamp was entirely dry during the droughts of 1816 and 1818–19.[22]

Porcher seems to have believed that had Greenland Swamp been used, vessels could have just passed from the Santee to the Cooper on an uninterrupted flow of water except for the extreme summit. He wrote: "It seems to me that if he had selected Greenland Swamp as his point of departure he would have had a navigable stream almost ready to his hands, and thereby making as direct a line as possible to Biggin Swamp, he would for the greater part of his line have had water flowing from perennial springs, and would have had, if not a shorter summit level to overcome, at least it would have been that level alone which would have been absolutely dependent upon reservoirs."[23] Again Porcher was in error. Mouzon's Greenland Swamp route had to cross the same ridge as did Senf's White Oak route, necessitating at least three locks to climb the ridge, and the same number that Senf employed to reach the level of the Cooper River from the summit. There were not sufficient springs along the Greenland Swamp routes to keep the canal flooded without depending on reservoirs and

FIGURE 4.3. Oak-hickory forest, Santee Canal environs, 2020. An oak-hickory forest similar to this would have been in the path of much of Senf's overland route. Photograph by Richard Dwight Porcher Jr.

locks. And the summit level reservoirs would have been dry during extreme droughts.

It is worth noting that Frederick Porcher never met Senf, so his opinion of Senf's "inordinate vanity" is somewhat suspect. No references have been found that described Senf with anything but respect for him as a gentleman and praise for his engineering skills. He was a founding member of the St. John's Hunting Club in 1800, organized by the planters of St. John's as their elite social club. Richard Porcher knows well the history of the club and does not believe the club would have let someone like the vain person so described to serve as a founding member.

Frederick Porcher also suggested that Ralph Izard, who owned White Oak and was well connected to directors of the Canal Company, persuaded Senf to start there. Izard apparently envisioned a trading post or town at White Oak to his financial benefit.[24] We may never know for certain. We have already referenced that the original subscribers intended the canal to begin at or near Greenland Swamp, presumably since they were aware of the burgeoning plantation culture of Middle St. John's and the value of the canal running through these prosperous plantations. A starting point at White Oak would have satisfied the original dictates of the subscribers.

During research for this book, the authors found no compelling archival material that supports Porcher's (or anyone else's) view that Senf was influenced by Izard or any other planters or merchants in choosing White Oak Landing for the starting point on the Santee River. Bennett and Richardson found that the canal's route "touched on the property of only five people directly involved in the company's operation over a period of fifty-five years."[25] Further, Senf would have had no problem with Izard planning a town at White Oak, and he even put the proposed town on his General Plan.[26]

The authors argue that Senf considered all possible options, read the landscape, considered the alternatives, and chose White Oak Landing as the route with the best possible chance for success, especially for obtaining surface water resources for the Summit Canal. Except for the drought years, the Santee Canal worked just like Senf planned. We argue he was influenced in his choice of the route above the lower Santee only by the technical aspects of building the canal and by having a reading or understanding—though later shown to be somewhat suspect—of the land along his proposed route.

History has validated Senf's route. Choosing a route through Greenland Swamp or other natural watercourses would have been more unreliable than his overland route starting at White Oak. Freshets in the Santee River, which happened more often than severe droughts, would have made a canal starting at Greenland Swamp unusable for extended periods. At the same time, Senf knew that the five-foot higher elevation at White Oak would reduce freshets flooding the canal. The upland route was the better choice. Senf planned his route well, making certain he had ample watersheds and reservoirs for holding water for the Summit Canal.

LAND ACQUISITION FOR THE CANAL ROUTE AND SUPPORT OF OPERATIONS

Land acquisition was critical to the success of the Santee Canal. Land that held lowlands that could be made into reservoirs was the main target for acquisition.

Senf knew well before construction started which tracts of land along the canal route would provide the necessary surface reservoirs of water and mapped his plans accordingly for land acquisition. Land was also needed to raise crops to feed the workforce, obtain lumber for construction, mine stone and clay, and provide numerous other supplies needed for what amounted to operating a large plantation. Senf included these acquisitions in his General Plan, which served not only as a plan of action to acquire the necessary lands but also as a historical document. Even after the canal was completed and Senf had left its employment, the Canal Company continued to buy lands as allowed by its charter that would provide additional water resources.

The Canal Company acquired land by exchanging with landowners parcels it owned, purchasing them outright, and claiming vacant lands, all three methods allowed by its charter. Even before the first tree was felled and the first shovel of soil moved, Senf was active in land acquisition. Unfortunately the archival record is not complete for all the land acquisitions or exchanges since records were lost over the years. There are enough records, however, to understand Senf's major acquisition goals as well as acquisitions by the company after Senf left its employment in 1803.

Henry Ravenel created a detailed plat showing the lands that had been acquired by the Canal Company at the Santee end of the canal in 1825 (fig. 4.4). Ravenel labeled the plat "Plan Exhibiting the Shape, Size and Situation of 12 Tracts of Land Owned by the Canal Company containing 5,684 1/2 Acres." The plat details land acquisitions by the Canal Company from the Santee River to Ray's below Frierson's Lock. This plat was not available to researchers prior to this book. Unfortunately the section along the Santee River with White Oak (1) and Big Camp (2) is missing. The plat is fragile and difficult to read since it has faded with age. Still it identifies most lands in the Pine Ville area acquired by the Canal Company during its existence. The legend concerning the twelve tracts on the plat reads as follows:

> No. 1 was purchased from Ralph Izard Esq. at different times and contains 404 acres.
> No. 2 was exchanged by Mr. Deveaux in 1822 for the Part A originally part of Lynah's Tract No. 4.
> No. 3 was called Foxhall, purchased from Jeremiah Candy 27 Sept 1794.
> No. 4 was purchased from Dr. James Lynah 15 March 1804.
> No. 5 was purchased from Mrs. Margaret Sinkler and James B. Richardson 25 May 1805.

No. 6 was purchased from Sheriff of Charleston District as the property of Mrs. Susannah Moreland 1 Apr 1805.

No. 7 was purchased from Mrs. Margaret Sinkler and James B. Richardson 25 May 1805.

No. 8 was exchanged by Mr. Glendkemp for the Part B originally part of Lynah's Tract No. 4.

No. 9 is a Tract of Vacant Land and contains 298 1/2 acres.

No. 10 from the Est. of Mrs. Hardcastle and contains 609 Acres.

No. 11 called Frierson's was purchased from T. Ford Esq. 18 April 1805 and contains 596 acres.

No. 12 is a Tract of Vacant Land called Weare's and contains 1897 acres.

The lands acquired by the Canal Company will be discussed in order from the Santee River to the end of the canal at Cooper River. The tracts under discussion can be seen on Ravenel's plat (fig. 4.4) and Senf's General Plan (fig. E3). There is no record for some of the lands acquired, so there are gaps in the company's land ownership.

The authors note that over the years property lines were not static. A tract was purchased and added to another, and the added tract's name was no longer used. Or tracts were divided, and new names were applied to the divided tracts. The property lines of Mexico are most difficult to ascertain for any one time because the Porchers (Samuel and William Mazÿck) kept adding to and trading parts of Mexico. When ownership of a tract of land changed, the tract was subsequently referred to on plats by the new owner's name, although it was the same tract. Pooshee is most often simply referred to by its name; Senf, however, referred to it as "Rene Ravenel," the owner. The authors tried to sort out some of the confusing entities on the plats used in this book.

White Oak (404 acres) was one of the most important tracts the Canal Company acquired, since it was the site of the starting point of the canal. Figure 4.2 shows White Oak in 1772 before work began on the canal. Authors were not able to find the exact date White Oak was obtained by the Canal Company. Ravenel's plat said that White Oak was purchased from Ralph Izard, Esq., at different times and contained 404 acres. Locks 1 and 2, two lockkeepers' houses, a dry dock, mill, and numerous other support facilities were situated on White Oak (fig. 5.9).

The next major acquisition was originally called Fox Hall (200 acres, no. 3 on Ravenel's plat), purchased by the company from Jeremiah Candy on September 27, 1794. On Senf's General Plan, Fox Hall is number 4. Fox Hall was

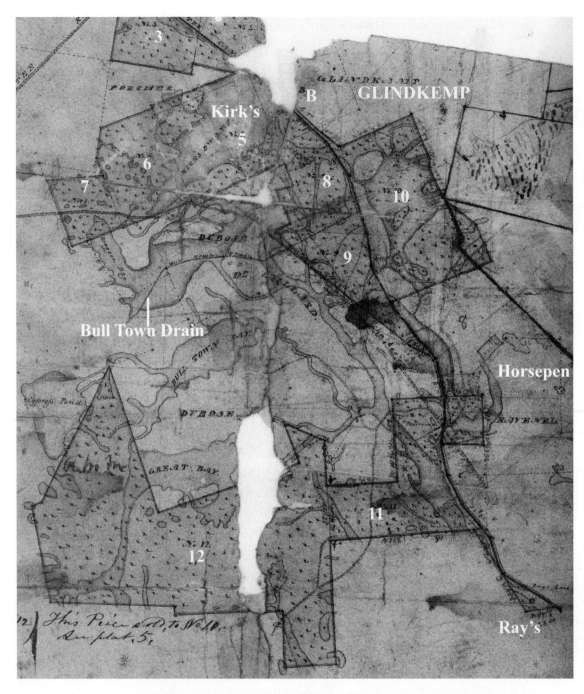

FIGURE 4.4. Henry Ravenel, "Plan Exhibiting the Shape, Size and Situation of 12 Tracts of Land Owned by the Santee Canal Company Containing 5,684 1/2 Acres." 1825. Courtesy of Theodore Keith Gourdin of Pineville, South Carolina. Keith inherited the plat from his father, but he does not know how his father came into possession of it. Copy in the personal archives of Richard Dwight Porcher Jr. The information

renamed Big Camp and became the main settlement for the Santee Canal Company's employers and laborers (fig. 4.5). The director's house, the overseer's house, the main support facilities for construction and maintenance of the canal, and the double lock at the beginning of the Summit Canal were located at Big Camp. There were numerous other structures present that were not shown on the plat: brick kilns, a blacksmith shop, housing for workers, and so forth.

FIGURE 4.4. (*continued*) on land acquisition on the Ravenel plat is different from the coverage of land acquisition detailed by other authors. Because the Ravenel plat has not been available to previous historians, the authors of this book suggest that it is the most reliable archival material to document land acquisition. Authors have added the numbers of the tracts corresponding to the numbers in the legend on the plat as well as other identifying features. The plat is cropped, and the accompanying legend is included in the text.

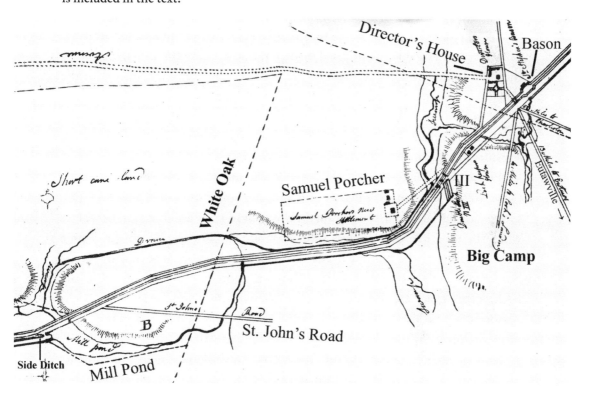

FIGURE 4.5. Section of plat of White Oak/Big Camp, ca. 1800. Courtesy of South Carolina Historical Society, Elias Ball Bull Papers (call number 376.02 (H) 01.08.01, box 22). There is no date or surveyor on the plat. Authors cropped the section with Big Camp and added Big Camp, White Oak, Director's House, Lock III, St. Stephen's Basin, Samuel Porcher's New Settlement (Mexico), Mill Pond, Side Ditch to Millrace, Road to Eutawville, and St. John's Road.

Choosing the Santee Canal Route and Land Acquisition ~ 57

Adjacent to Fox Hall was land owned by Dr. James Lynah, a native of Ireland, who attended to a large medical practice. The Canal Company purchased his tract on March 15, 1804. This tract is number 5 on Senf's General Plan and number 4 on Ravenel's plat, but it is mostly missing and labeled "Lynah" on the plat by the authors.

Glendkamp (Glindkamp) was adjacent to Lynah's tract.[27] It was once part of the Lynah tract, but we were unable to determine when it was cut off as tract B. According to the Ravenel plat of 1825 (fig. 4.4), Henry Glindkamp exchanged his ownership of number 8 to the Santee Canal Company for this tract. The tract also goes as Glen Camp and Pine Hill.

Tracts 5, 6 and 7 gave the company control of Kirk's Swamp, which became the Great Reservoir for the Summit Canal. According to Ravenel's legend, all three were purchased in 1805. This raises an interesting question: Why did the Canal Company wait until after the canal was opened in 1800 to purchase these tracts? The same question arises for other tracts that were purchased after the canal opened. Possibly the original incorporation act gave the Canal Company the right under eminent domain to use the necessary support lands with the understanding these lands would be purchased later.

Tract number 9 was vacant land containing 298.5 acres. No date was given for the acquisition, but it was a valuable tract since it bordered the canal for a considerable distance.

Pierce's Old Field (no. 10 on Ravenel's plat and 627 acres) shows on Senf's General Plan adjacent to the Santee Canal and south of Glen Camp (fig. E3). Elizabeth Clevland Hardcastle bought the tract in 1797, and it was in her estate when she died in 1808.[28] It was sold at public auction in 1822 to the Santee Canal Company, the highest bidder at $319.77, a valuable acquisition since it bordered the canal. A survey in 1859 shows that the tract belonged to Carlisle Richardson. It appears on later plats as "Richardson." More than likely Richardson bought it from the Canal Company after the canal closed in 1853. This property lies today mostly under the waters of Lake Moultrie.

Senf's third reservoir was Bull Town Bay. Ravenel's plat does not show its purchase. Bennett and Richardson state that the Canal Company purchased Philip Gadsden's tract in Bull Town Bay and later purchased lands of DuBose. With the DuBose purchase, the company owned the entire bay.[29] Ravenel's plat shows DuBose owning two tracts in Bull Town Bay, and Dr. Gaillard is shown owning one tract in Bull Town. Did Bennett and Richardson read the plats incorrectly and substitute Gadsden for Gaillard? Or did Gadsden purchase the tract from Gaillard before it was bought by the company? The Canal Company ultimately purchased all of Bull Town Bay for its third reservoir.

The Canal Company purchased Frierson's (no. 11 on Ravenel's plat), which contained 596 acres, from T. Ford Esq. on April 18, 1805. The tract bordered Frierson's Lock (fig. 5.23) and a smaller reservoir formed by damming Horsepen Swamp.

Weare's (no. 12 on Ravenel's plat), containing 1,897 acres, was vacant land purchased by the Canal Company. No date is available for this purchase.

In 1805 the company obtained 190 acres from Peter Ray Esq. (see the General Plan, figs. E3 and 4.4). This tract is number 16 on Senf's General Plan. The Santee Canal passes through the Ray tract, giving the company the canal and environs.

On March 27, 1819, the company received tract B from Maj. Samuel Porcher and gave Porcher tract A owned by the company (fig. 5.8). Because both tracts are so small, it is not certain why the exchange was made. The exchange was made well after the canal was open, showing that land acquisitions or exchanges continued after 1800.

No other lands along the canal's route were owned by the Canal Company until the purchase of Hope owned by the Simpson family (fig. E3). Lock number 10, called Hope Lock or Simpson's Lock, was located at Hope. Hope was identified as number 29 on the General Plan. According to Senf's letter to the Santee Canal Company directors dated November 11, 1800, he had not obtained title to all the land needed at Hope: "The lands reserved for canal use are sufficient for the requisite building, but the grounds for the pasturage of the horses or mules which must be stationed here to draw the boats is not marked out yet on the plans."[30] Simpson's basin and warehouse were located at Hope, as well as a water-powered mill, tollhouse, lockkeeper's house, pasture to keep horses and/or mules for towing, and a proposed village, which never materialized. Hope was the last recorded tract owned by the company along the canal's route from the Santee to the Cooper Rivers.

FIVE

Construction of the Santee Canal
THE WEDDING OF TWO RIVERS

The American Revolution and 1790 depression took its toll on the plantations of Middle St. John's and the adjacent English Santee.[1] Plantations in 1792 were at their lowest point of profitability. Indigo as a crop was greatly reduced because of the loss of the English bounty and market during the Revolution. Commercial rice production was minimal because the war years left the fields unattended, weeds had taken over the fields, and banks and water control structures had deteriorated to a point that it was not economically feasible to restore the fields. Commercial production of Santee long-staple cotton was just beginning, however, and planters would benefit from the canal as a convenient venue for their cotton to reach the Charleston markets. The more secure market also increased the value of their plantation lands. In the meantime, before construction could begin, Senf needed a labor force. Planters were more than willing to lease their idle enslaved workers to the Canal Company. René Ravenel of Pooshee recorded in his diary on January 1, 1796: "My Negroes return'd home from the Santee Canal after working three years," a period that must have rewarded him handsomely.[2] Samuel DuBose wrote about the planters leasing their enslaved workforce:

> Everyone availed himself to a greater or lesser extent of this opportunity of hiring their negroes; for men they received thirty and for women twenty pounds sterling per annum, besides their food. At times a thousand laborers were employed in this work, which was seven years in being completed. The enterprise, which was disastrous to those who had embarked in it, rescued a large number of planters from ruin.[3]

This was the situation in Santee Canal country in the early years of construction of the Santee Canal. Construction of the canal was no easy task—either in time, labor, or technology. Construction began in May 1793, seven years after incorporation of the Santee Canal Company, the seven years being devoted to planning, surveying, and obtaining financing. No on-site work on the canal was conducted from 1786 until 1793, or at least no record of what might have been done in the field during this period survives, since many records of the Canal Company have not surfaced.

Planters with lands along the canal route initially had concerns about the project. They feared their enslaved workers might use the canal as a means of escape or be influenced by passersby to commit depredations against the planters. The authors found no reports of any enslaved workers trying to escape while working on the canal or committing depredations. Senf, however, in his Final Report, stated there were twenty-eight runaways among seven hundred workers, so this was a problem he encountered in keeping a full workforce, albeit not a serious one.[4]

Only one lawsuit objecting to the canal's passage through or near a planter's land was found in the archives consulted, certainly not proof of widespread objection. The planter sued the Canal Company over the death of his enslaved workers killed by a lightning strike while working on the canal, but he was not suing in objection to the presence of the canal. In the end construction of the canal (and the introduction of long-staple cotton) saved many planters from financial ruin, and they ultimately welcomed its construction.

The canal was completed in 1800, seven years after construction started. That so short a canal (twenty-two miles) required seven years to complete reveals the difficulties of canal construction and technology in early American rural areas. Senf faced many problems. Constructing a canal like the Santee Canal through Lowcountry swamps, forested uplands, and waterways was no small endeavor. Heat and disease, especially malaria, took its toll. Malaria was a serious problem, since the route went through and next to swamps and abandoned rice fields, sites that breed mosquitoes, the vector of the illness. Twenty-four white people died from malaria, including two physicians. Enslaved workers died also, but no records of their deaths survive. Malaria made it hard to recruit skilled white tradesmen for summer work, a main time for construction.

No details were too small for Senf's attention. For example, he stated: "I have not marked on the Plans the quantity of lands reserved for the use of the Lock-keepers. There are near every lock small Slips of Land of little or no use to the Proprietors of the Land and will answer the purpose of the Lock-keepers to cultivate when obtained by Consent of the Owners."[5]

To ensure the canal operated as he planned, Senf drafted a series of guidelines that covered the role of the lockkeepers, keeping tradesmen employed by the company for infrastructure maintenance, care for the horses and mules, rules for the vessels to follow in transit, and keeping a staff of enslaved persons for labor.

Senf did his best to ensure planters were not inconvenienced with canal construction and operation. Planters along the canal lost a small quantity of land but received a safe and convenient passage for their goods to Charleston. In return for cutting off a few acres of Woodboo's rice fields, he made certain the canal bank would protect Woodboo's rice fields from freshets, while the fields would still receive water from Big Spring. Since the canal cut off its water supply from Big Spring, Senf arranged for Charles Johnston's Oakfield to receive surplus water from the canal during dry seasons through a floodgate. Owners of swampland near the Great Reservoir would receive just compensation if their lands were overflowed. And Senf reasoned that the lands of Samuel Porcher and Ralph Izard became more valuable as the canal gave an outlet to Charleston, just compensation for the loss of a few acres to the canal.

But there were issues with planters Senf had to contend with. When Daniel Ravenel III, Secondus of Wantoot, was informed by Senf that he would arrive at his rice mill on a certain date in July with a force of laborers to cut through Somerton Canal (see the General Plan for location of the rice machine) to construct a section of the Santee Canal, Ravenel sent a reply that he would be there, armed to protect his property. On the appointed day, Ravenel was at his mill as promised. Senf wisely postponed the cutting until a later date after Somerton Canal was cut, the law giving the Canal Company the right-of-way by proper process. Senf did arrange for Ravenel to flood his rice fields from the Santee Canal through an aqueduct, so Ravenel continued to grow rice.[6]

Senf was a superb engineer, and for more than seven years he and workers struggled through heat and storms, winter quagmires, labor problems, and summer fevers, overcoming all obstacles and making the Santee Canal a reality—but at what human cost? We may never know.

NEW ROME COMES TO SANTEE CANAL COUNTRY

The Santee Canal was the first summit canal in the new republic; it was not, however, the first summit canal in the world.[7] The authors argue that summit canal technology was well-known in Europe a hundred years prior to the Santee Canal. Senf certainly would have known of the Canal de Briare and Canal du Midi, both summit-level canals in France completed before he began construction of the Santee Canal. To craft the Santee Canal, he took existing summit-level technology and modified and tweaked it to conform to the physical landscape between the Santee and Cooper Rivers. He employed the water source of his canal to run a water mill, just like Pierre-Paul Riquet did on the Canal du Midi. That canal featured a horse path for pulling barges and side ditches along the exterior to carry excess water away from the canal, both features employed by Senf. Virtually all the major design elements of the Santee Canal are found in the Canal de Briare and Canal du Midi. At the same time, Senf added new or revised technology in his design. The history of technological achievement has always been based on existing technology, with others that follow adding their own improvements and adaptations. Senf did the same with the Santee Canal.

Canal de Briare

The Canal de Briare in France was initiated by Maximilien de Béthune, duc de Sully, with support from Henry IV, to develop grain trade and reduce food shortages. The first major summit canal built in Europe, it was hailed as an engineering triumph of its day. Construction started in 1604. The canal connected the Loire and Seine valleys. After Henry IV's assassination in 1610, work was halted in 1611. It began again in 1638, and the canal was completed in 1642, 158 years before the Santee Canal's completion in 1800. For centuries it was a lifeline for Paris, bringing food, timber, and coal to the capital by barge from the upper Loire and Allier valleys. By the mid-eighteenth century, more than five hundred barges were in use transporting wines.

The Canal de Briare was the protype for all French summit canals. It was also the first canal constructed at summit level using "pound locks," which feature a chamber with gates at either end to control the height of the water within. Before then locks were created with a single gate. The canal employed twelve locks on its rise and twenty-four on its fall. From Briare to Buges, it rose 135 feet from the River Loire over a ridge via the first twelve locks and then fell 279 feet via the next twenty-four locks to the River Seine. The canal was thirty-five miles long. Several artificial reservoirs were created to feed water into the locks. At the most precipitous location, Rogny, it was necessary to build a "staircase" of seven locks in order to navigate the fall of the canal. While it was without a doubt an outstanding feat of engineering, the staircase design caused huge holdups, as each vessel had to navigate all seven locks before the next was able to pass through. In the end the staircase of locks was abandoned, and the canal was rerouted to bypass them.

Canal du Midi

The Canal du Midi is a 150-mile-long summit canal in Southern France.[8] Originally named the Canal Royal en Languedoc, it was renamed by French revolutionaries as the Canal du Midi in 1789.[9] The canal is considered one of the greatest technical constructions of the seventeenth century. Like the Canal de Briare, it is a summit-level canal, passing over a mountain range between two water courses. It starts at Toulouse on the Atlantic Ocean and ends at the Mediterranean Sea at the port of Sète, a length of 150 miles. Along its route it crosses over the Seuil de Naurouze, the highest point (620 feet above sea level) of the canal. The Seuil de Naurouze was the watershed point identified by Pierre-Paul Riquet when he designed and built the canal. Water falling on the western side of the Seuil de Naurouze flows to the Atlantic Ocean, and water falling on the eastern side flows to the Mediterranean Sea.

The building of a canal to connect the Atlantic Ocean and the Mediterranean Sea was an old idea. Numerous and sometimes utopian projects were devised to build the connecting canal. The construction of a connection would save vessels of trade and the king's galleys from sailing around the Iberian Peninsula, which could take a month to complete. At that time ocean shipping was fraught with dangers, such as piracy and storms. Proposed projects were presented to the king in the sixteenth century. A first draft was presented in 1539, a second in 1598, and finally a third draft was proposed in 1617. These projects were abandoned because they did not give enough thought to the water supply for the canal, and a system for diversion of water from Pyrenees rivers was too complex or impossible to implement. In addition there was a fear of losing too much money and conviction of the human possibility to dig the canal. The major problem always remained: how to supply the summit sections with enough water to operate locks. This is the same issue that would confront Senf with the Santee Canal.

Riquet, a wealthy tax collector in Languedoc, proposed a more convincing project than his predecessors. Riquet, Baron of Bonrepos, was born in Béziers in 1604. He was responsible for collecting taxes on salt and thus gathered a considerable self-fortune that financed the canal. When Louis XIV received his proposal through the Archbishop of Toulouse in 1662, he saw the opportunity to deprive Spain of part of its resources and to mark his reign with an imperishable work. Riquet's plan solved the problem of obtaining the water supply at the summit to operate the locks. His obsessive vision led him to invest in a project that left its mark on his life and on the landscape and economy of France.

The Canal du Midi was a masterpiece of engineering. Work began in 1667 and was completed in 1681, 119 years before completion of the Santee Canal. For more than 15 years, almost twelve thousand workers were involved in digging the canal cut with pickax and shovel, a 150-mile route between Toulouse and Sète. The care that its creator, Pierre-Riquet, took in its design and the way it blended with its surroundings turned a technical achievement into a work of art that stands today. The diagram of the lock shows the detail of Riquet's engineering and understanding of the lay of the land traversed by the canal (fig. 5.1).

FIGURE 5.1. Locks on Languedoc Canal (Canal du Midi) in France. Note the angled gates (c) constructed to resist the water pressure in the lock chamber and the beams (b) used to open the lock gates. The same method was followed in the locks of the Santee Canal a century later. This sketch was first published in Denis Diderot's 1751 *Encyclopedie.*

Construction of the Santee Canal ~ 65

OVERVIEW OF CHRISTIAN SENF'S FINAL REPORT

The entire route of the Santee Canal as depicted in Senf's General Plan was outstanding in its detail. Senf outlined the main features of the canal in his Final Report. Since the canal was to be a summit-level canal with reservoirs to supply water, it was necessary to conserve as much reservoir water as possible to have an adequate supply during droughts. Consequently Senf designed a canal with diminutive dimensions (fig. 5.2). The canal was thirty-five feet wide at the surface and five-and-a-half feet deep, with four feet of water and twenty feet of usable water width for vessels. The locks were nine and a half feet to ten feet wide with sixty feet between the lock gates. Some locks were extended to sixty-six feet to allow for larger vessels. The small size of the locks would play out in the future when the canal could not compete with larger steam vessels on rivers. But Senf could not see into the future, so he constructed his locks and canal size on the small side to conserve water. In his Final Report, Senf wrote:

> The canal is twenty two Miles long—thirty-five feet wide, five feet and a half deep, four feet water, and a Drawpath, ten feet wide, on each side—and has two double—and Eight [seven] single—Locks—two large and two smaller Basons with Warehouses, Eight Aqueducts of different Size for small Streams of water to pass under the Bed of the Canal.
>
> The boats which navigate the canal carry from 20 to 22 tons and are drawn by horses. The boats rise, in a distance of 2 1/2 miles from Santee River to the Summit Canal, by two single and one double lock, 34 feet.

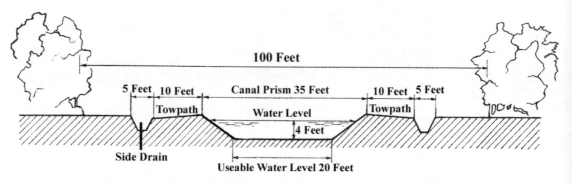

FIGURE 5.2. Santee Canal profile. This illustration by William Robert Judd is based on field studies of the extant sections of the canal and Senf's Final Report.

66 — THE SANTEE CANAL

The Summit Canal is 5 miles long, and is supplied from reservoirs and springs. The first reservoir lies higher than the canal and is 400 yards wide and 2,200 yards long. From the Summit Canal the boats descend, in a distance of 12 1/2 miles, by six single and one double lock, 69 feet, to the tide-water in Biggin Creek at Stoney's [Stony] Landing, which forms the head of the Cooper River. Stoney's [Stony] Landing is, by land, 33 miles from Charleston and may be 50 miles by water. Coasting vessels of considerable burden navigate as far as this point.

Over every lock of the canal is a bridge 16 feet wide, besides seven public and private communication bridges, without a single draw or turning bridge.

For a supply of water for the canal and to discharge the surplus water, there are in its whole length twenty-five flood-gates and overfalls. The locks, abutments, and walls of the bridges, and flood-gates are all built of brick and stone.[10]

Senf's water control for the canal has not been fully addressed by historians. He ingeniously created reservoirs and side ditches; built side chambers on locks to conserve water; used natural watercourses; cut off bends in Biggin Creek to make more direct routes and increased sediment removal; used the banks along the canal for "turning off from the canal the rain-water, particularly where the canal is cut deep";[11] incorporated springs for water; and constructed floodgates, overfalls, aqueducts, and a wing dam, all to ensure the canal had water. His system only failed during extreme droughts. At all other times his design adequately supplied water for the locks. Numerous examples of his water-control systems are still present in the two sections of the canal that were not flooded by Lake Moultrie in 1942 (see chapter 9).

There were eleven masterly crafted locks: two double locks, eight single locks, and the Tide Lock. The double locks and single locks were all made of locally formed brick and stone, with wooden gates, while Tide Lock was made of earth-filled wood cribbing, with brick and stone abutments at each end. A sixteen-foot-wide bridge passed over every lock except Tide Lock, allowing local passage across the canal. Seven additional public and private communication bridges crossed the canal. Locks 2 through 10 were ten feet wide and sixty-six feet long, enabling the passage of vessels fifty-six feet long and nine feet wide. The Guard Lock at the Santee entrance was seventeen feet wide and seventy-two feet long to allow larger river vessels to enter the canal. The river entrance leading to the Guard Lock was one hundred feet wide to allow ferry boats to lay in without interrupting navigation. The ferry system Senf planned, however, never materialized (see chapter 9). Tide Lock, at the entrance to Biggin Creek, was also seventeen feet wide and seventy-two feet long (fig. 5.38). White Oak Lock (not flooded by the Santee Cooper Project) is the only lock in which the brickwork survives in reasonable condition. No wooden structures survive except portions of the gates found preserved underwater at Tide Lock. At White Oak Lock (fig. 5.11) and from the photograph of Black Oak Lock (fig. 5.29), one can still see and appreciate the detail of the locks' brick construction.

Four basins, Santee, St. Stephen's, Black Oak, and Biggin, provided sites where wagons from surrounding farms and plantations could bring goods to be loaded onto or unloaded from the canal vessels. Turning basins were constructed, where larger vessels could pull out of the way so the smaller canal vessels could pass. Senf constructed two dry basins (dry docks in today's terms) where vessels could be repaired (figs. 5.8 and 5.15).

Seven brick aqueducts allowed natural watercourses to flow under the canal (figs. 5.27 and 5.28). There were towpaths ten feet wide on both sides of the canal chamber for mules and horses (fig. 5.16).[12] The towpaths were carried across the aqueducts (fig. 5.28).

The first three locks enabled traffic to negotiate a rise of thirty-four feet from the Santee River to the five-mile-long Summit Canal; the next seven locks negotiated a fall of sixty-nine feet to the Cooper River (fig. 5.3). Tide Lock was at the level of the Cooper River at high tide. It took a vessel about half an hour to pass through a single lock and two days to pass through the canal.

There were twenty-five floodgates and overfalls placed along the entire length of the canal. No floodgates or overfalls have survived in the sections of

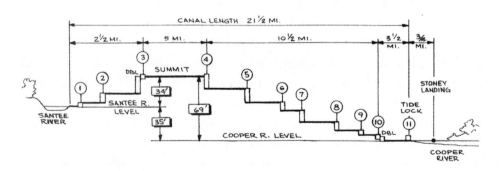

FIGURE 5.3. Elevation profile of the Santee Canal. Illustration by William Robert Judd.

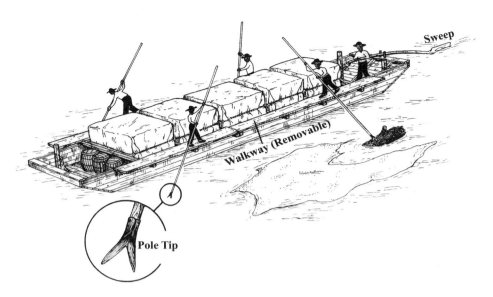

FIGURE 5.4. Canal vessel. In this sketch the boat is depicted in the river as evidenced by the poles, which would not have been allowed in the canal for fear of damaging the canal chamber. Each pole was supplied with a wrought iron tip for traction. Note the sloped ends of the vessel. The sweep was laid aside when the vessel entered the canal since steering was not necessary. The walkways were removed to allow vessels to pass through the locks. Illustration by William Robert Judd.

the canal not flooded by the lake. Side ditches were strategically placed along the outside to drain off excess water (fig. 5.8) and to pass water into the canal, while the banks created with fill from digging the canal prevented outside rainwater from flowing in. There were numerous warehouses and lockkeepers' houses (figs. 5.30 and 5.31), two toll receivers, and other support buildings along the route. At White Oak Lock there was a mill powered by water carried by a ditch alongside the canal to the mill (fig. 5.9). A similar mill was built at Hope Lock.

The first three locks of the canal and a short distance past the Great Reservoir lay in St. Stephen's Parish; from this point locks 4 through 10 lay in Middle St. John's Parish (fig. E3). The segment from Hope Lock to the Cooper River, including Tide Lock, lay in Lower St. John's Parish.

Canal vessels were specially constructed nine feet wide and fifty-four feet long to fit within the lock. Two sketches of a canal vessel have been found in the archives, one depicted by Andrew Gibbes's sketch of Black Oak Lock (fig. 5.30) and the other in Charles Fraser's *A Bason and Storehouse Belonging to the Santee Canal* (fig. 5.36). The vessel diagram depicted in figure 5.4 is based on these two sketches and excavations at Tide Lock.

Construction of the Santee Canal ~ 69

Some canal boats were constructed so they could be reused. The two visible side planks were shifted, that is, butt joints of one row of planks were centered on the plank below, increasing side strength. The ends and sides were tapered. The tapering profile and sturdy construction added credence to Frederick Porcher's assertion that some vessels were reused. On a return journey, one vessel could be nested on top of the other so that they might make a return journey as one vessel—thus paying only one toll.[13] These sturdy vessels were called *cotton boats* to distinguish them from other types of vessels. Vessels not intended to be used again were dismantled for their wood once reaching Charleston and were not as refined as other vessels.

OPERATION OF A TYPICAL LOCK ON SANTEE CANAL

The diagram of the lock in figure 5.5 demonstrates how Senf's ten chambered locks operated and does not necessarily represent any one of the eleven locks. The locks were the most prominent technological feature of the Santee Canal. Although there are discernible differences in their structure, they all functioned basically the same (except Tide Lock). When a vessel approached from the lower canal to be raised to the next level, the double gates of the lower canal were opened, and the vessel (1 in diagram) entered the empty lock chamber (2). Water in the upper canal had been kept out of the lock chamber by the angled gates (fig. 5.5b). Attendants pushed on the beams attached to the lower canal gates to close them against a sill, making the chamber watertight. The lower gates were also angled (fig. 5.5b), so pressure of the water inside the filled chamber would press against them, making a tight seal and holding water in the lock chamber. Water was let into the lock chamber from the upper canal through two sluices (see also insert, fig. 5.11), until the water level inside the lock chamber equaled the water level in the upper canal, raising the vessel (3). The gates of the sluices were raised by turning a grooved crank attached to the sluice gate (fig. 5.6). Since the water pressure now was the same in the lock chamber and the upper canal, the upper canal gates could be easily opened by pushing on the beams. The vessel exited the lock chamber (4) and proceeded to the next lock.

When a vessel came from the upper canal side, a different method was applied, since the chamber was full of water after the previous vessel exited the lock. Because the water levels of the lock and the upper canal were equal, a vessel entered the lock and the upper canal gates were closed. The lower canal-side gates could not be opened easily since the water pressure in the lock chamber

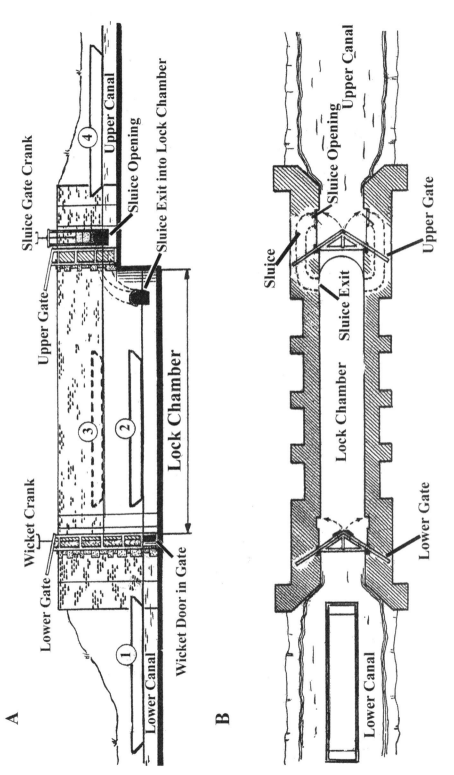

FIGURE 5.5A–B. Operation of typical Santee Canal lock. Illustration by William Robert Judd.

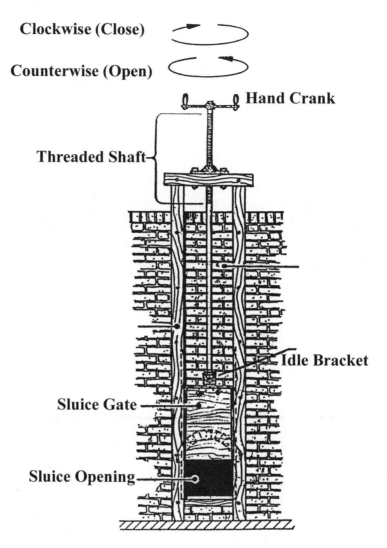

FIGURE 5.6. Conceptualized diagram and operation of sluice gates. Illustration by William Robert Judd.

pressed against the angled gates (fig. 5.5b). At the base of each gate was a small wicket gate (fig. 5.7), which was raised by a crank. The crank could be easily turned, raising the gate upward and letting the water slowly out of the lock chamber into the lower canal. When the lock chamber was empty and there was no pressure on the gates, the lower canal-side gates of the lock were easily opened, and the vessel exited the lock. The water pressure in the upper canal kept a tight seal so no water would enter the lock chamber until ready for the next vessel.

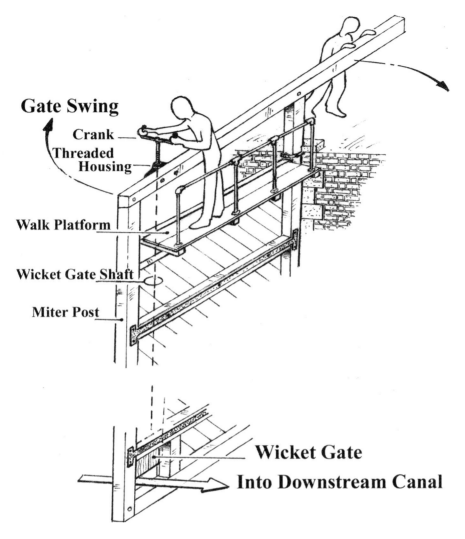

FIGURE 5.7. Conceptualized diagram and operation of wicket.
Illustration by William Robert Judd.

CONSTRUCTION OF THE SANTEE CANAL, 1793–1800

Before actual construction could begin, Senf had to put a labor force in place. He began work on the canal in May 1793 with 10 workers; by July that number had increased to 150; and by the end of 1793, the total number had swollen to 1,000. Senf chose to supervise the workers directly through overseers rather than hiring contractors and paying an agreed sum per cubic yard excavated. He wrote to the directors that "I have never been able, from the first beginning

Construction of the Santee Canal ~ 73

of the Works to the present day, to meet with a Tradesman nor any Person to assist me, who had been actually employed at any similar works."[14] He chose to hire an overseer for each twenty laborers, who reported to and were paid by the company. All the workers were put on like terms. It was probably not too difficult for Senf to ride the length of the proposed canal by horse to check on progress and give the overseers directions. He also reasoned that it would be easy to move an overseer and his twenty workers to other sites when needed. His method of labor worked, although Frederick Porcher was critical of this method, stating it took much longer to build the canal than if done by contractors.[15]

The process of constructing a canal followed a logical pattern. Once the labor force was in place and the initial surveying for the route completed, Senf had to provide infrastructure and to secure sites for reservoirs. Big Camp was the central headquarters for canal operations. Housing had to be provided for laborers and overseers, and the director's house at Big Camp needed to be built. Blacksmith shops, saw pits, brick making facilities, and a variety of other structures to support the workforce had to be constructed. Senf had to find a source for building material, since there were no commercial suppliers for the type of material needed for a canal in Santee Canal country in the 1800s. Cypress and pine could be obtained for the nearby forests and swamps but required a specialized labor force to saw both into lumber. Shells as a lime source for mortar were brought from the coast.

Frederick Porcher described Big Camp as a pleasant, village-like assemblage of support structures:

> The road from Pineville led across the Santee Canal at Big Camp where we had a pleasant view of the village-like assembly of houses. First on the right of the road was the superintendent's house; and directly opposite that of the overseer; then the large brick store in which goods were deposited that had come by the Canal, or were to go by it. A little further to the north was the residence of the lock-keeper, and further north in full view was Mexico, the homestead of my uncle, Major Samuel Porcher.[16]

Once Big Camp was established, Senf was ready to begin actual excavation of the canal bed. First he had to clear the trees from the proposed 150-foot-wide route. Tree clearing finished, excavation of the canal chamber began. But where did he start? Ulrich Bonnell Phillips states that "digging was begun at both ends of the canal."[17] Phillips does not give a source for this statement, so it is somewhat suspect. No other source in the archives the authors consulted mentioned that digging began at both ends. Bennett and Richardson wrote that "it makes sense that he started his canal at the summit, [because] this allowed him to calculate the fall of each lock and to establish the correct for each of these."[18] Here again there was no citation for their statement. It seems likely that Senf knew where the locks were to go prior to excavation of the canal's bed, since he had already surveyed the canal's route and established his levels. Senf wrote on April 2, 1787: "I have traced the Course of the Canal upon the Plan and marked (from No. 1 to 11), where about the locks may be fixed. The number of Locks will be eleven, their falls will be from eight—to eleven—feet, more or less, as the situation of the Ground may admit of."[19] Determining the sites for the locks would seem to have been part of his initial survey of the canal's route. The authors argue that Senf knew well where he planned to place the locks before he began excavation of the canal's bed, but changes probably resulted as he began actual construction.

Senf wrote about where he began excavation: "Here begins the Summit Canal and is carried on the slope of the hill between made Banks for 400 feet—(which is the first work of the Canal in May 1793)."[20] Was he referring to establishing Big Camp as the "first work," or the actual start of digging? This statement is too unclear to establish the Summit Canal as the site for the first digging of the bed. The authors conclude that no archival material is clear enough to state where Senf began the first digging for the canal chamber and leave the issue unresolved. In the discourse on the canal's construction to follow, for the readers' convenience, we will proceed as if excavation began at the Santee River and continued to the Cooper River.

At the river's entrance, Senf built three or four embankments of "large and heavy Stones"[21] to divert water to the opposite shore to prevent undermining the bluff on the canal side. Because of low river water during droughts, he constructed a wooden wing dam just downriver from the entrance. The wing dam was a simple solution to low water in the river. Water hitting the wing dam would swell or rise, creating a higher level of water at the entrance of the canal, which allowed vessels to pass from the river into the canal and not be grounded.

The canal began at White Oak Landing (fig. 4.2), used since the early colonial period. The entrance of Outside Creek was located at White Oak Landing. A woods road ran from the landing, presumably all the way to the Pine

Ville–Eutawville Road. Senf may have converted the woods road at the river's edge into a basin 100 wide at its mouth, so that ferry boats could lie in it without interrupting navigation of the canal boats. Construction of the canal cut continued along the woods road since it provided a partially treeless path. Workers used shovels and wheelbarrows supported on planking to excavate the canal's cut. The Guard Lock was located at the end of the river basin 150 feet from the river. Guard Lock (see fig. 9.7) was 17 feet wide and 60 feet long, with a lift of 5 feet. Senf built it wider than the other locks so larger riverboats coming down the Santee could pass into the canal. When the water level in the Santee was exceptionally high from freshets, the gates on the Guard Lock were left open, and vessels could pass directly to Santee Basin. Senf made the canal 40 feet wide with a water level 6 feet deep between the Guard Lock and Santee Basin (fig. 5.8) so river vessels could pass to the basin, where they could unload their cargo to the smaller-draft canal vessels. Riverboat traffic stopped at Santee Basin. Senf constructed a brick overfall in the wall of the basin, which maintained the water depth of 6 feet.[22] See figure 5.16 for explanation and diagram of an overfall.

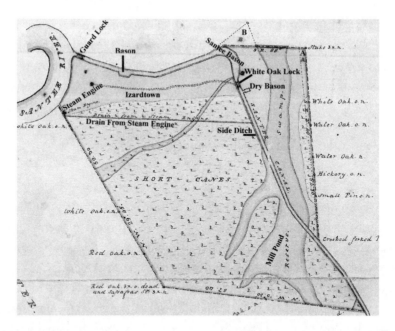

FIGURE 5.8. Plat of White Oak, St. Stephen's Parish. Watercolor map created by Henry Ravenel, 1822. Authors added White Oak Lock, Guard Lock, Basin, Izardtown, Santee Basin, Dry Basin, Steam Engine, Mill Pond, Side Ditch, tracts A and B, and Drain from Steam Engine. Map courtesy of the Georgetown County Digital Library/Georgetown County Library (digital collection, 02-1822-04), Georgetown, South Carolina.

Immediately past the Guard Lock, according to his General Plan and Final Report, Senf constructed a small basin, a widened section of the canal bank, where a vessel "may turn out of the way" to allow another vessel to pass (fig. 5.8).[23]

At the head of Santee Basin was White Oak Lock (fig. 5.8). White Oak Lock was the standard ten feet wide and sixty-six feet between each pair of double gates (figs. 5.9 and 5.11). Once through this lock, vessels were fifteen feet above the Santee River. The Summit Canal supplied water for this section of the canal that first passed through Big Camp Lock.

The tollhouse, lockkeeper's house, mill, and pastureland for tow animals was located at White Oak Lock (fig. 5.9). White Oak Lock was the toll lock for

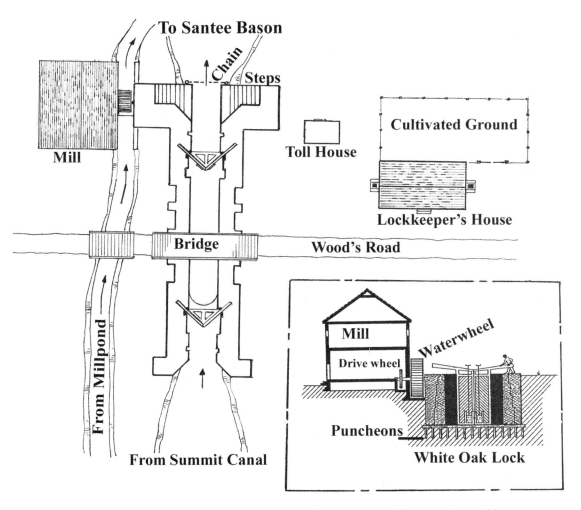

FIGURE 5.9. White Oak Lock and environs. Illustration by William Robert Judd.

Construction of the Santee Canal ～ 77

FIGURE 5.10. Steps on White Oak Lock (date and photographer unknown). The image is cropped from the original. Steps on the left went to the tollhouse; steps to the right might have gone to the adjacent mill. Courtesy of the South Carolina Historical Society, Elias Ball Bull Papers (VM 376.00, box 6, folder 21, Santee Canal).

vessels entering the canal from the Santee end. Senf constructed steps on the Santee end of the lock so a vessel operator could ascend to the top of the lock and go to the tollhouse (figs. 5.9 and 5.10) to pay the toll. The brick steps were originally framed in wood based on the presence of pockets in the brick wall, which received the timbers on which the wooden steps were attached.

With the completion of the canal, the company ordered Senf to install chains across the entrance to White Oak Lock (see fig. 5.9) and Hope Lock, so that, "for the present, No Boat, Flat, or other vessel, loaded wholly or in part, be suffered to pass either chain, without paying a Toll of *One Dollar* for each chain they pass."[24] Actual tolls were much higher: Senf recommended a toll of five pounds (about twenty-one dollars) for all vessels traversing the canal. The company, however, adopted a sliding payment based on the breadth of the vessel. A vessel six and a half to seven and a half feet wide paid fifteen dollars, while a vessel seven and a half to eight and a half feet wide paid twenty dollars.[25]

Senf constructed an undershot water mill at White Oak Lock (see fig. 5.9). In his Final Report, Senf wrote of the mill: "Next to this Lock, is connected a Mill Seat for an Undershot Wheel, six feet tall, 4 feet width, and 3 feet Millhead with a Brick Wasteway—And 443 yards from this a Floodgate, to turn the Water away from the Mill Race."[26] Senf supplied water for the mill via a side ditch (fig. 5.8) running parallel to the canal from a millpond. He explained how the millpond was created, an ingenious use of the terrain: "Here the bottom of the canal is 3 feet higher than the natural [grade] for the distance of 586 yards. This interfered with the natural drainage of the land and formed a pond. Instead of permitting this accumulation of water to pass under the bed of the canal it was carried at less expense alongside the canal [in the side ditch] to the afore-mentioned mill-seat."[27] When Senf elevated this section of the canal three feet above natural grade using fill, water backed up, forming the millpond.

FIGURE 5.11. White Oak Lock, 2021. Note the quoin (one quoin is missing) where the gate was hung and the sluice openings to allow water to enter the lock chamber. The insert shows one of the openings of the sluice into the lock chamber, and arrows show the location of the openings (hidden) within the lock chamber. All wooden structures have deteriorated. Note the raised brick abutments that supported the bridge over the lock. Photograph by Richard Dwight Porcher Jr.

Senf did not state the type of mill (corn? wheat?) or who it supplied. Perhaps he expected Izardtown to flourish and the mill to supply products to the town, or perhaps it would process grain for workers. The Canal Company owned the mill and would have received the revenue.

The mill shown in figure 5.9 shows a construction method used to build locks and/or buildings on soft soil: puncheons driven into the ground to support the weight of the structure. To construct a lock, a layer of timbers was laid on top of the puncheons, on top of which the brick walls of the lock were constructed. A brick floor was laid between the walls on the timbers. An examination of the Guard Lock after the walls had collapsed revealed puncheons under the walls. The puncheons appeared to be cypress, about three to eight inches in diameter and approximately eight feet long.[28] Use of puncheons was a common construction method when heavy structures were built on swamp soil, and more than likely all the locks except Tide Lock were built over puncheons.

White Oak Lock demonstrates two additional features of lock construction: quoins and a recess in the lock wall to allow the gates to lie flat within the wall, out of the way of vessels (fig. 5.12).[29] The recess had two levels, the deeper

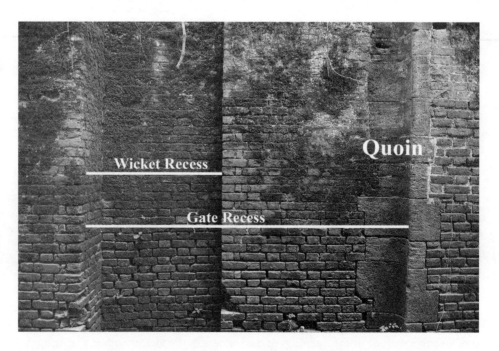

FIGURE 5.12. Chamber wall of White Oak Lock, 2021. Note the quoin, which accepted the gate post, and the recess in the wall, where the gate and wicket were housed when opened. Photograph by Richard Dwight Porcher Jr.

one at the end for the wicket, which projected off the gate, and the entire recess for the gate and wicket.

Lock gates were hinged into the quoins on either side of the lock. White Oak Lock has three intact quoins. Each quoin (figs. 5.12 and 5.13) consisted of a series of individual quoin blocks stacked to the height of the lock. There was no standard size or shape to the individual blocks that comprised a quoin. Each block was attached to the one below and the one above by an alignment bar (fig. 5.13). The entire quoin was attached to the brick wall by a series of tie bars, making a secure structure that could support the weight of the wooden gate.[30] Each quoin block had a square-shaped hole to receive the alignment bar, and a recess was chiseled into each block to receive the square-shaped end of the bar (5.13). This allowed each block to sit flush on top of the block below. The combination of alignment bars and tie bars pinned the entire quoin together. The blocks fit together so tight that mortar was not needed to seal them, a testimony, again, to the skill of the workers.

Senf devised an ingenious method to prevent leaking where the gates were hinged in the quoins. The pins that held the gates in their sockets at the base

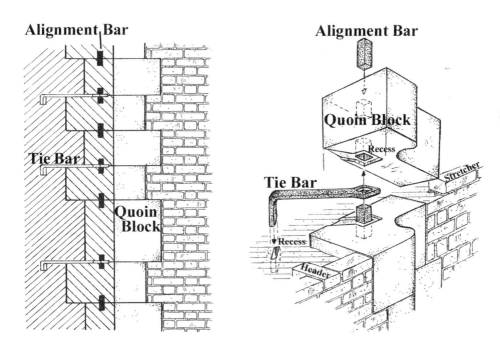

FIGURE 5.13. Construction of quoins. This illustration also shows the brick pattern, which was Flemish bond, where each course alternates stretcher and header to produce a basket weave. Illustration by William Robert Judd.

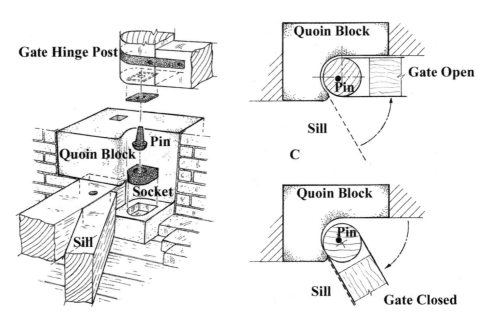

FIGURE 5.14. Gate attachment to quoin. Illustration by William Robert Judd.

and top were offset, so when the gates were closed against the sill, it forced the edge of the gate tightly against the quoin (figs. 5.14b and c). Leakage was kept at a minimum.

White Oak Lock is the best site to dispel one of the myths of the Santee Canal. Two references state the chamber walls of the locks were lined with marble facing. The original reference came from a "Report of the Secretary of the Treasury" in 1807: "The locks, made of brick faced with marble, are 60 feet long and 10 feet wide."[31] In August 1971, citing that same report, Crowson wrote that the locks were "faced with marble."[32] The authors examined the walls of locks 1 and 2 and saw no signs of marble facing or means where marble facing was attached. Senf did not mention marble facing in his Final Report. He was meticulous in his work and his account of construction of the locks, and he certainly would have discussed the use of marble facing. The authors do not believe marble facing was used by Senf. The source of the Secretary of the Treasury's note of marble facing is unknown. It may be that other canals in the country had marble facing and the author of the report simply assumed the locks on the Santee Canal were also faced with marble. The authors do not believe that the writer of either report ever visited the canal.

Senf employed the common canal technique of puddling to seal the canal chamber and bed from leaks. Puddling consisted of mixing local clay with water to form a watertight paste. The paste was then tamped (packed down) by hand on the chamber walls "for at least 3 or 4 feet in height."[33] Puddling a chamber of even a few miles would have been a major task. Senf, however, used every means at his disposal to ensure the Santee Canal retained an adequate water supply.

Senf stated there was a "Dry Bason for the purpose to repair boats—the bason is 30 feet by 60 feet sufficient to admit two boats at a time."[34] This dry basin does not appear on Senf's General Plan, but it shows on figs. 5.8 and 5.15 as rectangular in shape. The lidar image (fig. 9.9) confirms the dry basin's shape and its location.[35]

The lidar image shows the dry basin (dry dock in today's terms) set back from the canal with the east bank angling toward the entrance to the basin, creating a flooded forebay (1). The forebay allowed a sixty-four-foot-long vessel from the canal to maneuver into position to enter the basin (2). Once inside the basin, the vessel would be floated over a cradle. The entrance would be closed by an undetermined structure, preventing additional water from the canal from entering the basin. Water from inside the basin would be drained by opening a floodgate at its rear wall, expelling the water through a drain into an adjacent low area. The drain is shown in figure 5.15. As water flowed out of the basin, the vessel settled on the cradle, allowing workers access to the bottom of the vessel. Once repairs were completed, the floodgate at the rear was closed, and water was let into the basin from the canal, refloating the vessel. The vessel passed out of the basin through the forebay into the canal. The basin would remain flooded and open to water flow when not in use to keep its puddle lining from drying out.

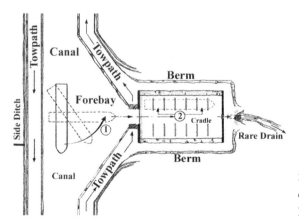

FIGURE 5.15. Dry basin and environs. Illustration by William Robert Judd.

The entrance into the basin bisected the towpath. How this problem was solved is unknown. A field examination did not reveal any clues to the issue. Possibly a removable plank bridge could have spanned the entrance.

Senf utilized overfalls for another type of water control. No physical remains or diagrams of the overfalls survive, only a reference in the Final Report: "For the supplies of the water for the Canal, and to discharge the surplus water, there are in its whole Length twenty-five Floodgates and Overfalls. . . . The Overfall . . . consist of a brick wall in the Bank and Pavement; that whenever the Water in the Canal should rise higher than 4 feet, the surplus water runs over—[.]"[36] An overfall acted as a safety valve to discharge excess water caused by heavy rainfall or from some other source. It ran through the towpath and was made of brick and wood. A wooded bridge allowed animals to cross over it (fig. 5.16). The top of the towpath was one and a half feet above the water surface of the canal. When water rose above the floor of the overfall, it flowed through the overfall and did not flow over the top of the towpath, where it might have caused erosion. Excess water flowed through the overfall into an adjacent wetland. Each level section of the canal running between two locks had an overfall, which maintained a constant four-foot level of water within that section of the canal chamber.

A small side drain ran along the inside of the towpath (figs. 5.2 and 5.16). Rainwater coming down the inside of the canal bank would run into this side drain and not across the towpath into the canal chamber, preventing erosion of the towpath. The side drain carried the water to the nearest overfall, where it would exit into a low area. This process kept the water in the canal at an even level. Rainwater on the towpaths, which were sloped toward the side drain, would drain into the side drain and be discharged.

Big Camp Lock was a double lock, with each lock having a lift of nine and a half feet for a total lift of nineteen feet.[37] Senf equipped Big Camp Lock with a side chamber to conserve water. (See the account of Frierson's Lock for discussion of the side chamber.) Once through Big Camp Lock and in the five-mile Summit Canal, vessels were thirty-four feet above the Santee River and sixty-nine feet above the Cooper River.

Big Camp housed an animal-powered pug mill that mixed sand, clay, and water to make bricks (fig. 5.17). Animal power turned the spur wheel, which in turn rotated the lantern wheel. The lantern wheel was connected to a shaft, on which were placed angled blades that rotated in a narrow tub as the shaft turned. The rotating blades mixed the clay, sand, and water into a pug. The pug was placed in molds to dry, then into kilns and fired to make bricks. Because

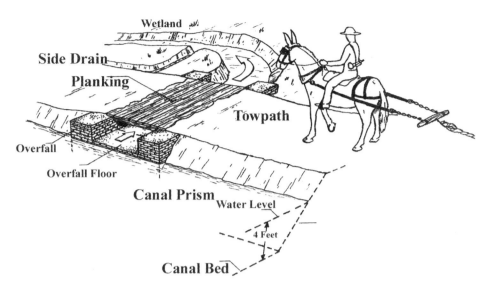

FIGURE 5.16. Conceptualized diagram of overfall through the towpath. Illustration by William Robert Judd.

ends of the walls of the locks were angled, Senf had molds made that formed angled bricks (see fig. 5.17 and, for Black Oak Lock, fig. 5.29).

Mortar was made at Big Camp from shells brought from the coast. David Ramsay, president of the board of directors at the time, noted in an article in the *Charleston City Gazette and the Daily Advertiser:* "Two boats of shells, containing eighteen hundred bushels, in Santee river, and the company's boat with twelve hundred at Stony landing, were unloading. Shells and more black bricklayers are wanted to expedite the work."[38]

The road from Pine Ville to Eutawville (today's Highway 45) crossed the canal on a bridge.[39] The towpaths and side drains passed under the bridge (fig. 5.18). The side drains were carried under the bridge through a bypass. The towpaths were reduced to five feet under the bridge. The canal chamber was reduced to ten feet since it had to accommodate the floodgate on the bottom of the canal under the bridge (fig. 5.19). Although the Eutawville–Pine Ville bridge is the only bridge mentioned in Senf's Final Report or Drayton's diary in any detail, the authors of the present work suggest that all seven communication bridges over the canal had this narrowing of the canal chamber.

Senf installed a floodgate to lie in the bottom of the canal, "which can easily be raised to stop all the Water in the Canal, in case of Accident, or that part of the Canal towards the Double Lock [Big Camp Lock] required to be dry."[40]

Construction of the Santee Canal ～ 85

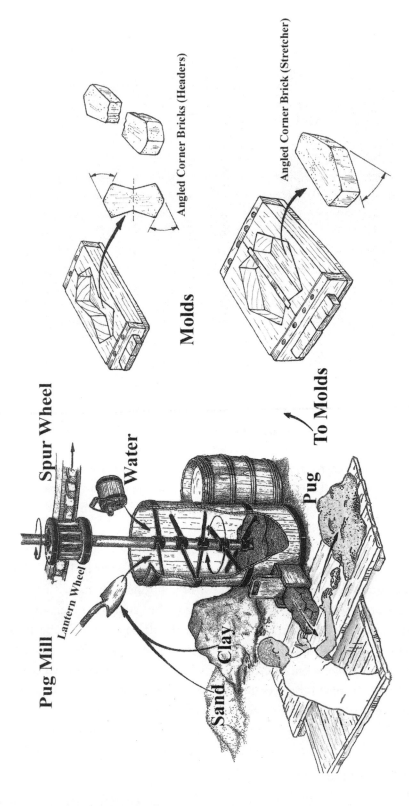

FIGURE 5.17. Pug mill (left) and brick molds (right). Pug mill illustration by William Robert Judd based on description from Charles Drayton's diary, Drayton Hall, National Trust for Historic Preservation, Charleston.

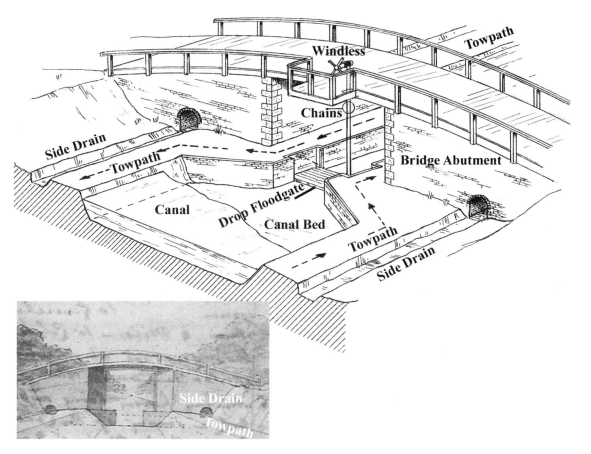

FIGURE 5.18. Bridge on Pine Ville–Eutawville Road (present-day Highway 45) across Santee Canal. Illustration by William Robert Judd based on a sketch from the diary entries of Dr. Charles Drayton, May 6, 1794 (see insert). Judd made changes in his diagram where it was determined Drayton had not been accurate. He also added a windlass and the drop floodgate. As Drayton made his sketch in 1794, Senf may have made changes to his final plan for the bridge. Drayton's diary is from the collection of Drayton Hall, National Trust for Historic Preservation, Charleston.

No diagram of the floodgate survives. A conceptualized diagram of it is seen in figure 5.19 based on floodgates of similar use in the archives and Senf's Final Report. Some type of windlass must have lowered and raised the floodgate. The canal floor was recessed so the gate could lie on the bottom of the canal when lowered so as to not obstruct boat traffic. When the windlass turned counterclockwise, it unwound chain (b). At the same time, it pulled chain (a), which was attached to the floodgate and lifted it to a vertical position. A ratchet wheel and pawl on the drum of the windlass locked the gate in place against the

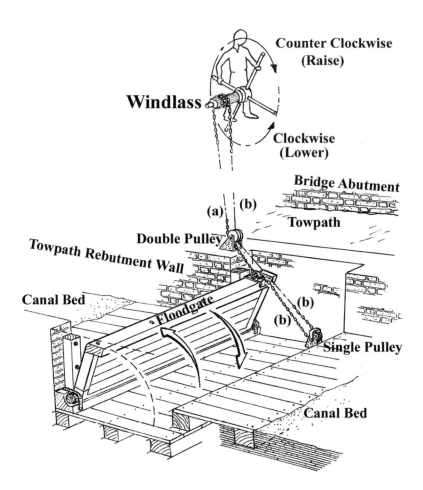

FIGURE 5.19. Conceptualized diagram of floodgate under bridge that crossed the Pine Ville–Eutawville Road. Illustration by William Robert Judd based on Senf's Final Report.

vertical timbers within each side wall recess. The pressure of the retained water in the Summit Canal pressed against the gate, further sealing the gate against leakage. When the windlass turned clockwise, it unwound chain (a) and at the same time pulled on chain (b). Chain (b) was attached to the gate, pulling it down into the recess on the floodgate floor, clear of passing vessels. The chains were probably disconnected when not in use so to be out of the way of northbound vessels. The side drains passed through the bridge abutments in brick aqueducts.

South of the bridge, Senf created St. Stephen's Basin (fig. 4.5). Planters from the adjacent plantations used the canal to ship cargo to Charleston and needed a wide place to load their cargo from wagons onto the canal vessels.

The five-mile segment from Big Camp Lock to Frierson's Lock was the summit level of the canal. A three-mile section between Big Camp Lock to Frierson's Lock had to be a hundred feet wide by fourteen to sixteen feet deep where it crossed the highest point of the ridge between the Santee and the Cooper. A portion of the deep cut can be seen from White Bridge Road just past St. Stephen's Basin.

Senf's water control system has not been fully addressed by historians. It was brilliant the way he constructed upland reservoirs to fill the Summit Canal; used side ditches and side chambers on locks to conserve water; used natural watercourses; incorporated artesian springs for water; and constructed floodgates, overfalls, aqueducts, and a wing dam, all to ensure the canal had water. His system only failed during extreme droughts. At all other times, the system supplied sufficient water for the locks.

The Summit Canal depended on three rain-filled reservoirs: Great Reservoir, Greenland Swamp, and Bull Town Bay. All three reservoirs appear on Senf's General Plan, although part of Bull Town Bay is not seen because of damage to Senf's original plan. Gillmore's 1881 copy of Senf's plan was made before the 1800 General Plan was damaged.[41] A section of the Gillmore plat (fig. 5.21) is used to show the three reservoirs and surrounding area. (Greenland Swamp was virtually inundated by the present Lake Marion and the Diversion Canal, and the Cross Generating Plant and Diversion Canal obliterated most of Bull Town Bay.)

The main reservoir was the Great Reservoir created by damming Kirk's Swamp. It was cleared of trees prior to flooding, a seemingly hard task given the size of the reservoir and the denseness of the swamp trees. Senf constructed a dam running along the canal that was four hundred yards long, seventy feet wide at the bottom, and forty feet wide at the top, which raised the level of water in the reservoir (fig. 9.11). He wrote "in its bank (the dam) are two strong Floodgates, with an Iron Grate, arched over and enclosed in a small strong Brickhouse—through which the Canal may be supplied with Water—the surface of the Canal is two feet lower that the Bottom of this Reservoir" (fig. 5.20).[42] The iron grating protected the floodgates from floating debris. Opposite the floodgates was an overfall leading into Deep River, which carried off excess water in the Summit Canal to the Santee River (fig. 5.21). Black Oak Road west of the reservoir acted as a second dam, preventing water from the Great Reservoir draining into Bull Town Bay (fig. 9.12).[43] No traces of the floodgates or brick house are present. A modern culvert installed in the dam destroyed the floodgates.

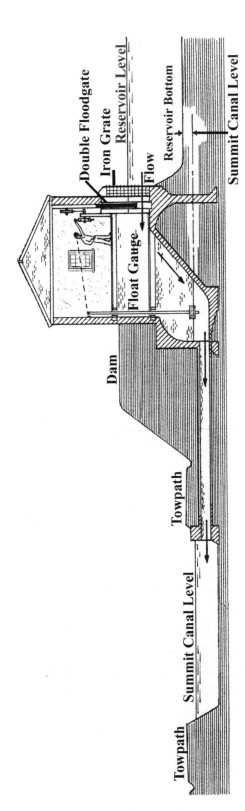

FIGURE 5.20. A conceptualized diagram of a double floodgate that controlled water flow from the Great Reservoir through the dam into the Summit Canal. Illustration by William Robert Judd, based in part on Senf's note in his Final Report. Since the water level in the Great Reservoir was higher than in the Summit Canal, water flowed by gravity once the floodgates were open. A float gauge may have helped workers know when to let water into the canal.

Greenland Swamp was the second reservoir (fig. 5.21). The swamp flowed north into the Santee River (indicated by arrows in fig. 5.21). Senf used the head of the swamp for water to supply the Great Reservoir. He constructed a dam (labeled D___D in fig 5.21) to hold back the waters that drained into the swamp, forming a reservoir (B). Senf constructed an upland drain (C, identified by a broken white line) that carried water from the swamp's reservoir to the Great Reservoir. Senf wrote on April 2, 1787: "Kirk's Swamp (A) will serve as the first Reservoir into which the Water from the second reservoir (B) at the head of Greenland Swamp, may be drawn as Occasion shall require, by a Drain (C) all other smaller Drains and dams to supply the Reservoirs with more water."[44] The head of Greenland Swamp appears to have been fed by numerous upland tributaries and springs, so a good supply of water fed the Great Reservoir through the upland drains from the swamp reservoir.

Kapsch states that water for the canal between White Oak Lock and Big Camp Lock "was supplied with water from a reservoir in Greenland Swamp immediately west of the canal."[45] The authors believe this to be impossible. Figure 5.21 shows that Greenland Swamp drained into the Santee River with one small tributary coming from the general area of the canal near Big Camp Lock. Water flow in this small tributary would have drained into Greenland Swamp, away from the canal. Senf does not mention this reservoir in his Final Report, and it does not show on his General Plan. There is no way Senf would not have discussed this reservoir if indeed it was one of his. Kapsch gives as his source an 1823 report from the state superintendent of public works cited by David Kohn and Bess Glenn in their *Internal Improvement in South Carolina, 1817–1828* (1938). We could not find the source for the reservoir in Kohn and Glenn's work. It is possible that an attempt was made to obtain water from Greenland Swamp after the main reservoirs went dry in 1816 and 1818–19, but it would have required some sort of canal or drain from above Senf's dam on Greenland Swamp. There is no evidence in the field of such a structure, and no plats were located showing a possible water route to the canal from Greenland Swamp. The authors conclude there never was an attempt to divert water from Greenland Swamp to the Santee Canal between locks 2 and 3.

Bull Town Bay (figs. 5.21 and fig. 5.22) was the third reservoir to supply the Summit Canal. In his Final Report to the directors, Senf wrote:

> In the following inserted Report I made in April, 1787, I recommended the First Reservoir to be at Kirk swamp; the second at the head of Greenland Swamp. I am yet of the same Opinion. But, when I made the Survey

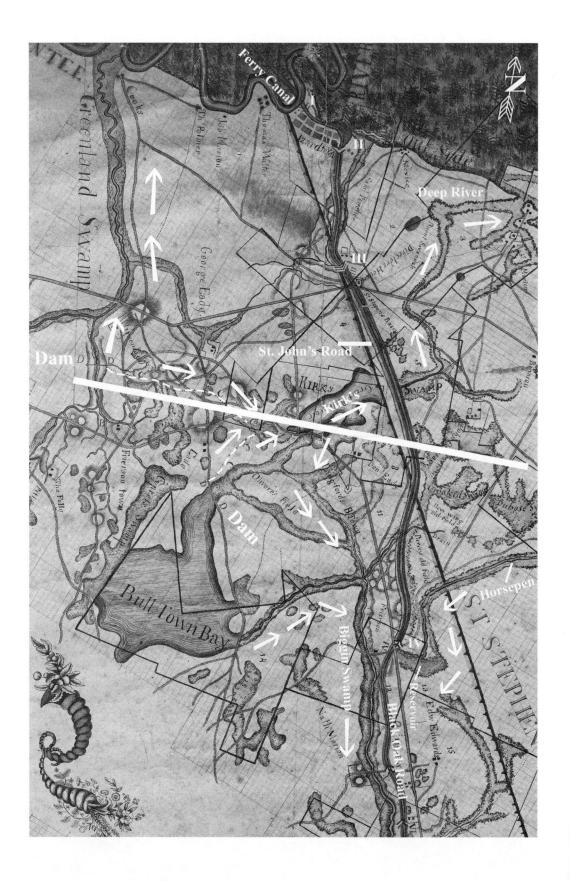

LEFT: FIGURE 5.21. Section of the Gillmore 1881 copy of Senf's General Plan. Arrows indicate the directional flow of water. The two major drains are indicated by a series of broken white lines (– – – –) and letters (C). Both upland drains emptied into the Great Reservoir. Note Horsepen Swamp feeding water into the reservoir at Frierson's Lock (IV) and the flow of water in Biggin Swamp toward the Cooper River. Authors added Locks I–IV, Black Oak Road, Kirk's, Dams, Reservoir B, St. John's Road, Biggin Swamp, Deep River, and Ferry Canal. The solid white line represents the approximate location of ridge between the Santee and Cooper Rivers.

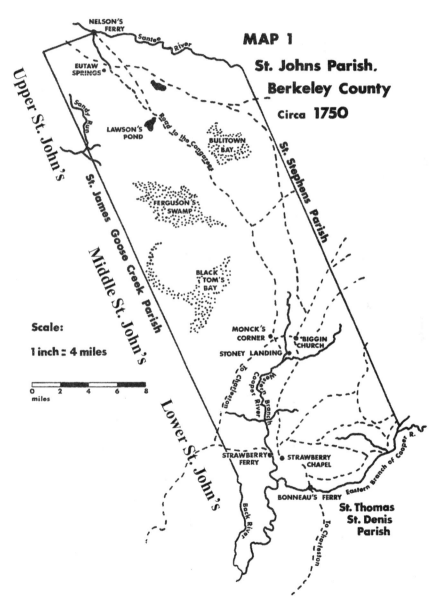

FIGURE 5.22. St. John's Parish, Berkeley County, ca. 1750. Courtesy of Terry, "'Champaign Country.'"

and Level it was in the month of March, when all Watercourses, Ponds and Swamps were full of Water, the Season prevented me in many places from more accurate Observations. Much of the Information concerning Biggin Swamp were given to me by the Inhabitants at and near it—My surveys were necessary to be done, before the Legislature adjourned, who was at that time assembled, to have all the supplies of Water, which can be conveyed to a Work of such great Consequence to the Country, that even in the dryest Seasons the Canal may always have a supply of Water. And from further Examination I recommend a third Reservoir of a Swamp called Bull Town Bay, from whence with less Expense, than from the Head of Greenland Swamp, Water may be conveyed to the third [first] Reservoir. This Bay has high Ground round it, and at the outlets the Water may be retained by Banks and Floodgates. On the General Plan all these Places are marked—(C) shows the Drains and (D) the Dams, and (E) to let off the Surplus Water of the first [Great] Reservoir into the Head of Biggin Swamp.[46]

This last sentence is significant. It indicated that the Great Reservoir was on the break of the ridge between the Santee and Cooper Rivers. Excess water from Kirk's flowed south toward Biggin Creek.

Bull Town Bay was identified in colonial times as shown on an early plat of St. John's Parish (fig. 5.22). The site has gone by numerous names, including Bull Town and Bulitown. A pre–Santee Cooper aerial photograph shows what seems to be a treeless area, so it might have originally been a low shrub or herbaceous wetland.

Senf constructed a dam to hold the water in Bull Town Bay and keep it from flowing uncontrolled into the Great Reservoir. Water flowed from Bull Town Bay through an upland drain that joined the drain from Greenland Swamp's reservoir; the two drains fed water into the Great Reservoir when needed. Viper Road (State Road S-8-708) uses the original dam as its roadbed. Viper Road and the dam are intact since the Cross Generating Station did not impact them.[47]

Bull Town Bay was a sprawling wetland system. Since most of it is under the lake or obliterated by the Cross Generating Station, ground-truthing is impossible. Based on the 1881 Gillmore plat, Bull Town was along the general line of the elevation break between the Santee and the Cooper (fig. 5.21). When the connection between Kirk's and Bull Town Bay was dammed, it raised the level of Bull Town, creating Senf's third reservoir. To the west, some of Bull

Town's waters drained into tributaries of Greenland Swamp, contributing to the reservoir created by damming Greenland Swamp. To the east it drained into Kirk's Swamp. Water easily could be flowed into Kirk's. To the south, Bull Town drained into Biggin Swamp (fig. 5.21) via a small tributary. Senf determined that not enough water was lost passing Biggin to matter. Here one must admire and credit his skill, where he read the land's topography and channeled the various watercourses to supply water for the Summit Canal.

Frierson's Lock and locks 5 through 10 were flooded by Lake Moultrie in 1942 (fig. E3). Consequently we have only Senf's Final Report and several archival photographs to document the flooded locks and associated infrastructure of the canal. One exception is Frierson's Lock, which was exposed during the lake drawdown in 2007–8. This lock, which marked the end of the Summit Canal, was ten feet wide and sixty feet long with a ten-foot fall and was fed by water from the Summit Canal. Once through the lock, a vessel was fifty-nine feet above the Cooper River. Black Oak Road crossed Frierson's Lock. Figure 5.23 shows a bridge over the abandoned lock in the 1930s. This is not the original bridge constructed by Senf's workers.

Senf built counterforts on the outside of the lock to support the walls when the lock was flooded (fig. 5.24). Counterforts are also visible on White Oak Lock and Hope Lock (fig. 5.35).[48]

A small reservoir on the northern side of the lock supplied water for the canal below the lock (fig. 5.21). The reservoir was formed by damming Horsepen Swamp, which flows west into the headwaters of Biggin Swamp from its elevation break near Pine Ville. It flows east from the elevation break as Crawl Branch to the Santee River. Excess water from the reservoir passed under Frierson's Lock in a unique, curving, brick-lined aqueduct that opened into Biggin Creek on the opposite side. Since the opening of the aqueduct in the reservoir was higher than the opening into Biggin Creek, water flowed by gravity from the reservoir through the aqueduct to the creek. A floodgate was installed at the head of the aqueduct to control the flow of water from the reservoir into the aqueduct. A second floodgate must have been installed to control the water flow from the reservoir into the canal below the lock.

Senf described the circular aqueduct at Frierson's Lock as different from the other six he constructed:

> Over the lower end of this Lock crosses the main St. John's Road—and under the upper end of it passes an Aqueduct 6 [feet] by 6 [feet] (in a curving Shape) from the left to the right Bank and under the Road from

FIGURE 5.23. Frierson's Lock, ca. 1930s. The bridge (not original) allowed Black Oak Road to cross the lock. Courtesy of the Historic American Buildings Survey, Prints and Photographic Division, Library of Congress, Washington, DC.

FIGURE 5.24. Frierson's Lock during the Lake Moultrie drawdown in 2008. Note the counterfort. Courtesy of Norman Sinkler Walsh.

Santee River along the Right Bank of the Canal (which ends here); and the main of St. John's Road—this Aqueduct is in case the Water from the Reservoir may not be wanted in the Canal below this Lock the Floodgate in the Ditch passes the water through the Aqueduct—Or in case of rainy seasons to receive no more Water in the lower Canal than wanted.[49]

The aqueduct opening into Biggin Creek, exposed during the drought of 2007, is seen in figure 5.25.

Like Big Camp Lock, Frierson's Lock had a side chamber to conserve water. The side chambers at Big Camp Lock were destroyed, and the one at Frierson's Lock was not found. A possible explanation of the operation of the side chamber is diagrammed in figure 5.26. Most vessels using Frierson's Lock were going from the Santee to the Cooper River, and the lock lowered a vessel. A vessel entered the lock from the Santee end when the lock's chamber was full. Next the lock had to be emptied so the vessel could exit. Figure 5.26 shows that the upper half of the lock's usable water was exited (1) through a sluice into a side chamber.[50] A crank was turned that raised the sluice gate. Remaining water in the lock was released through wickets at the bottom of the two gates into the

FIGURE 5.25. Opening of circular aqueduct into Biggin Creek, 2008. Courtesy of Drew Ruddy.

Construction of the Santee Canal ~ 97

canal below the lock (not shown), leaving only the permanent level of water necessary to float the vessel so it could exit the lock. The gates of the lock were opened, and because the water level in the lock was now the same level as in the Cooper River side of the canal, the vessel exited the lock. When an ascending vessel came from the Cooper River side, the vessel entered the lock and the lock gates were closed. The water in the side chamber (2) was released through the second sluice into the lock. This filled the lock chamber only half full above the permanent water level. To fill the lock all the way, the sluice gates outside the upper gates in the lock walls (see White Oak Lock for description) were opened and water flowed into the lock chamber from the Summit Canal. The Santee-side gates were opened, and the vessel exited the lock. Each time the lock operated when a vessel passed from the Santee side to the Cooper side, half of the water that would have been discharged down the canal and ultimately lost was saved for the next operation of the lock.

Frierson's Lock was the beginning site of the access road called St. John's Road. St. John's Road shows on the 1881 copy of Senf's General Plan (fig. 5.21). St. John's Road ran from Frierson's Lock to White Oak Lock and gave workers ready access to this section of the canal.

Flint's Lock (V) was next of the seven locks flooded by the lake. In 1800 Flint's Lock was on land owned by Capt. Peter Ray. In 1805 the Canal Company acquired the land from Ray under its charter. Flint's Lock had a ten-foot fall. Once through Flint's, a vessel was forty-nine feet above the Cooper River. Since this lock depended on water from the Santee side, it was the first to go dry during droughts. Flint's Lock had a bypass measuring five feet wide coursing around the east side of the lock and into the lower canal to supply water when needed. See figure 5.30 for Black Oak Lock and discussion under Black Oak Lock for operation of the bypass.[51]

Hepworth Lock (VI) was next, located on Hepworth (later incorporated into Chelsea), and had a five-foot fall. The distance between Flint's Lock and Hepworth Lock was 0.66 miles. Again the uneven terrain required fill to elevate the canal bed six feet over natural grade. Once through Hepworth Lock, a vessel was forty-four feet above the Cooper River. The lock had a bypass that carried excess water around it.

Senf described the "beginning of low ground" past Hepworth Lock.[52] He installed brick aqueduct number 5 with "two passages each four feet high and four feet wide owing to the great quantity of water in rainy seasons to pass under the Canal" (figs. 5.27 and 5.28).[53] This was the first of two double aqueducts he installed on the Santee Canal; the remaining five were single aqueducts.

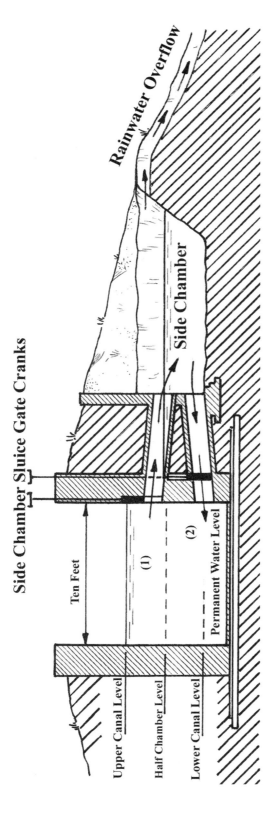

FIGURE 5.26. Conceptualized diagram of a side chamber. Diagram and operation based on Senf's description in his Final Report. Illustration by William Robert Judd.

The top diagram of figure 5.28 shows three ways Senf carried the bed of the Santee Canal through its entire twenty-two-mile length. When the canal's bed did not have to be excavated except for just the depth of the thirty-five-foot cut, there would have been a minimal bank on the side of the canal (top right). When the canal had to be carried over a wetland, fill had to be applied to raise the bed (middle top), and there would not have been a bank on the side

FIGURE 5.27. Double-arched brick aqueduct under Santee Canal. The photograph is from the Samuel Lord Hyde Papers, 1901–1939, College of Charleston Libraries, Mss. 0089. Hyde did not label the photographs in his collection, so it cannot be ascertained if this aqueduct was between Hepworth/Black Oak or at Wantoot Lock, the only two locations with double aqueducts. The double aqueduct at Wantoot Lock passed under the upper part of the lock. From the photograph this aqueduct does not appear to pass under a lock, so the authors conclude it was the aqueduct between Hepworth and Black Oak Locks.

RIGHT: FIGURE 5.28. Conceptualized diagrams of double aqueduct. Illustrations by William Robert Judd based on figure 5.27 and archival material on aqueducts. The canal was carried over a wetland by filling the wetland with earth and constructing the aqueduct at the base of the wetland, carrying water from one side to the other. Whether Senf carried the canal bed wide enough for two vessels (as diagrammed) to pass across the aqueduct is unknown. In Europe engineers narrowed the bed so only one vessel could pass, saving resources.

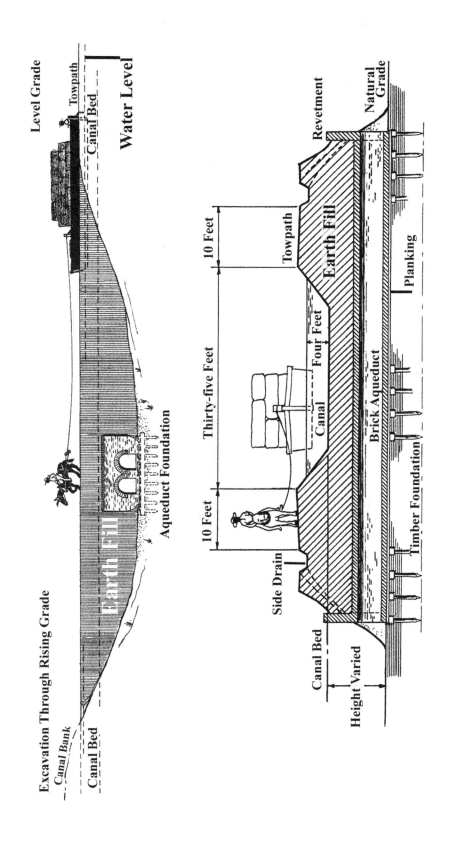

of the canal. When the bed had to be cut much lower than the natural ground level, the excavated fill was piled on either side of the canal, creating a high bank, which also acted to keep rainwater from running into the canal (top left).

The seventh lock, Black Oak Lock (fig. 5.29), was about three miles down from Hepworth Lock and located at Black Oak. This lock had a drop of ten feet and a bypass built down the right side (fig. 5.30). The bypass was a unique construction that Senf created to pass surplus water around a lock. Senf described the bypass at Flint's Lock, which operated the same as the lock at Black Oak: "This lock has a ten-foot Fall—and has an overfall (s) [bypass] on the right side round the lock to the lower Canal five feet wide, for the purpose, that from the surplus water of the upper Canal the lower Canal is constantly supplied."[54] The bypass operated in conjunction with an overfall in the upper canal. When water in the upper canal was higher than the top of the overfall floor (fig. 5.16), the excess water that could not pass through the overfall would flow against the lock's closed gates, causing the water to back up and flow through

FIGURE 5.29. Santee end of Black Oak Lock. Date and photographer unknown. Note the angled bricks and recess in the lock wall for the gate. Edward L. Green Collection, South Caroliniana Library, Photographs 11170.15.

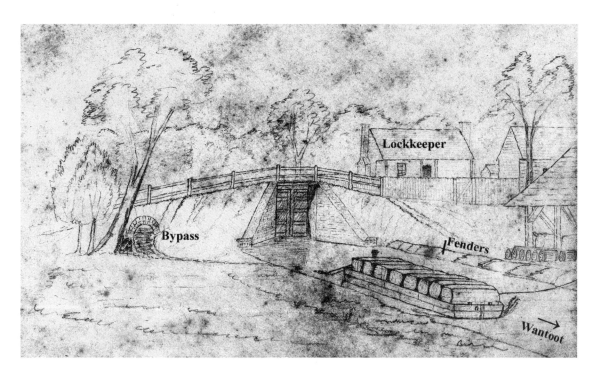

FIGURE 5.30. "A Cotton Box at Black Oak Lock," by Andrew Gibbes. Gibbes sketched the lock in 1852 when traveling the canal. Note the opening of the bypass on the left (right side of the lock). The lockkeeper's house sits on the side of the canal. The vessel loaded with cotton bales has just passed through Black Oak Lock on the way to Wantoot Lock. Note the fenders next to a loading/unloading dock that protected the canal chamber when boats were docking. Courtesy of the Charleston Museum.

a bypass that ran around the lock into the downstream canal. The bypass was lined with brick but was otherwise an open conduit, and water flowed directly into the lower canal. The bypass opening in Black Oak Lock is seen in figure 5.30. In this way excess water could be passed from the upper canal into the lower without having to open the doors of the lock and increase wear on them.

Senf constructed a lockkeeper's house at each lock. These houses sat alongside the canal, giving the lockkeeper a close view of happenings in and around the lock and canal. Based on the sketch (fig. 5.30) and photograph (fig. 5.31), they were small (thirty by sixteen feet), two-roomed, weatherboard houses with a chimney at each end. The lockkeeper's duty was to inspect the canal daily. After every rain shower, he inspected a certain distance along the canal on either side of the lock, and if there was any damage, he immediately had it repaired by the company's workers. The lockkeeper was also responsible for checking the side drains and overfalls to make certain they were kept clean.

Construction of the Santee Canal

FIGURE 5.31. Lockkeeper's house at Black Oak Lock. Date and photographer unknown. Courtesy of the South Carolina Historical Society, Elias Ball Bull Papers (VM 376.00, box 6, folder 21, Santee Canal).

A remarkable photograph (fig. 5.31) shows the lockkeeper's house sometime in the early 1900s before it burned. A bridge over the lock is also visible, although undoubtedly not the original. Richard Porcher remarks that his father, Dwight, must have passed over this same bridge many times on his way to Cedar Spring from Pooshee, both family properties. Dwight Porcher was born in 1900, a young man on the move when the bridge was still passable.

Once through Black Oak Lock, a vessel was 34 feet above the Cooper River. As indicated on the General Plan, Senf constructed a turning basin at Black Oak Lock called St. John's Basin. The basin measured 150 feet long by 100 feet wide. It was situated below the lock and provided a place for boats from the surrounding plantations to moor and load or offload goods. The bridge over Black Oak Lock connected a network of five roads on each side of the canal that came through Black Oak.

Wantoot Lock was 0.2 miles from Black Oak Lock and had a ten-foot fall. Once through Wantoot Lock, vessels were twenty-four feet higher than the Cooper River. Senf constructed a double-arched brick aqueduct under the upper section of the bed of the lock to allow water to pass under the canal into Biggin Creek. A second aqueduct further down allowed Daniel Ravenel III to flow springwater under the canal to his rice fields on the opposite side and to power his "rice machine." Edmund Ravenel described Wantoot's rice fields as being supplied by water from an artesian spring: "The water here issues from the marl which is about two or three feet below the surface at this spot. This water passes south and is carried under the Santee Canal in a Brick-Aqueduct, to be used on the Rice-Fields of Wantoot Plantation."[55]

Woodboo Lock, with a fall of nine feet, owned by Stephen Mazÿck II, was next, 1.5 miles from Wantoot Lock. Once through Woodboo, a vessel was fifteen feet above the Cooper. The lock was supplied with water from Woodboo's Big Spring (also called Mazÿck's Spring; see fig. 5.32), one of the many artesian springs that fed the canal along its lower course. Senf placed floodgates in the canal bank so Mazÿck could flood his rice fields with water from the canal during dry seasons. Francis Simmons Holmes commented on the springs at Woodboo:

> Woodboo plantation . . . is remarkable for two springs, the vent of one or perhaps two of these subterranean streams. The waters flow from openings in the marl, four or five feet in diameter, at the bottom of a basin, the area of which is several hundred feet . . . and so beautifully clear and transparent are they, that the trout, bream, and other fish, and indeed objects of the smallest size, may be distinctly seen at the depth of twenty or thirty feet. The bluish tinge of the water, too, casts a sombre [*sic*] but agreeable hue on all around; the general effect is not a little enhanced by the willows and cypresses extending graceful arms above its surface, and studding the banks of a considerable stream which, flowing from the basin in a winding course, empties, at the distance of nearly half a mile, into the Santee

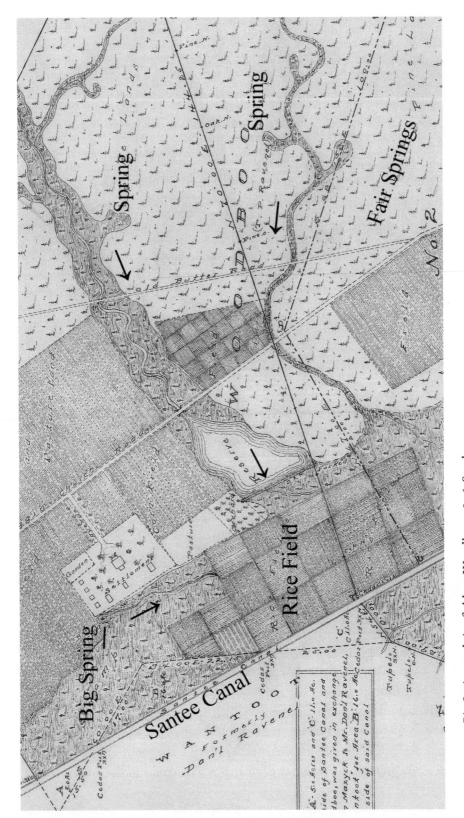

FIGURE 5.32. Big Spring and rice fields at Woodboo, 1806. Stephen Mazÿck could flood his rice fields from the Santee Canal through floodgates Senf constructed. Arrows indicate flow of water from Big Spring and from upland springs to the rice fields.

Canal, the lower sections of which are dependent upon it for their supply of water.[56]

Santee Canal left the highland at Woodboo Lock and entered Biggin Swamp. Senf constructed an elevated bank on the eastern side of the canal to prevent floodwaters from overflowing into the canal. The bank also protected Mazÿck's rice fields.

Senf had to contend with the ubiquitous artesian springs of Middle and Upper St. John's and St. Stephen's, both as sources of water and as routes for water under the canal for use by adjacent plantations. Artesian springs formed because of the unique geology of the coastal plain. The sandhills of the state, a belt of sand that runs from Aiken to below Columbia and through Bennettsville into North Carolina, represent the former ocean shoreline at the base of the fall line some two million years ago. When the present coastal plain was under the ocean, shells of marine organisms settled to the ocean floor, forming layers of shell deposits. As the ocean began retreating about two million years ago from the fall line during the Pleistocene Epoch and reached the continental shelf about sixteen thousand years ago, the shell deposits were turned into limestone and marl formations. Sand carried down from the Piedmont and mountains formed a layer over the limestone and marl formations, forming the coastal plain. An impervious layer formed between the sand and the marl and limestone. The limestone is porous and outcrops at the fall line. Water enters the outcrops at the fall line and flows through the limestone, under pressure, and exits at the continental shelf. If a break occurs in the impervious bed, water, under pressure, will force its way through the sand and bubble into a pool in the sandy soil (fig. 5.33). This is an artesian spring (fig. 5.34). Artesian springs laced Middle St. John's because of the underlying Santee limestone formation that ran to Eutawville.

Hope Lock was a double lock three miles from Woodboo Lock and located on Hope. Each chamber of the double lock had a fall of seven-and-a-half feet for a total of fifteen feet. Hope Lock was a gigantic structure, just like the Guard Lock on the Santee River. A photograph of the lock during its destruction to install the hydroelectric plant is seen in figure 5.35. Counterforts to brace the lock's walls of each chamber are visible. Once through Hope Lock, a vessel was at the level of the Cooper River at high tide.

Senf constructed Biggin Basin immediately north of Hope Lock for vessels to maneuver. Charles Fraser immortalized Hope in *A Charleston Sketchbook* with a sketch of Biggin Basin and storehouse belonging to the Santee Canal

FIGURE 5.33. Origin of an artesian spring. D. Johnson, *Mysterious Carolina Bays*, 54.

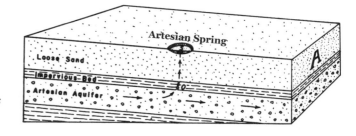

FIGURE 5.34. Artesian spring at Indianfield, 1921. From album titled "Northampton Hunting Trip, 1921," Charleston Library Society. Copy in personal archives of Richard Dwight Porcher Jr.

Company (fig. 5.36).[57] In the background is the lockkeeper's house. Biggin Basin had a ten-foot overfall on the southern side, which drained excess water into an adjacent creek. Senf built a two-story brick storehouse on the northern side, more than likely the building in Fraser's painting. The General Plan shows a layout of a town identified as Hope on land owned by the Canal Company. Nothing is known of this town, and it never prospered or became a reality, just like the proposed Izardtown.

Senf constructed a water-powered mill at Hope similar to the mill at White Oak Lock, recording that "on the East side of the Lock is a Millrace six feet wide and Mill Seat nine feet fall, clear of the Water in the lower Canal, and four

FIGURE 5.35. Hope Lock. Date and photographer unknown. Note the man next to the lock, showing the massive size of the double lock and the size of the counterforts. Courtesy of South Carolina Public Service Authority, Moncks Corner, South Carolina.

FIGURE 5.36. Charles Fraser, *A Bason and Storehouse Belonging to the Santee Canal,* 1803. Courtesy of the Gibbes Museum of Art, Charleston, South Carolina.

feet head, and a constant supply of Water."[58] He again did not state which type of mill it was or whether it was for the Canal Company.

Senf also constructed a dry basin at Hope: "On the west side [of Biggin Basin] the small dry bason, similar to the one near Santee Bason, will be very useful in repairing boats with ease and dispatch."[59] His use of the word *small* suggests the dry basin may have accommodated only one vessel at a time since it was attached to Biggin Basin and would not have required a forebay.

The Tide Lock was the last lock in the chain of eleven locks. According to the General Plan, Senf constructed a two-mile section of the Santee Canal, called the Biggin Canal (fig. 9.13), from Hope Lock to the Tide Lock, because, as he reported: "If conducted in as straight a course as the Nature of the Ground and situation will admit of, the Velocity of the Current will, with a little aid carry almost all the Sediments with it, and will deposit it on useless deeper places—And by a straight course the flood Tide counteracting with more force the Current, will swell the Water for a Sufficient Depth."[60] Senf read the landscape, and by avoiding the natural watercourse of Biggin Creek, which was tortuous and had many obstructions, he kept Biggin Canal clean of silt and debris and at the same time ensured sufficient water in the canal. Biggin Canal was difficult to excavate because of an underlying hard limestone substratum. An access road (fig. 9.3) paralleled the canal on the south side from Hope Lock to Biggin Road, as indicated in the General Plan.

Along this section of the deep cut is the line between Keithfield and Tibbekudlaw, where the two plantation property lines crossed Biggin Canal. Somewhere along this section, Senf reported "several large teeth and bones, a tusk, a large rib and smaller bones, part of them petrified, were found in digging the canal, in a bed of sand, surrounded by a kind of limestone, 9 feet under the surface of the ground. Some of these teeth and bones may be seen in the library room."[61] In his *A View of South Carolina* (1802), John Drayton illustrated the fossils (fig 5.37). These illustrations were the first published figures of South Carolina vertebrate fossils in an American museum.

So where are the fossils? The "library room" was the Charleston Library Society. The fossils are not at the Library Society today. In its accession records titled "Items donated to CLS in the CLS Accession Book 1798–1818," the fossils were not noted, and there are no other records of the fossils having been at the Charleston Library Society. As best as can be determined, they were transferred from the "library room" to the Charleston Museum.[62]

Senf's General Plan clearly shows Biggin Canal and Tide Lock where the canal entered the natural flow of Biggin Creek. Vessels entered Biggin Creek through Tide Lock and moved the short distance to the Cooper River, where they continued the water journey to Charleston. Senf built Tide Lock seventeen feet wide and seventy-two feet long so larger river vessels could pass from Biggin Creek through the lock into the Biggin Canal and go to Hope Basin, where cargo from the smaller canal vessels could be transferred to the river vessels or vice versa. Tide Lock had a composite construction. Its walls were cribbed. A double layer of parallel timbers was constructed, and the space between was filled with soil (fig. 5.38). This cribbed construction caused historian Frederick Porcher to call it a wooden lock, but this is not technically correct. Why Senf constructed the walls of wood between the two brick abutments that house the gates is not recorded. The most obvious reason is a considerable saving in bricks made at Big Camp that had to be brought to the lock.

Tide Lock was built over a bed of limestone. Timbers were laid on the limestone bed and cross planking laid on the timbers. A layer of bricks was laid on the planking, creating a tight seal (fig. 5.38). The walls and abutments were built on top of the flooring. The wooden gates were angled toward Hope Lock.

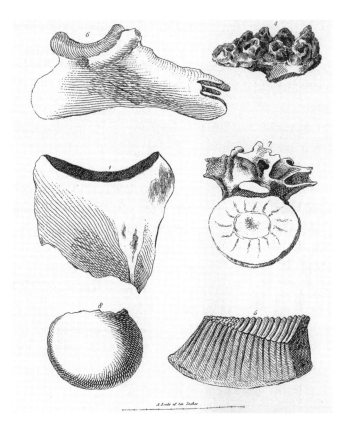

FIGURE 5.37. Vertebrate fossils found in Biggin Canal in 1795. From J. Drayton, *View of South-Carolina*, opposite 40.

Construction of the Santee Canal ~ 111

At high tide both gates were open, and the canal was flooded all the way to Hope Lock. Vessels could pass directly from Biggin Creek to Hope Lock or pass from Hope Lock to Biggin Creek. At low tide the outer gate was closed, conserving water in the lock and Biggin Canal. Water pressed on the gates from inside the lock, and the angled gates would have been pressed tight, holding water in the lock and Biggin Canal.

When a vessel needed to pass from Biggin Canal to Biggin Creek at low tide, the vessel entered the lock from Biggin Canal and the Hope-side gates were closed, trapping water in the lock. Since the creek-side gates could not be opened because of the water pressure inside the lock, wicket gates in the Biggin Creek gates were opened and water flowed from the lock into the creek. When the water level in the lock and creek were equal, the creek gates were opened and the vessel moved into the creek, its journey down the Santee Canal over.

Senf planned an ingenious method to clean Tide Lock of sediment. Biggin Canal severed off a section of Biggin Creek between Hope and the Tide Lock, abandoning a long section on its west side. Senf planned to connect the two severed ends of Biggin Creek with a "new course" thirty feet wide at the bottom, forty-eight feet at the top, and nine feet deep. He outlined the new course in red on his General Plan. He planned for it to tie into the abandoned section of the creek, which would junction with Biggin Canal at Tide Lock and enter it through a turning floodgate twelve feet wide installed in the lock's wall. Water coming down the new course would enter the lock through the open floodgate and carry away sediments in the lock and canal. Like Senf's ferry canal, the new course was never excavated, and the floodgate was never constructed in the Tide Lock.[63] The only record of his grand plan is the red line on the General Plan.

Senf may have used a backup plan, whereby the natural flow of water through Biggin Swamp east of Biggin Canal would be let into the canal upstream from the Tide Lock and its force carried away sediments through the open lock. No record was found if this plan was ever put into operation.

The distance from the Tide Lock to the Cooper River was three-quarters of a mile. This section of Biggin Creek is intact, but water from construction of the Tailrace Canal in 1942 has kept the water considerable higher than in the 1800s, and the precise route that a vessel would have traveled is uncertain.

Biggin Creek made a sharp loop just before it entered the Cooper River. The General Plan indicates that Senf cut a canal at the base of the loop to make a more direct route for traffic. In his Final Report, he stated:

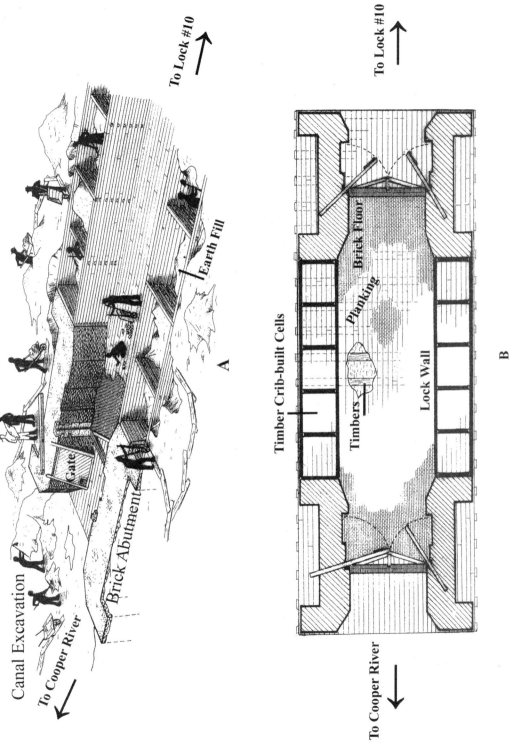

FIGURE 5.38. Conceptualized diagram and construction of Tide Lock. Illustration by William Robert Judd based on an archaeological survey of the lock.

At Stoney [Stony] Landing it was necessary to cut off a short turn of the Creek, which retarded the Flood very much, from gaining that height in the Canal which was absolutely wanted—and at the same time to give more Velocity to the Tide by as a direct Course as possible, with the additional Current of the fresh water of the Creek, to keep the short part of the Creek and the Canal clear of the Sediment, which not alone along Biggin Creek, but the inferior runs of water may bring in it in rainy Seasons.[64]

Senf suggested another method to force the creek's waters to move more swiftly and carry away sediments: "Several parts of the Creek should be made narrower by projections in an obtuse Angle with the currents. The projections may be easily made by a rough Frame of any kind of Logs and filled with that kind of Limestone of which the Creek abounds."[65] None of these frames survives today in Biggin Creek. Construction of the Santee Cooper Project and accompanying Tailrace Canal raised the water level in the creek, virtually destroying all traces of Senf's work.

For fifty-three years Senf's engineering marvel operated (except for three years of drought) just as he had planned. It ceased operation because of competition from railroads and steamboats, which could never have been foreseen in 1793 when construction on the canal began.

SIX

Grand Opening of the Santee Canal, Buford's Inaugural Passage, and Life along the Canal

On May 20, 1800, the following appeared in the *Charleston City Gazette:* "The Directors of the Santee Canal were yesterday informed by Col. Senf, that the Canal was completely filled with water, from one end to the other, and ready in every respect to receive boats."[1]

The evening before the Santee Canal was officially opened, Senf went with some friends to spend the night with Gen. Moultrie at Northampton. Moultrie invited his neighbors to meet and breakfast with the esteemed engineer and accompany him to the site of his triumph. Senf spoke of the Santee Canal as a great and crowning effort of engineering skill (which it was). The next day at Hope Lock, he intended for a worker to divert the water of Biggin Creek from its natural flow into the straight channel (Biggin Canal) dug from Hope Lock to Tide Lock. To turn a river from its bed into another was to Senf a great work to be admired by all. He had sent a German worker to Hope Lock early in the morning to see that no oversight occurred in the preparations and then sat down to enjoy Moultrie's breakfast with admiring friends. After breakfast the party set out to witness the diverting of the river. On reaching Hope Lock at noon, they found the river flowing in its new channel as though it had never known any other. The servant did not know the diversion was to be the last scene in Senf's act of self-glorification and had already opened the gates of Tide Lock. The preparations had been so perfect that they did not need Senf's hand to finish. This did not satisfy Senf; he saw himself robbed of fame by his presumptuous servant and dismissed the man from his service. Not many years afterward, the servant, Henry Glindkamp, was superintendent of the canal.[2]

BUFORD'S INAUGURAL PASSAGE

Upon the official opening of the Santee Canal, the *Charleston Times,* on May 28, 1800, reported that planter William Buford was the first person to pass through the Santee Canal to Charleston on a commercial venture: "William Buford, who lives on the banks of the Broad River, arrived in this city, through the Santee Canal, with his own boat, built on his own land, and loaded with his own crop, after safely passing over all the falls and shoals that are between his plantation and Charleston."[3] Newspapers far and wide reprinted the *Times*'s report, including the *Salem (MA) Impartial Register,* the *Hudson (NY) Balance,* and the *Windham (CT) Herald.*

Through landscape plats, Senf's Final Report, and his 1800 General Plan, archival and contemporary photographs, and contemporary field studies, let's ride with Buford on his epic trip along the Santee Canal and experience the natural history and burgeoning plantation culture of English Santee and Middle St. John's Parish that he witnessed.

It is not known how long it took for Buford to travel from his plantation on the Broad River to the Santee before he entered the twenty-two-mile-long Santee Canal at White Oak. During the two-day journey through the canal, though, Buford would have witnessed unparalleled natural beauty and burgeoning plantation opulence as he passed leisurely through thirty-five plantations in English Santee and Middle St. John's (fig. E3 and Senf's General Plan). He would have experienced the closeness and majestic beauty of a swamp, accompanied by sounds of swamp creatures and boat hands.

Buford's first sense that he was approaching the canal's entrance would have been the high bluff where botanist Thomas Walter had lived surrounded by his botanical garden. Passing by the high bluff, Buford would have approached the wooden wing dam Senf built to swell the water level at the entrance and allow boats to cross the sill of Guard Lock. A flurry of activity likely greeted Buford as attendants made ready to receive the vessel and guide it into the Guard Lock. Once through the lock, a rope from the tow mule or horse would have been attached to Buford's vessel for the pull to the next lock.

Undoubtedly, Buford would have found that there was something wonderfully appealing about being pulled along an artificial waterway by a mule or horse, and perhaps he thought it unnatural to float uphill, but that is what vessels did on the way to the Summit Canal. He next entered the Santee Basin, where riverboats too large to pass through locks 2 through 10 unloaded their cargo into the narrower canal vessels, turned around, and went back through the Guard Lock for the return trip up the Santee River. Numerous canal vessels could be loaded from a larger river vessel that brought plantation products down the river. Buford, however, came down the Santee in a canal vessel and was the only one on the canal.

Buford next approached White Oak Lock, which was the toll lock. One imagines that he departed his vessel and climbed up the stairs to the tollhouse and paid the toll. The lockkeeper would have explained the rules of the Santee Canal, which included no loading or unloading cargo except at public landings and no stopping anywhere except public landings. If his vessel was delayed and unable to reach a public landing, he was to stop at the next lock and stay there before proceeding the following morning.

After Buford returned to his vessel, the Santee-side gates would have opened, the vessel entered the lock, and the gates were closed. The tow mule, which had been routed around the lock, waited on the towpath on the far side to pull the vessel to the next lock. As Buford waited in his vessel for the lock to fill, the mill adjacent to the lock might have caught his attention (fig. 5.9). The *swish, swish, swish* as water hit the floats of the waterwheel surely mesmerized him. Quickly, though, he would have been brought back to the present—the gates of the lock opened and his vessel passed out of it, where the tow mule and attendant waited.

Traveling past White Oak Lock, perhaps Buford noticed the side ditch between the canal and adjacent St. John's Road, which fed water to the millrace (fig. 5.8). Did he see men in the ditch clearing branches that were blocking the passage of water to the mill? If puzzled for a moment at their activity, he would have quickly realized they were removing a beaver dam. Maybe he would later learn from workers that beavers were a problem anywhere water flowed, such as the side ditches. Beaver activity plagued the canal during its entire active operation but was mostly a nuisance since their dams could be easily removed from the narrow side ditches.

To the east of the lock, Buford might have noticed the stable and pastureland Senf provided for the horses and mules that drew the vessels along the canal. The horses and mules leisurely grazed on the abundant switch cane, common along the woods and swamps of the Lowcountry. Workers burned this natural pastureland to promote new growth every year. This was a scene that might have reminded him of the land around his Upcountry plantation, since switch cane was also common in the Piedmont (although a different species than on the Santee Canal).

While passing through Samuel Porcher's Mexico, Buford would have seen in the distance the commodious plantation house surrounded by numerous outbuildings that supported Porcher's enterprise. Porcher, seeing Buford's vessel, might have ridden up on horseback to chat briefly as the vessel passed by Mexico house. Porcher watched for seven years as the canal was constructed and probably was delighted to finally see a vessel loaded with Upstate cotton. Like his fellow planters, he had leased his enslaved people to the Canal Company to help himself overcome the depredations and financial setback of the Revolution. The canal gave him a more expeditious route to Charleston for his plantation crops, further helping him (and his fellow planters) to recover financially.

As Buford continued along the canal, he probably noticed one of Senf's overfalls (fig. 5.16). The overfall was a brick structure built into the towpath. It allowed excess water from the canal to flow into the adjacent wetland and prevented water from flowing over the towpath and causing erosion. The planks allowed the mules to cross the overfall. Buford never would have encountered a structure like the overfall except on his passage along the canal. The *clack, clack, clack* of the mule's hooves on the wooden overfall echoed through the woods, blending with the natural sounds of the woods and forests.

Buford next passed through Big Camp Lock, a double lock that raised vessels nineteen feet into the Summit Canal, taking him thirty-four feet above the Santee River and sixty-nine feet above the Cooper River, his destination. The Summit Canal was the highest elevation during his journey. It was five miles long, ending at Frierson's Lock. The passage on it took Buford through primordial oak and pine forests with little signs of habitation. This soon changed, because the construction of the Santee Canal would bring renewed activity along the canal's route.

As Buford's vessel passed out of Big Camp Lock, he was in the heart of Big Camp, the central headquarters of the canal's operations. To his left he may have seen a couple on the steps of the lockkeeper's house. He would have known immediately they were Colonel Senf and his wife, Gertrude. Senf would have been aware of Buford's passage, and after he and Gertrude shared the trials and tribulations of overseeing the canal's construction for seven years, perhaps they wanted to share this moment of triumph together. Buford might have wondered how Gertrude could possibly have endured living so many years in the solitude of Santee Canal country, removed from her New York social life before she married Senf. Perhaps the lockkeeper and several others assigned to Big Camp joined them in celebration of Buford's passage. It was a historic moment, and Buford would have been delighted to be a participant. Perhaps he tipped his hat politely to the esteemed engineer and his wife as he passed along the canal.

Buford may have seen a bustle of activity among a complex of buildings, including the overseer's house, workshops, lockkeeper's house, brick kilns, a brick warehouse, and numerous other support buildings that serviced the canal. One pair of laborers worked an implement that Buford may have never seen before—a mill used to mix sand, clay, and water into a mix called pug (fig. 5.17). The pug was placed in molds to dry, then the molds were fired in kilns to make bricks. Even though construction of the locks and associated structures was complete, Senf knew bricks would be continually needed for repairs, so he kept a supply on hand.

As Buford passed along the canal past Big Camp Lock, he might have noticed a stone marker on the bank (fig. 6.1). Engraved in the marker were these words:

> Constructed
> By Ch. Senf Colonel of Engineers and Director in Chief
> of the Santee
> Canal.
> February the 2? Th 1794.

Buford might have been amused that either Senf or someone else placed the marker in 1794, six years before the canal was completed.[4]

Buford was next at Burnt Savanna, owned by Robert Marion.[5] Cattle were grazing on the new growth of grass and forbs (broadleaf plants). Local owners burned their pinelands in the spring for cattle to graze on the succulent vegetation that grew in response—hence the name Burnt Savanna. Buford could not help but admire the herd of free-roaming cattle as he gazed over the canal bank.

He then passed under the bridge of the road leading from Pine Ville to Eutawville (fig. 5.18) and traveled into St. Stephen's Basin, where local planters and farmers would later bring their plantation wares to load on canal vessels. Since he was the first planter to come down the canal, locals had not yet begun to use the basin, but it would become a busy place in future years as nearby Eadytown (fig. 7.4) became more important to the canal as a commercial stopover.

FIGURE 6.1. Stone marker. The photograph of the marker is located at the South Carolina Historical Society (call number 30-16-6, Santee Canal).

Buford's next point of interest was the Great Reservoir (or Kirk's Reservoir by some accounts since it was created by damming Kirk's Swamp). Shortly after Kirk's Swamp was cleared of woody vegetation to make way for the reservoir, a variety of aquatic plants covered the surface, especially waterlily with its large floating leaves and beautiful white flowers. Kirk's fed water to the Summit Canal. Flooded in May, the reservoir teemed with waterfowl feeding on the rich aquatic life and vegetation.

Leaving the Great Reservoir, Buford crossed into Middle St. John's Parish and soon arrived at Frierson's Lock. Once Buford entered Frierson's Lock, he began his sixty-nine-foot descent to the Cooper River. He was now "floating" downhill, which seemed more natural than floating uphill. Buford could not help but admire the side chamber Senf constructed at Frierson's Lock to save half the water that would have passed down the canal and ultimately been lost to the system. On the eastern side, Buford saw a reservoir that fed the canal between Frierson's Lock and Flint's Lock, his next destination.

Buford passed Edward Edwards's Fountain Head (later renamed Woodlawn) east of the canal and the Marion family's Stewarton on the western side. Game such as deer and turkey were common on Fountain Head and throughout St. John's (fig. 6.2). The canal paralleled the eastern side of Biggin Swamp (the second route that Mouzon first laid out but Senf rejected; see fig. 4.1), which was fed by some of the many artesian springs of St. John's. Buford passed through Hepworth Lock and thereafter by the widow Ravenel's elegant and commodious Chelsea House to the south, built by Daniel Ravenel in 1714. Perhaps he witnessed young men and women arriving in carriages and horses for a "harring party" at Chelsea's spring.[6] Buford had fought at the Battle of Eutaw Springs and may have heard of a British cavalryman who had hacked at the front door of Chelsea with his sword trying to gain entrance but had been denied by widow Ravenel. The hack marks remained until the house fell into disrepair years later. He thought he might stop by and visit on his way back since the house sat close to the canal. Now, however, he had to get to Charleston by a certain date to meet with his broker, so the visit would have to wait.

Buford was now sojourning into the heart of Middle St. John's, which was becoming the "land of opulence," and many of the structures he saw that day would be replaced by plantation houses built on a much grander scale. He knew he was passing through a burgeoning plantation community because signs of agriculture abounded.

He would have observed a tributary of Biggin Swamp that passed under the canal by a double-arched brick aqueduct, one of seven aqueducts Senf constructed to allow natural watercourses to flow uninterrupted (figs. 5.27 and 5.28). Buford could not help but admire Senf's engineering and the brickwork so masterfully crafted by the enslaved workers from the adjoining plantations as his vessel was pulled across the aqueduct in an elevated stream of water.

FIGURE 6.2. Deer and turkey in St. John's. Courtesy of Karl Beckwith Smith.

Grand Opening of Santee Canal ~ 121

As Buford passed into Pooshee, he was in a stand of longleaf pine trees. Perhaps he saw a lone worker cutting a cavity at the base of a pine across the canal bank (fig. 6.3). This was the box method of harvesting crude turpentine from the tree, the original method practiced since the early days of the Lowcountry. Boxing involved cutting a cavity a few inches wide and several inches deep into the tree base. The crude turpentine flowed into the cavity (the box), where it was collected in a bucket, hauled to a distilling shed, and distilled into spirits of turpentine and rosin.

Two other products of the pines were tar and pitch, which were the basis of the naval stores industry that abounded in Santee Canal country. The naval stores and turpentine industry in the United States were closely identified with the economic development of the South and Santee Canal country wherever longleaf pines grew. Obtained from tar kilns (fig. 6.3), tar and pitch were among the earliest exports, and the industry was the main source of livelihood in the early days of the thinly settled piney woods of the Carolinas and Santee Canal country. At first the products were chiefly used in wooden sailing vessels, a fact that gave the industry its name. Tar was used to coat the rigging of ships, and pitch was used to caulk the seams of hulls. The dominant market for naval stores was England, whose mighty navy sailed the oceans on caulked hulls from Santee Canal country.

Buford would have next arrived at Black Oak Lock (fig. 5.29), which joined René Ravenel's Pooshee. Ravenel was one of the many plantation owners who

FIGURE 6.3. (Left) Box cutting near Ocilla, Georgia, 1903. Courtesy of US Forest Service, Forest History Society. (Right) Burning a tar kiln in North Carolina. *Harper's New Monthly Magazine,* May 1857, 74.

FIGURE 6.4. Northampton. Photographer and date unknown. Historic American Buildings Survey, Prints and Photographs Division, courtesy of the Library of Congress.

leased enslaved workers to the Canal Company. Buford was in the heart of Black Oak, a community center that was beginning to gain prominence as the location where so much of the social, political, and agricultural life of St. John's would occur. Nearby was a muster field of the St. John's Militia, warehouses that supported the canal, and a voting precinct. Looking west from the perch of his vessel, Buford would have seen Northampton in the distance, where Gen. Moultrie first experimented with Santee long-staple cotton in 1793. Green rows of cotton plants filled fields, each flower waiting to produce fiber that would adorn European royalty. Workers were in the field hoeing weeds from around the young stalks. Santee long-staple cotton, a strain of *Gossypium barbadense,* replaced rice and indigo as the main money crop after the Revolution in Santee Canal country. Planters had a ready market to ship their cotton overseas after canal completion. Northampton House (fig. 6.4), built in 1715 by the St. Julien family, with its array of support buildings, would certainly have been of interest

Grand Opening of Santee Canal ⁓ 123

to Buford, visible in the distance across a field of cream-colored cotton flowers. He was used to the white blossoms of short-staple cotton in the uplands, so the cream-colored flowers of Santee long-staple cotton surely commanded his attention.

While Buford waited for the lock to fill, he might have struck up a conversation with the lockkeeper, who had returned to his house (fig. 5.31) overlooking the canal after his daily inspection of the canal and lock. Did the lockkeeper playfully tell him to watch out for the cymbees or water spirits that enslaved people believed resided in the local springs?[7] Cymbees were part of local folklore from the beginning days of the parish, a holdover from African homeland and culture. These supernatural beings were believed to assume forms like a web-footed goose or a long-haired water nymph.[8]

Docking his vessel in St. John's Basin, Buford would have retired at Black Oak for the evening. The trip through the canal from the Santee to the Cooper River was a two-day event, so travelers had to spend one evening in quarters. Buford's workers camped on the canal bank for the evening. Maybe he dined on venison from the nearby woods and drank water from one of the many springs of the area. In late afternoon he might have taken a walk to the vicinity of Wantoot spring, whose waters passed under the canal in a double-arched brick aqueduct into Biggin Creek. Again, Buford admired the craftsmanship of the enslaved people that built the aqueduct, its graceful arches complementing the lights and shadows of nature's land. Women were filling containers with the cool spring water for home use and chanted in a dialect unfamiliar to Buford. From the conversation with the lockkeeper, he knew that the women were careful to leave the spring before dark, lest their chanting caused the cymbees to "dry up the spring." He watched them leave, balancing baskets on their heads and chanting in unison as they returned to the road. Buford was truly in a different world from his home in the Upcountry.

The next morning, Buford's crew would have had the vessel waiting and the tow mule ready for the passage to Hope Lock. Buford traveled along an elevated section of the canal, skirting the rice fields of Daniel Ravenel III's Wantoot before passage through Wantoot Lock. Rice plants were just beginning to pip, stretched in neat, green rows across the fields. The rice fields of Wantoot would have looked different to Buford than the rolling clay fields of his own plantation in the red hills of Carolina. Enslaved workers were shaking rattles and cracking whips to "mind off" the ricebirds gorging on the unsprouted seeds, or perhaps shooting them, for ricebirds (also known as bobolinks) were a delicacy.[9]

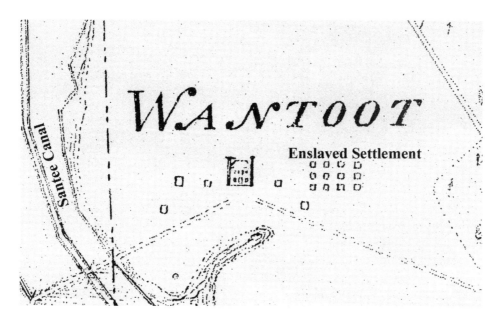

FIGURE 6.5. Wantoot. Sketch of the Wantoot House was cropped from "A Plan of Wantoot, Somerton and Hogswamp Plantations," by Isaac G. Wiare, Surveyor, 1795. Copied by J. Palmer Gaillard, 1915. Courtesy of the South Carolina Historical Society, Gaillard Plat Collection, 1835–1989 (bulk 1900–1980, call number 375.00, G-785).

To the east was fortlike Wantoot House, built in 1712 (fig. 6.5). Wantoot was one of the three sites in 1715 where forts were built in Carolina to protect early settlers from perceived hostilities by Native Americans. Directly to the western side, Buford saw Ravenel's water-powered pestle rice mill, stilled at the time since it was not processing season (fig. 6.6). The mill was a sign of the early prosperity of Huguenots of St. John's.

From the elevated perch on his vessel as he crossed an aqueduct built over Wantoot Lock, he could see Hanover House across Wantoot's rice fields and the open fields of Hanover (fig. 6.7). Huguenot Paul St. Julien built Hanover House in 1716. Viewing both Wantoot and Hanover might have impressed Buford with the achievement of the Huguenots, who had come from persecution, starting with nothing in the New World except their indomitable energy and will to succeed, and prospered in the face of prejudice and unseemly obstacles. Porchers, Ravenels, Mazÿcks, and St. Juliens all found a new home in Middle St. John's. During the Revolution, Hanover was owned by Henry Ravenel (1729–1785), known as Henry of Hanover. His son, Capt. Henry Ravenel Jr., fought for independence with Buford at the Battle of Eutaw Springs, so

Grand Opening of Santee Canal ⁓ 125

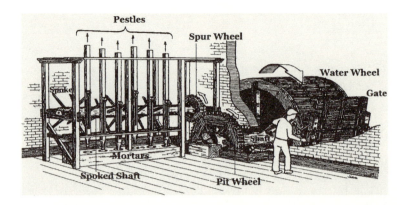

FIGURE 6.6. Water-powered rice mill. Illustration by William Robert Judd, illustrating what a water-powered rice mill may have looked like in the Carolina rice fields based on archaeological remains from abandoned mills in the Lowcountry. Senf's General Plan features a "rice machine" on Daniel Ravenel III's Wantoot located on a small canal or stream. Water turned a waterwheel, which turned a pit wheel attached to a spoked shaft. Attached to the shaft were pestles that were lifted and then dropped into the mortars, pounding the rice to remove the hull and bran, after which it was winnowed to clean it. Ravenel's rice machine may have looked like this illustration.

FIGURE 6.7. Sketch of Hanover House by artist Karl Beckwith Smith. Used by permission of the artist.

Buford might have felt a connection to Hanover as he viewed the house in the distance.[10]

Buford next came to Woodboo Lock. The canal skirted Stephen Mazÿck's rice fields that were fed by Mazÿck's Spring (later called Big Spring). Mazÿck's house and plantation buildings were directly behind the spring and rice fields (fig. 5.32). Woodboo, after a Native American word meaning "large water," was named for the spring.

Once through Woodboo Lock, the canal entered the natural watercourse of Biggin Swamp. Again Buford would have observed a cypress swamp unlike anything he had experienced in the Upcountry red hills. The canal followed the swamp to Hope Lock. On the way his vessel passed by Daniel Ravenel III's Somerton (Summertown on the General Plan) and Somerset and through Charles Johnston's Oakfield and William Simpson's Hope. Near Hope the canal passed into Biggin Basin. A storehouse stood on the bank of the basin, and one might imagine the watercraft depicted in Fraser's watercolor as Buford's vessel (fig. 5.36).

Hope Lock was a double lock with a fall of nineteen feet. Once through the lock, Buford's vessel would have been in Biggin Canal, which was at the same water level of Biggin Creek at high tide. At high tide water from Biggin Creek flowed all the way to Hope Lock. Buford's vessel followed the two-mile canal to the Tide Lock. Tow animals were not used between Hope Lock and Tide Lock; vessels were either poled or carried by the current. Although Buford passed through Keithfield,[11] Glebe Land, Tibbekudlaw,[12] Kent,[13] and Fairlawn, he would not have seen the highland houses through the swamp trees. Biggin Canal ran through Biggin Swamp, which carried Buford through moss-draped cypress trees and swamp hardwoods (fig. 6.8), a sight that even today never fails to inspire. Buford passed under the bridge on which the Biggin-to-Charleston Road was carried and next passed through the Tide Lock. He was then in the natural flow of Biggin Creek (fig. 6.9).

It was May, and a bluff close to the creek's edge was alive with spring wildflowers. Trillium, bloodroot, wild azalea, all in flower, may have reminded Buford of the rich hardwood forests he knew in the Upcountry where his farm was located. Shortly he passed Stony Landing, and about three-quarters of a mile farther, where Biggin Creek joined Fair Forest Creek (today's Wadboo Creek), he entered the West Branch of the Cooper River, his journey down the Santee Canal over. Buford flowed on his watery way to Charleston, the burgeoning commercial hub of the Lowcountry.[14]

FIGURE 6.8. Cypress swamp, 2018. Photograph courtesy of Richard Dwight Porcher Jr.

FIGURE 6.9. Biggin Creek, 2020. The water level is much higher in 2020 than it was in 1800 because of the Santee Cooper Project, but the view in 2020 was not too unlike what Buford would have experienced in 1800. Photograph by Richard Dwight Porcher Jr.

off on a chestnut horse; Edel identified the man as Samuel Sloan, a post rider, his route being from Camden to Charleston. Edel offered a reward for return of the pistols. No report was found if the pistols were ever recovered.[17] Edel was probably careful in the future with whom he shared his hospitality.

In 1803 several workers on the canal were killed while huddled in a shack during a violent thunderstorm. Theodore Gourdin II sued the Canal Company for loss of his enslaved workers.[18] The Honorable Jacob Drayton, a stockholder in the company, presided over the hearing. The Judgment Rolls recorded the incident: "Slaves were killed by the falling of several large trees on or near the bank of the said canal, which the said company had carelessly and negligently left standing after having deprived them of their roots, whereby they were exposed to tempestuous weather . . . and were blown down and killed the said Negroes."[19] Drayton, in favor of the Canal Company, ruled that the trees falling was an act of God.

In the same year, an unusual cargo must have surprised the locals along the canal's route, since they were accustomed to seeing only cotton bales on the vessels. The *Charleston City Gazette* of April 22, 1803, reported that Mr. Lawrence of Granby brought the following cargo down the canal: ninety-two bales of cotton, nine hogsheads of tobacco, five tons of hemp, and a considerable quantity of tallow, wax, lard, and butter.

On a Sunday morning, those traveling on vessels in the canal would have seen activity in and around Black Oak Lock. Planter families from all over Middle St. John's would be arriving for services at Black Oak Church. The land for the church, carved out of Pooshee by René Ravenel, bordered the canal adjacent to Black Oak Lock. Within sight of the canal, planters built the first church building in 1808.

René Ravenel reported from Pooshee on weather conditions at the canal that must have tried St. John's souls. On September 10, 1820, he recorded: "A severe Gail of Wind from E. and N. E. with a great fall of Rain, a higher fresh in the Swamps than had been for several, broke the Santee Canal bank in several places."[20] Weather events like this were common.

In May 1821 Joe, a leader of a maroon band, led a raiding party down the Santee River to George R. Ford's plantation on South Island.[21] Ford, a wealthy planter, was shot and killed while attempting to apprehend the raiders, who were reportedly stealing his cattle. For two years or more, Joe eluded capture and continued plundering. He found refuge in the vast swamps at the confluence of the Congaree and Wateree Rivers and the eastern banks of the Wateree and Santee Rivers from Manchester to Nelson's Ferry. In response to the threat,

Buford's successful passage proved to other planters that the Santee Canal was a viable, safe, and expeditious route to market. For example, the *National Intelligencer and Washington Advertiser* wrote:

> To those who feel an interest in the prosperity of our State, it might be highly gratifying to notice, that the Santee Canal proposes to shortly become the medium of conveyance for the rich produce of the interior country. Several boats laden with provisions, &c. arrived during the last week; and we are informed that most of the planters are building boats for the purpose of sending the whole of their crops through the canal.[15]

On March 18, 1802, the *Carolina Gazette* reported:

> Mr. Reuban states he came to this city on Friday by way of the Santee Canal in a boat from Lincoln County, N.C., 300 miles by land. 600 by water. His boat is calculated to carry 25 bales of cotton or 4 hogsheads of tobacco. The part of Lincoln County he came from is on the Broad River 10 miles from the mountains. He navigated his boat with one other person, met no impediments on the way where the rivers were up. Several other boats lately built on the river were to follow him shortly. The river was low when he first left so he did not carry a full load as it was a voyage of experiment. He is satisfied with the amount he carried.[16]

From 1800 forward newspapers continually reported on activities on the Santee Canal, in particular arrivals from the Upcountry. The articles proclaimed that the canal was open for business.

LIFE ALONG THE SANTEE CANAL

Life was not always uneventful on the canal. Each day brought something different. In a timeless activity, kids from the nearby plantations would hitch a ride on a vessel as it passed from Black Oak Lock to Wantoot Lock, a distance of only two-tenths of a mile. Such innocent fun, riding on cotton bales, was not unlike hayrides of later times.

One planter must have thought he was in the Wild West. On a May morning in 1802, at Bull Town, a young man on horseback rode up and asked for a drink of water. He was let in the house and, while there, stole a pair of horseman's pistols and brass locks. The owner, Francis Edel, said the horseman rode

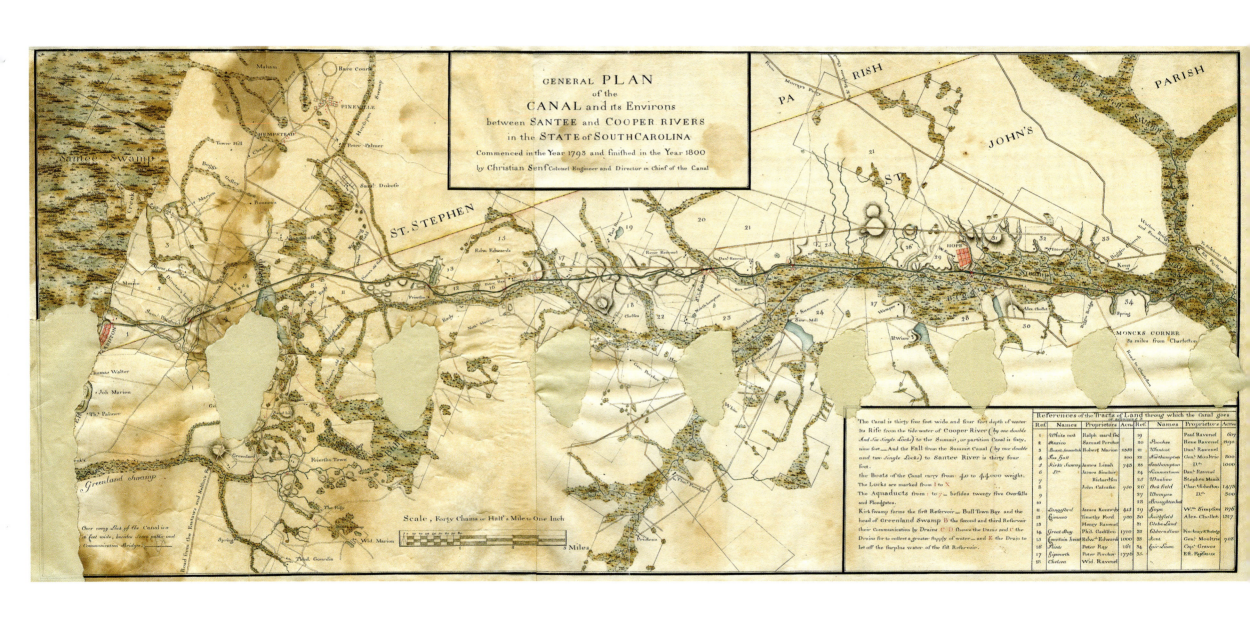

a group of local planters formed the Pineville Police Association to deal with Joe and others that might follow.[22] Their plan was simple: divide and conquer by offering rewards or bribes to a certain enslaved person to reveal Joe's hiding place. Before the association's men were able to commence their task to kill or capture Joe and his band, twenty-three men from the neighborhood of Manchester in Clarendon County conceived a similar plan to lure the raiders out of hiding. They had Royal, an enslaved boatman, attempt to trade with Joe and his band and hid in Royal's boat. Royal was directed by Joe's men to his camp in the swamp just above the canal. He followed Joe's orders, and when the boat was near to shore, the search party showed themselves and fired, killing Joe and two other members outright and shooting a fourth man who had jumped into the water. The search party then attacked Joe's maroon camp, killing men, women, and children. As for Joe, "his head was cut off and stuck on a pole at the mouth of the creek, as a solemn warning to vicious slaves."[23] The warning was implicit: this land belonged to planters, with complete domain, and their plantation system would forever prosper from the labor of the enslaved. Furthermore, they intended to reclaim and govern the swamp along the Santee River where Joe's band had escaped capture for two years. When enslaved boatmen in the future navigated down the Santee Canal to Charleston, they would pass by Joe's impaled head along the creek bank and the decomposing bodies of other members of his band.

In January 1822 onlookers must have been amused by an innovative manner by which vessels were routed around Black Oak Lock, as reported in the *Southern Patriot*. An extraordinary accumulation of water occasioned an accident that closed the lock. The *Patriot* did not specify the damage to the lock, but more than likely it was done to the brickwork by a vessel, and the lock had to be repaired. Timbers were obtained "for the purpose of rolling cotton barges and other freight" around the lock. The operation of the canal was not interrupted, and the lock was soon repaired.

The *Charleston Gazette* on Tuesday, May 17, 1824, reported:

> A Canal Boat, belonging to Mr. Samuel S. Saylor, with a valuable cargo of merchandize [*sic*], was blown up in the Santee Canal, near the plantation of Dr. Ravenel [Dr. Henry Ravenel of Pooshee, son of René Ravenel], on Friday last. The boat, and most of the cargo, including an elegant new piano forte, were destroyed. The crew, which consisted of five negro men, were all more or less injured by the explosion, some of them dangerously. From the statement of the patron, it appears that a carboy of either, or

vitriol, must have burst in the hold—on hearing the explosion, he opened a slide between the cabin and the hold, and on putting in his lantern to discover the cause, fire was instantly communicated by the candle to the foul air. The crew hastened to get off the hatches, but while in the act of doing so, a quantity of gunpowder, which was below, exploded and literally blew the boat to pieces.[24]

No record was found about Ravenel's reaction to the boat's exploding near Pooshee.

Although the canal was primarily used for agricultural products, occasionally it was used otherwise. Frederick Porcher wrote that in 1831, as dinner was being served at the nearby St. John's Club (fig. 6.10), members' attention was directed to a crowing of cocks in the canal. Upon inspection they found a vessel in Black Oak Lock laden with coops holding gamecocks. "On inquiring we were told that they belonged to a gentleman from the upper country of high social position, but of a decidedly sportive tendency." The gentleman had heard that the governor of Havana was a lover of the cockpit, and he was going to Havana to try his fortunes. Professor Porcher said the club invited the gentleman to dinner, after which he continued his trip to Havana.[25] Whether the gentleman reached Havana or how his cocks fared in the cockpit, the authors know not.

FIGURE 6.10. Clubhouse of the St. John's Hunting Club, built 1811. Courtesy of Karl Beckwith Smith based on an archival description.

The sky of St. John's was on one occasion aglow with burning cotton bales. In November 1833, the *Charleston Courier* reported "a cotton boat, belonging to Mr. McMillan, with 94 bales Cotton on board, took fire, and 40 or 50 bales of Cotton were destroyed. The boat is also stated to be much injured."[26] The incident must have been spectacular to the enslaved people and planters, who were not used to such pyrotechnics prior to the Civil War.

On June 28, 1834, the *Charleston Courier* announced that "Mathew Crawford's boat, from Columbia, with 105 bales of Cotton consigned to Boyce Henry & Walter, being overloaded sunk in the Santee Canal, a day or two since. The Cotton all saved but in a damaged state."[27]

The canal at Black Oak was a meeting place on Saturday mornings at nine o'clock in the fall and winter months. Somebody was certain to be there with dogs and drivers, prepared to hunt. The baying of hounds as they chased the wily fox through the woods and fields could be heard around Black Oak and up and down the canal. Or one might hear the sounds of Parker shotguns as hunters on stands fired at the fleeing deer chased by hounds.

Frederick Porcher related an incident in 1837 concerning a freshet, which were common on the Santee. Imagine the surprise of Samuel Porcher of Mexico "that in the great freshet of 1837 a canal boat was washed over the [Canal] bank and stranded in Major's corn field."[28]

The Santee Canal also attracted agricultural reformer Edmund Ruffin during his agricultural and geological survey of South Carolina in 1843. He touted the use of lime to restore depleted agricultural fields. Construction of the Santee Canal revealed significant limestone and marl deposits in St. John's. From February 4 through 6, he left the vicinity of Biggin Church ruins and "from the elevated bridge which crosses [Biggin Creek] this above the lower lock [Tide Lock], the whole lower section of the canal [Biggin Canal] is in view, having a straight course for nearly three [two] miles. My route was along the margin [bank], for five miles to Wantoot. For that distance, & some higher, the canal passes through the very large Biggin Swamp."[29] Ruffin met with numerous plantation owners in and around Black Oak and attended a meeting of the Black Oak Agricultural Society, all the while touting the use of limestone on agricultural fields.[30]

For three days, from October 31–November 2, 1843, the sounds of gunfire were heard along the canal. The shooters were Maxcy Gregg and his friends Robert Pringle Mayrant and Bob Myers from Columbia, along with two servants, boating down the Santee Canal on their way to Charleston from Columbia.[31] Gregg was on one of his many outings as an amateur ornithologist and naturalist. In two boats, the larger *John Moore* and the smaller *Nimrod,* they entered the canal on Tuesday. They had hewed off the gunwales of the *John Moore* so it could pass though the locks. They slept at night along the canal banks and shot game as they passed down the canal. The open water of Kirk's Reservoir was especially abundant in waterfowl, and Gregg shot at ruddy ducks and ringnecks. At Black Oak, and at two other locks, they had to haul the *Nimrod* around the lock on rollers. At dusk the third day they reached Biggin Creek and then the Cooper River, where they boated to Charleston. It is doubtful if any others during the canal's history repeated Gregg's adventure.

Black Oak was the community center of Middle St. John's. The first Episcopal church in the area was built here in 1808 within sight of the Santee Canal. In 1846 those traveling on vessels through Black Oak Lock might have been witness to the original church building being rolled from Black Oak to nearby Macbeth after it was given to Rehoboth United Methodist Church. Others might have witnessed the replacement church being built in 1847. Dr. Henry Ravenel stated in his diary on January 1, 1847: "The new Church at Black Oak was consecrated this day."[32] The building was made of wood (probably local cypress or pine) and measured approximately thirty by sixty feet. The church, except for the Egyptian effect of its window treatment, was severely plain, both on the exterior and interior, in striking contrast to the appearance of other coastal chapels and churches. Its design was in keeping with the sensibilities of the planters of the parish, who were rarely given to ostentatious displays of wealth or position, letting their deeds define their community. The church served Santee Canal country until the coming of the lake in 1942. Families coming from west of the canal would cross the lock on the Black Oak–Bonneau Road and have a wide-open view of the canal and vessels moored or passing through. Black Oak was the community center of Middle St. John's, and those on vessels passing through Black Oak would have seen a variety of activities, including political meetings.

Perhaps those on the vessels passing down the canal in the vicinity of Northampton noticed a lanky man walking the bank or in the nearby fields, head down looking at the ground, oblivious to all around him. This was the botanist William Henry Ravenel, who owned Northampton until he sold it in 1853 and moved his family to the drier air of Aiken for health reasons. The canal bank and adjacent St. John's were ideal for collecting Ravenel's specialty, the fungi of South Carolina, and any variety of vascular plants that caught his interest. Within sight of the canal, he collected a specimen of *Eriocaulon* he did not recognize, which he sent to Alvan Chapman, who was working on his *Flora of the Southern United States.* Chapman determined that it was a new species of pipewort and named it in Ravenel's honor, and today it is known as *Eriocaulon ravenelii* Chapman, Ravenel's pipewort. Ravenel's collection site is now under the waters of Lake Moultrie, and his pipewort has not been found in South Carolina elsewhere since his collection.

Imagine seeing a parlor on a barge coming up the canal. It might have happened, if what William Cain Jr. (1908–93) wrote in an undated letter to Elias Bull was factual: "I have always understood that Mr. [Charles] MacBeth brought up all the stock of the Canal when it was going out of business and that the last thing floated up the Canal was the Parlor of our village house [in Pinopolis], which had been a beach cottage on Sullivan's Island. I cannot vouch for the accuracy of the comment."[33] Since the Santee Canal passed by Pinopolis, it would have been relatively easy to move the parlor to the summer house if it was small enough to pass through Tide Lock. Such were the days along the Santee Canal—days of serenity and peacefulness broached by all sorts of interruptions—some comical, some not so.

SEVEN

Attempts to Solve the Water Deficiency of the Santee Canal

The Santee Canal was plagued throughout its history with difficulties in obtaining an adequate supply of water in the Summit Canal and lower reaches to operate the eleven locks along its length. Numerous attempts were made, and numerous plans suggested, to secure the water supply. The following are five attempts to address the canal's water deficiency.

STEAM ENGINES

As early as 1809, as low reservoir water became more of a problem, steam engines were considered as a source of water for the Santee Canal. On June 20, 1809, the board of directors advertised in the *City Gazette* that they considered "erect[ing] a Steam Engine on Santee River, for the purpose of furnishing an abundant supply of water to the summit Canal, in the driest seasons."[1] The directors requested that "any person disposed to contract for any part of the Machinery . . . please send in their proposals." There is no record of any responses to the advertisement, and this early use of steam engines was never implemented.

During the drought of 1816 and 1818–19, when the Summit Canal went dry, the Santee Canal ceased operations. The Santee Canal Company petitioned the General Assembly for thirty thousand dollars to buy two steam engines "to provide a resource for water in the driest seasons . . . of a capacity sufficient to raise from the bed of the Santee River and throw up to the level of the Summit

Canal."[2] Two steam engines were installed sometime in March 1819, one at Big Camp (fig. 7.1) and one along the river (fig. 7.2).[3] The engine on the river was intended to pump water into the canal between White Oak Lock and Big Camp Lock, and the second engine was intended to pump water from between White Oak Lock and Big Camp Lock into the Summit Canal. With great fanfare, the company announced in *Miller's Weekly Messenger* that the engines "were put into operation on Saturday last, and they fully answered the expectation entertained of their utility. In a few days the Canal will be filled, and boats will hereafter be able to pass at all seasons, without difficulty or delay."[4]

Despite the boastful announcement, however, the engines were a failure:

> Two engines were erected, one at White Oak to lift the water from the river, and one at Big Camp to lift it to its summit level. After a great expenditure of time and money the engines began to play. That at White Oak barely furnished water to fill the leakage; that at Big Camp . . . commenced its operations by lifting up a boy who was recklessly leaning upon the beam, but fortunately doing him no damage except to frighten him, and continued working for half an hour, when it stopped and never worked again.[5]

Porcher's reference to a beam indicates that the engines were some type of walking-beam steam engines, common in England to pump water from mines.[6] The horizontal steam engine that became common to drive rice mills was not available until around 1825 and would not have been used in 1816 or in 1818–19.[7] There were different designs of walking-beam engines, but a fundamental feature of one that would have operated on the river was a rod connected to a plunger attached to the beam. As the beam was forced down by steam power, the plunger was forced down a pipe or well (fig. 7.2) to the water table (which was shallow since the engine was on the bank of the Santee River). When the beam was raised it raised the plunger, bringing up water from the water table. A mechanism must have been available to divert the water into a nearby drain that ran to the side ditch along the canal. The drain shows in figure 5.8 and is still present today.

The second engine, also a beam engine, was at Big Camp. A plat by Henry Ravenel, dated September 1822, shows the location of the steam engine southeast of Big Camp Lock (fig. 7.1). Its location indicates it pumped water into the Summit Canal from between White Oak Lock and Big Camp Lock.

Attempts to Solve the Water Deficiency ~ 137

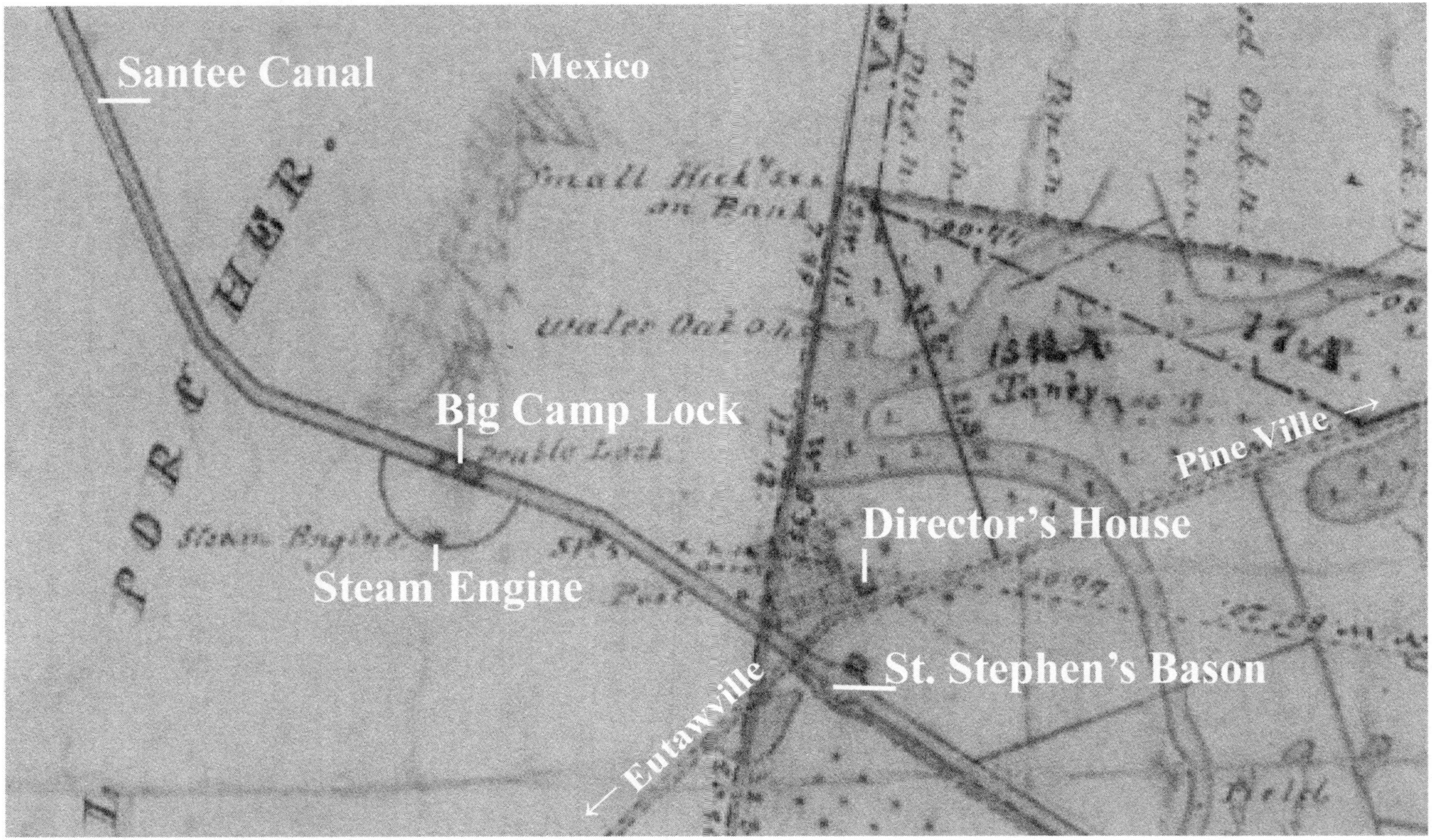

Santee Canal
Mexico
Big Camp Lock
Steam Engine
Director's House
St. Stephen's Bason
Pine Ville
Eutawville

LEFT: FIGURE 7.1. Plat titled "The Above Plan Represents Several Tracts of Land in Saint John's and Saint Stephen's Parish Belonging to the Santee Canal Company and Containing Together Eighteen Hundred and Eighty (1880) Acres," surveyed in April 1822 by Henry Ravenel. Authors include a cropped section of the plat with the steam engine site. Porcher is Samuel Porcher, who owned Mexico. No remains of the engine or engine foundation were found. Plat courtesy of the Georgetown County Digital Library/Georgetown County Library (digital collection, 02-1822-04), Georgetown, South Carolina.

The engines were not retained by the Canal Company after they quit working. They were advertised for sale by Mr. LeQueux, superintendent of the canal, on March 19, 1830, in the *Southern Patriot*:

> Steam Engines. By Wm. Payne & Son. ON Tuesday, 15th of May, at 11 o'clock, at the Exchange in Charleston, will be sold The Two Steam Engines, said to be sixteen horse power each; they will be sold as they lay at the Santee Canal, in St. John's, and may be examined by any person in the mean time, on application to Benjamin Lequeux, Esq. Superintendent of the Santee Canal; the same to be moved by the purchaser in twenty days after day of sale. Conditions—one-third cash; balance in note with approved endorsers, adding bank discount; payment in 6 and 12 months.[8]

FIGURE 7.2. Steam engine mount and pipe, Santee River, 2020. Photograph by Richard Dwight Porcher Jr.

Attempts to Solve the Water Deficiency

It would have been hard to sell these engines in 1832 except for scrap, since they were beam engines and the horizontal steam engine, introduced around 1825, was the engine of choice in the burgeoning rice industry. The authors did not find a notice stating the engines had been sold.

The remains of the brick steam engine mount and the pipe that functioned as the well can be seen on the bank of the Santee River (fig. 7.2). The drain from the engine site to the side ditch (fig. 5.8) is visible and easy to follow. The side ditch carried water to the millpond where the water was stored. From the millpond water could be released back into the side ditch when needed to operate the mill at White Oak Lock, or it could be fed into the canal to operate the locks.

ABRAM BLANDING'S INSPECTION OF THE SANTEE CANAL, 1823

The Santee Canal always commanded attention, since it was a vital link in the extensive statewide river-navigation network—but it also served as its weakest link. Its closing during droughts caused the Committee on Internal Improvements to request that Abram Blanding, the state's superintendent of public works, to develop recommendations for improving the water supply of the canal so it that would remain open continuously.[9] On a larger scale, this was just one study in the beginning of an extensive survey on the importance of inland navigation to the state's economy.[10] In May 1823 Blanding inspected the Santee Canal along with stockholder Henry Ravenel and Henry Glindkamp, superintendent of the canal at the time.[11]

Blanding reported on two main problems he saw with the canal: the Summit Canal went dry during droughts, so that the passage of boats was suspended, and the locks were only sixty feet long and ten feet wide, too small to be used by larger river vessels that could carry larger cargo loads and thus were more commercially profitable. The reservoirs that fed the Summit Canal, Kirk's Reserve, Greenland Swamp, and Bull Town Bay were completely dry during 1816 and 1818–19. So severe was the drought that corn was grown in Kirk's Reserve. The reservoir at Frierson's Lock was also unable to supply water to the canal below the lock. All methods the company tried to supply the requisite water failed. Furthermore, Blanding reported, the only plan that promised success was pumping worked by steam engines; he explained why a recent attempt with steam engines failed: "This experiment was not, however, fairly made; for the engines turned out to be worthless; and the pumping establishments were so badly planned, that with the best engines, they must have failed. But I am of the opinion, that had these works been conducted on the very best plan, they would not have furnished the requisite water to all levels, which in dry seasons, fail; the whole extent of which is a little more than nine miles."[12]

Blanding said that depending on machinery to pump water into the Summit Canal and on surface reserves to solve the water supply would always be limited, and he recommended three changes to provide the necessary water for each level of the canal. The first recommendation was to lower the bed of the Summit Canal four feet between Big Camp Lock and Frierson's Lock. Even during droughts of 1816 and 1818–19, Blanding observed that the Summit Canal had eighteen inches of water from seepage from the surrounding groundwater. No part of this water was supplied from the surface, since all the reservoirs and feeders were dry. Whenever the eighteen inches of water was drawn off, it rose again to the same level in less than six days. Blanding wrote: "The wells in the vicinity of the summit canal, which were 14 feet deep, did not fail in these years. . . . The water table of the country, through which this level passes, when reduced by drought to its lowest point, is 18 inches above the present bottom of this part of the canal. Lower this bottom four feet and the whole country becomes the reservoir of the canal."[13] Blanding calculated that in the driest seasons the water would rise nine inches in twenty-four hours: "If these conclusions be correct, it follows that the reduction of the summit 4 feet, will give, in the driest season, four times the quantity of water at present required for all the transportation of the country."[14] He addressed the opinions voiced by some who said the summit level should be changed to pass through Greenland Swamp: "The only difference in level between the ridge on that rout [sic], and the ridge where the canal now exists, is five feet. The whole length of the new canal will be about 8 miles; and at last, the prospect of water from the surface of the earth is not rendered any better; for this swamp in 1816, 1818, and 1819, was entirely dry. And of course the only water to be depended on, for the new canal, must be derived from percolation through its banks and bottom."[15] Reasoning that changing the canal to Greenland Swamp would be expensive and without any certainty of success, Blanding recommended lowering the level of the present summit as the best option. He next addressed how two additional levels could "at all times be supplied without depending on water from the summit level."[16]

The level between Frierson's Lock and Flint's Lock, which was one and three-quarters miles long, had no feeder springs. The feeder was a rain-fed reservoir (fig. 5.21) made from Horsepen Creek that went dry in droughts. Two springs, Frierson's and Gaillard's, were a short distance from this level and were about four feet eight inches lower that the water table of this section of the canal. Instead of lowering the present bed, Blanding recommended cutting a new canal on the right side of the present one between locks 6 and 5 four feet eight inches lower than the present canal bed. This would allow water from Frierson's and Gaillard's springs to supply the new level. The present bed, Blanding noted, ran on rising ground on the left of Frierson's Swamp (which Senf and Mouzon called Biggin Swamp), and very little cut entirely within the soil. The new cut to the right for a short distance would carry it entirely out of the ground, and the ditching would not average more than three feet. The lock at the south end of this level, which had a ten-foot fall (lock 5), would then have a six-foot fall, and a new lock with a fall of four feet, eight inches, would be located a short distance below lock 4. The summit level would still supply the water for lock 4.

The level between Hepworth Lock and Black Oak Lock was three miles and failed in dry seasons. Its bed was about two feet four inches higher than Ravenel's Spring (Pooshee Spring), which had a never-failing supply of water. Lowering this level by two feet four inches would allow water from Ravenel's Spring to flow into this section. Lowering the section would not be a difficult task, since the canal bed here was generally formed by an embankment and had but one short, deep cut. Blanding also realized that if Senf had made Hepworth Lock with a ten-foot rather than five-foot fall, the deeper bed below the lock would always have had water. The section of the canal below Black Oak was fed by springs at Wantoot and Woodboo, so no changes in these sections were needed.

Blanding summarized these suggestions for the changes on the three levels as follows: "These are all the changes, that under any circumstances can be required to give this canal a sufficiency of water at all times, according to the view I have taken of it."[17] He devised a work plan that would not stop the passage of vessels through the canal while work was being done in the Summit Canal between the first of November and the first of May, the busy season. A new canal would be cut on the east side of the present Summit Canal from lock 4 north to where deep cutting began. This could be done more cheaply than cutting the old bed four feet deeper. This new cut would later become the canal, and the original section abandoned. While the work was proceeding, vessels could continue to use the Summit Canal. In May the Summit Canal would be emptied, and the excavation of the new deep cut carried on until November. If the work had not been completed by November, the present canal would be filled, and work stopped until May. The next summer the work would be completed.

Blanding then gave this assessment on the outcome of the proposed changes to the Summit Canal: "Should it [the changes] answer all the purposes contemplated, and be found adequate as a feeder of the other levels, the whole work of supplying water is done. If it is only adequate to its own supply, then the work on the other levels must be undertaken. But if it is found to give no adequate supply of water to the Summit Canal, all further efforts should be stopped, and the canal left to its fate."[18] He gave a price of $48,453.47 for completing work on the summit.

To allow river vessels to use the canal, Blanding recommended enlarging the locks to sixty-five feet long and sixteen feet wide. River vessels loaded with 250 bales of cotton could pass through the new locks. Since these larger vessels could now make the same passage as two canal vessels carrying only 100 bales each, Blanding reasoned that enlarging the locks would increase the canal's capacity by twenty percent. Also, even though the river vessels were larger, several turning basins along the canal would allow them to pass each other, and more could be constructed with little expense.

Lastly Blanding suggested that steamboats with a lesser draft than normal could pass through the reconfigured canal towing three boats, each carrying 750 bales of cotton, and could descend from Columbia to the Santee Canal in less than two days. In three more days, the towed boats would be in Charleston. The same towed boats would return from Charleston and through the canal in three days and be towed to Columbia in five, the entire trip taking sixteen days or fewer. The same boats on a trip via the Santee by ocean took a month, so the savings in time would be significant.

Blanding's recommendations did not stop with just the technical aspects of the canal. He argued that there was another important advantage of enlarging the locks: "The risque [sic] of navigation, by the larger boats, would be vastly diminished . . . between the mouth of the Santee and Charleston."[19] He reasoned that the loss of boats and cargo in the ocean or bays over twenty years would be more than equal to the expense of reconstructing the locks of the Santee Canal. In time of war, he noted further, boats in the ocean between the Santee River and Charleston would be constantly exposed to capture, and traffic between the Upcountry and Charleston would be interrupted. The inland route of the redesigned canal would never be exposed to the enemy except under occupation.

Blanding also proposed using steam pumps to feed the canal from the river and installing water-saving locks (possibly similar to Senf's locks with side chambers). Steam pumps had already been tried and had failed, however; the

Canal Company did not have the resources to make these improvements and the state declined to fund them, so they were never implemented.

Blanding understood the Canal Company would never have the financial resources to pay for the changes to the canal he recommended. The company was in debt; its major assets were 110 enslaved people and six thousand acres of land. Moreover, it could not dispose these assets to pay off its debts, because they were necessary to maintain and operate the canal. Blanding suggested that the state "loan to the Company $50,000 in a 5 per cent. stock, to be issued as it might be wanted, which shall be expended exclusively on the summit canal. The re-payment should not be required until after the expiration of three years. At the end of that time, if the company are receiving more than 6 per cent. profit on their stock, estimated at $150,000, the surplus over 6 per cent. shall be paid to the state, in extinguishment of the loan, and interest on it."[20] He proposed that if the company accepted the loan, it would be subject to the following conditions: (1) if the work on the Summit Canal supplied sufficient water to the Summit, then water should be supplied to the other levels; (2) the locks should be reconstructed to make them seventy by sixteen feet; and (3) the thousand shares of stock of the company should be estimated at less than $150.00 each so that the whole stock might be regarded as worth $150,000.00.

When the sky opened, the welcome rains came, and the reservoirs were full, all consideration of Blanding's recommendations was ignored, and life on the canal proceeded as if there would never be an end to the good times. Those good times would last only until 1853.

BULL TOWN DRAIN

Henry Ravenel's plat of 1825 (fig. 4.4) is the earliest mention the authors found of Bull Town Drain (in some references called Bull Town Ditch). It does not show in Senf's Final Report or on his General Plan. If Senf had constructed the drain, he surely would have mentioned it in his Final Report to the Santee Canal Company when he discussed the three reservoirs he created. The authors conclude that Bull Town Drain was not part of the original construction of the Santee Canal. Blanding's 1823 report also did not mention the drain. Thus, the authors conclude that Bull Town Drain was constructed sometime after 1823 but before 1825 (the date of the Ravenel plat).

Blanding went into too much detail concerning the water supply for the canal not to have mentioned the drain's value in supplying water for the Summit Canal. Why it was not mentioned by Gillmore in 1881 is unknown, because it was in use by 1825. The authors found no mention of the drain in the archives they consulted, and neither Kapsch nor Bennett and Richardson mention the drain.

Richard Porcher and friends walked the entire length of Bull Town Drain to assess if any infrastructure still exists. The drain is four miles in length and empties directly into the Summit Canal as shown on the 1825 Ravenel plat and the 1979 topographical map (fig. 7.4).[21] In the topographical map, the entire drain is shown. The drain in the field looks similar to how it appears in figure 7.3 for most of its length. More than likely it was created during or just after the drought of 1818–19 to provide the Summit Canal with water. It passes through four swamps that could have provided a source of water, possibly even during moderate droughts. In constructing the drain, workers placed fill from the excavation mostly on one side, making a higher bank on that side (fig. 7.3). Whenever it traversed through swamps, breaks in the drain's bank allowed water to flow into it, which then flowed into the Summit Canal. The drain ran south of and parallel to the elevation break in the landscape, allowing its waters to easily

FIGURE 7.3. Bull Town Drain, 2020. Note the high bank on the southeast side. Photograph by Richard Dwight Porcher Jr.

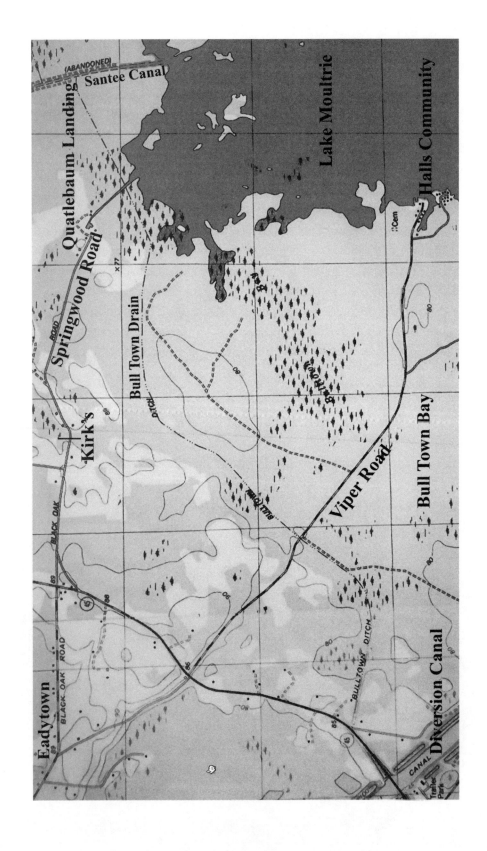

LEFT: FIGURE 7.4. USGS Quad, 1979. Bull Town Drain is called Bultown Ditch in this quad; they are one and the same. The Santee Cooper Cross Generating Plant and fly ash deposit site were created after Bull Town Bay was obliterated in 1979. The main site of Bull Town Bay is where the authors placed the label, not where Bultown Bay is labeled on the topographic map. Black Oak Road today is called Springwood Road. The drain is easily seen where it crosses Viper Road. Note the location of the old settlement of Eadytown (top left). Authors added Halls Community, Lake Moultrie, Viper Road, Quattlebaum Landing, Springwood Road, Kirk's, Bull Town Drain, Bull Town Bay, Diversion Canal, Eadytown, and Santee Canal.

flow into the Summit Canal (fig. 7.4). Floodgates were probably located at the breaks in the bank to control water into the drain, but no remains were found. It is certainly possible that the Canal Company constructed the drain, but the authors found no archival records in support of the company's role.

Two additional theories might be explored by future historians. Did adjoining landowners construct the drain to open up their wetlands to planting, while at the same time assisting the Canal Company in its endeavors to keep the Summit Canal supplied with water? Or did they construct the drain on their own and use the Summit Canal to rid the excess water from their lands without input from the Canal Company? The present authors found no records to document either possibility. We argue that the drain was constructed to supply the Summit Canal with water during future droughts when the reservoirs that normally feed it might become dry again—but by whom was not determined.

Bull Town Drain must have been constructed by enslaved labor, since at the time there would have been no other source of labor sufficient to create this four-mile long drain. Even today the authors are in awe of this historic structure that may have been an integral part of Santee Canal's history after Senf left— one overlooked by historians who later wrote about the history of the Santee Canal.

PLANKING THE CANAL BED TO STOP LEAKAGE

Porcher and Judd documented an attempt to fix a leak in the canal bed just past the Guard Lock (figs. 7.5 and 9.5). A conceptualized reconstruction of the planking is seen in figure 7.6. The bulkheads that enclosed the planking were ten feet apart, and backfill (soil) came right to the outside wall of the bulkheads. Timbers were laid crosswise and planking timbers laid lengthwise on top of the cross timbers. A series of carved stones were laid end to end on either

FIGURE 7.5. Planking on Santee Canal, 2021. Note the scattered bricks from the floor. Photograph by Richard Dwight Porcher Jr.

side of the planking ten feet apart. The walls of the bulkheads were attached to uprights anchored into notches of the carved stones. The bulkheads were stabilized by tiebacks. A brick floor was laid on the lengthwise planking, creating a tight seal and preventing leakage.

Senf stated that the canal from the Guard Lock to Santee Basin was seventeen feet wide, so river vessels, which were wider than the nine-foot-wide canal vessels, could pass through to the basin, and the canal bed was forty feet wide from the Guard Lock to the basin. Why, then, was the planked section only ten

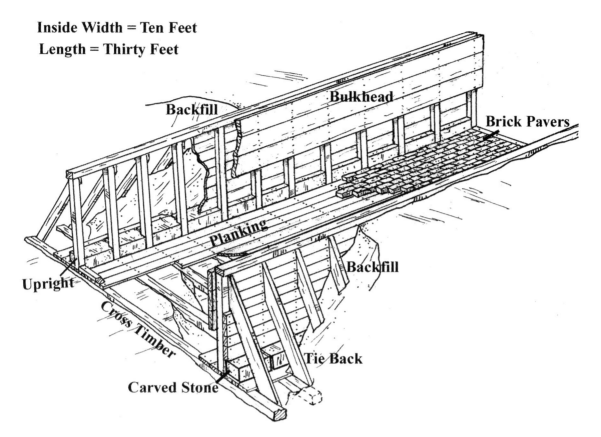

FIGURE 7.6. Conceptualized planking, Santee Canal bed. Illustration by William Robert Judd based on field survey of ruins in figure 7.5.

feet wide, which would have precluded the larger river vessels from reaching the basin? The only explanation authors have is that the planking section was done well after Senf constructed the original canal, and the Canal Company had abandoned allowing river vessels to pass to the basin—hence a bed ten feet wide was adequate, since this was the same width of the locks. The authors found no explanation why the Canal Company would have abandoned river traffic to Santee Basin. After planking reduced the canal's width to ten feet, river vessels must have unloaded their cargos into canal vessels in the river basin at the Guard Lock.

In 1844 Frederick Porcher wrote that water leaked from the short reach from Black Oak to Wantoot Lock. A wooden floor (probably cypress) was laid at the canal bottom nearly the entire way to Wantoot Lock, which succeeded in containing the water.[22] Porcher wrote that the "leak was found to proceed

Attempts to Solve the Water Deficiency ～ 149

from the sinking of a portion of the lower rock upon which the whole country lies."²³ The authors found no other references to planking in the archives that were consulted. One other set of planking remains was observed at the base of the inner gate of the Guard Lock. These remains were so deteriorated that no meaningful description or diagram was considered useful.

HOW TO KILL THREE BIRDS WITH ONE STONE

An article titled "How to Kill Three Birds with One Stone" appeared in the *Charleston Daily Courier* in 1852.²⁴ The article outlined an audacious plan to ensure (1) the continuing operation of the Santee Canal; (2) a supply of freshwater to Charleston from the Santee River; and (3) the irrigation of the Cooper River via water from the Santee River to extend rice production into heretofore unused brackish marshes. The plan was based on a false premise touted by the article's authors that the South Carolina legislature would not allow the Canal Company to close the canal.

> As long as the property of the Company, or that which they may have over and above the earnings at any time, remains unexhausted; the obligations of the Company can be discharged, and will be enforced. An attempt to escape from them will be strenuously opposed; and in the present temper of our Legislature towards corporations, it is probable that their answer would be—"Your first duty is not to divide your property, but to discharge your obligations. Exert your energy to render your Canal more useful, and it may return you a profit more creditable, far, than any to be gleaned by an abandonment of your duty to your community, and the petty dividend to be gleaned from your remaining moveables [*sic*]."²⁵

The plan was based on the recommendation of the Blanding report. Starting at the Santee River, a thirty-five-foot-deep new canal would be excavated all the way to Black Oak Lock, eliminating locks 2 through 6. The new canal would cut through the ridge that separated the Santee and Cooper Rivers. A new guard lock would lower vessels from the Santee down thirty-five feet to the new level. Vessels would then flow uninterrupted, without locks, all the way to Black Oak Lock. Local springwater would permanently keep the rest of the canal filled, and vessels would always be able to reach the Cooper River. The new excavation would not be fed by the three reservoirs, so they could be sold, and the funds would be used to pay for the proposed work.

Excess water from the Santee would flow through the new canal to Black Oak and thereby through a new smaller channel to the Cooper River. A series of reservoirs along the channel would store water to be let out at will to supply Charleston. There would also be an abundant supply of water from the Santee to keep the Cooper River fresh during droughts and keep the salt point downriver, making extensive brackish marshes suitable for rice cultivation.

The Santee Canal Company surrendered its charter a year later, despite the pronouncements of those who wrote the article. Such were the dreams of men, some of which, like the original Santee Canal, were brought to fruition; others, like this plan, never left the paper they were printed on.

US ARMY CORPS OF ENGINEERS 1881 REPORT ON REOPENING THE SANTEE CANAL

The Rivers and Harbors Act of 1880 sought to survey various rivers and canals on a national basis to assess their role in national defense and inland navigation and rekindle hope for canals in the states.[26] The survey was under the supervision of the secretary of war and conducted by the Army Corps of Engineers. The 1880 act included a cost-benefit assessment of reopening the Santee Canal.[27] The assessment was completed under the auspices of Lt. Col. Q. A. Gillmore, with field work and the 1881 report carried out by Capt. James C. Post and his assistant, Mr. H. Fisher. Although the canal was never reopened, the report contained an important historical account of the canal, including a transcript of Senf's Final Report to the directors of the Santee Canal Company, several letters by Senf on the canal's construction, and a copy of Senf's General Plan.[28]

For almost twenty years, the "Big Ditch" lay abandoned from the Guard Lock to Wantoot Lock, frequented by waterfowl, mosquitoes, kids swimming, and people fishing its waters when the land was not in drought. The section from Wantoot Lock to Biggin Creek was used for a short time by locals after the canal officially closed in 1853. The Great Reservoir that had fed the hungry locks was invaded by swamp vegetation because there were no workers to maintain its open nature. The towpaths were grown up in briars and canes, and the canal banks were cut in several places by adjacent owners to drain their wetlands for farming. Weirs, floodgates, overfalls, lock gates, and aqueducts were in a dilapidated state. The lock chambers, however, were in good condition, a testimony to the engineering skills of Senf and the craftsmanship of the enslaved workers. Even the lower section of the canal was abandoned for local traffic by 1880 because the former planters were not able to raise sufficient crops to make use of it. Tide Lock was destroyed. But the canal was fortunate in one respect: Union troops did not deem it important enough to do any further damage as they moved through Santee Canal country. Had the canal stayed in operation up to the Civil War, Gen. Edward E. Potter's troops certainly would have destroyed the canal's infrastructure since they decimated any institutions in their path that might support the South's war efforts.

The 1881 report first noted that without any changes or improvements, a reopened canal would suffer under the same disadvantage as when it was operational: a serious lack of water for the Summit Canal during droughts. The report stated that "recent examination has failed to discover, within practicable distances, any new sources [of surface water] from which the summit level might be supplied during the dry season. The expense of putting the Santee Canal into complete repair, but without providing for the adequate water supply, was estimated by Assistant Fisher at $76,825.95."[29] Since the estimate did not provide engineering and other contingent expenses, Post suggested a budget of $100,000.00. He noted that this sum "will not, however, put the canal into full working order as it will not secure any [new] water supply."[30]

In light of the lack of new water supplies to operate the canal, Post submitted that there were three methods that might make the canal serviceable: (1) lowering the summit level so that it can be fed directly from the Santee River; (2) using steam pumps to keep the summit level supplied with water drawn from the Santee; and (3) restoring the old reservoirs to furnish water to the summit level when a sufficient supply was available, augmented by the pumps during the dry season. Post concluded that the third method did not offer any advantages over using the pumps to supply all the water, so he did not give an estimate of the costs for this method and dismissed it.[31]

The first method involved lowering the bed of the Santee Canal from the Santee River to Wantoot Lock between thirty to forty feet. This section would then be fed directly from the Santee River, since the low-water level of the Santee River at the Guard Lock was about thirty-five feet above low water at Tide Lock. Below Wantoot the water level of the canal was about seven feet below the low-water level of the Santee. Feeding the canal directly from the Santee all the way to Wantoot Lock entailed doing away with the reservoirs. From Wantoot Lock to Biggin Creek, the canal would be fed by springs and/or runoff. A new lock would be required at the Santee River entrance to lower vessels to the new canal bed, while locks 2 through 7 would be eliminated. A new lock of about seven-foot fall would replace lock 8. Locks 9 (Woodboo) and 10 (Hope) and Tide Lock would be preserved or repaired. The length of the new cut would be about fourteen miles, and at many places the bottom of the new canal would be about thirty to forty feet lower than it was previously. Once through the new Guard Lock, vessels would pass directly to lock 8, where they would be lowered to pass on to lock 9.

The cost estimate in the 1881 report was $810,000.00, including $750,000.00 for excavating 5 million cubic yards of soil and $60,000.00 for new locks, bridges, basins, and support buildings and the purchase of additional land. Ten percent was added for engineering and incidental expenses, bring the total to $891,000.00.[32] The 1881 report did not address how the new cut would affect adjacent landowners. Presumably, if the new cut were to be made, this issue would be addressed, and adjacent landowners would be consulted. The report also did not address if any new support land had to be acquired.

The second method involved establishing three steam pumps to force water from the Santee River to the Summit Canal, not unlike the method tried in 1819 with two steam pumps when the drought rendered the canal inoperable. The 1881 report stated:

> To make an approximate estimate of the cost of this plan, it is necessary to compute the probable quantity of water that is required for the service of the canal.
>
> In years when navigation was suspended in the canal from want of water, it was dry for about 14 miles of its length. The pumps must be therefore powerful enough to fill a canal [chamber] of that length, and when filled to provide for all losses from filtration, evaporation, leakage at locks and lock age.[33]

Fisher and Post would have placed a steam pump at locks 1, 2, and 3.[34] The first pump would draw water from the Santee River and discharge into the canal between locks 1 and 2; the second pump would draw water from the canal between locks 1 and 2 and discharge it into the canal between locks 2 and 3; the third pump would draw water from the canal between locks 2 and 3 and discharge it into the Summit Canal; water from the Summit Canal would reach as far as lock 8 (Wantoot). Total cost for the pumping plant was estimated at $44,770.00, and repair of the locks was estimated as $100,000.00. Added to this were annual expenses of $20,400.00. Capital was equal to $340,000.00, the interest from which would pay these annual expenses. Total cost of securing operation of the canal by pumps was estimated at $484,770.00.[35]

Attempts to Solve the Water Deficiency ~ 153

Apparently the 1881 report failed to consult Abram Blanding's study of 1823. Blanding noted that the Santee Canal locks should be widened so that they could handle steam traffic, a transportation mode that was becoming more prominent on the rivers of Carolina fifty-eight years earlier. Why Post neglected this aspect of vessel traffic is unknown, but in the end it would have made no difference, since other factors worked against reopening the Santee Canal.

Scattered throughout the 1881 report are reasons why the reopening of the Santee Canal by either of the two methods would not be cost-effective or advisable: (1) neither of the methods found a never-failing source (besides the reservoirs already in use) of adequate water; (2) the canal was given up nearly thirty years ago because its business was taken away by the South Carolina Railroad, and the situation had grown worse with the addition of the North East Railroad, which crossed the canal; (3) railroads also had the advantage of speed in getting produce to Charleston or other markets, for which growers were willing to pay a premium in order to shorten the term or their crop loans; (4) the state was unwilling to fund removing the obstructions of the rivers that fed traffic into the Santee Canal, and the canal's success was tied to success of river navigation; and (5), there was no new country to be developed or resources to be gained by the canal at that time, and "if it could not pay its expenses in 1850 it certainly will not do so now."[36] No attempt was made to reopen the Santee Canal as a result of the adverse recommendations of the 1881 report. This would not be the end, however, of efforts to wed the waters of the Santee and Cooper Rivers. Looming in the distance was Santee Cooper.

EIGHT

End of Commercial Operation of the Santee Canal

The Santee Canal bridged the gap between arduous land traffic and the advent of railroads and steam ships. The fact the canal closed in 1853 does not lessen its importance to the early economy of the state after the Revolution. It provided for half a century (not including the times it was dry) a venue for goods from the Upcountry to reach Charleston. Plantation products from Santee Canal country and the Upstate filled the coffers of bankers, merchants, and shipping companies in Charleston. It provided planters along its route needed funds by leasing enslaved people to the Canal Company after the Revolution when money was needed to get plantation operations going again, and it probably saved some from financial ruin. The canal came at the time when Santee long-staple cotton was developed as a crop, which was a financial boon to the planters of Santee Canal country as a replacement for rice and indigo, whose production declined after the Revolution. The canal served as a venue of communication, transportation, and commerce between the Upcountry, the two parishes, and the port of Charleston. The canal created new service centers in Middle St. John's and the surrounding area. The community that became Black Oak resulted from the infrastructure that supported operations of the canal, much like Eadytown, Pinopolis, Pine Ville, and Moncks Corner. That the planters of Santee Canal country welcomed the Santee Canal is evident by the existence of only one lawsuit against the company during its sixty-year history of construction and operation. Indeed it appears that the Canal Company and planters functioned as an amiable agricultural and social society. And this social society, fueled by wealth from their cotton reaching the Charleston market via the canal, produced some of the most educated and productive citizens in the state, including, for example, the theologian William Porcher DuBose; educators such as Rev. Octavius Theodore Porcher Sr.; the distaff planter Isabella Sarah Peyre; the botanist Henry William Ravenel; physicians Francis Peyre Porcher, Joseph Palmer Cain, and Edward Porcher; Lt. Gov. William Cain; historian Frederick Porcher; and Congressman Theodore Gourdin, all educated with "canal money." Numerous others could be cited.

The men who organized and financed the Santee Canal Company in 1785 hoped for great profits. The project took so long to complete, with initial construction costs of more than a half-million dollars (way over what was budgeted for originally) and proved so costly to operate that it became a financial burden to its financial backers. William Loughton Smith, its chief shareholder, struggled for many years merely to regain his initial investment.[1] Little did Smith and other investors know that the Santee Canal was destined to financially fail its investors. The locks were too small to allow steam vessels to pass, and a reliable source of water for the Summit Canal was always going to be problematic. Senf knew this, so he was compelled to make the locks only ten feet wide to save water, but, the authors argue, he had no other choice given the limitations of water sources. Steam vessels were in the future and unknown to Senf when he started the canal. That the Santee Canal operated as it did is a testimony to his engineering skills—and the skill of all those in his employ.

It might be argued the success of the canal contributed to the Civil War. Santee Canal country's planters and politicians were rabid secessionists and did not want to lose their enslaved labor force that worked the cotton fields, which were made profitable by the canal. Men of Santee Canal country quickly volunteered for the Confederate forces, assured of victory, little realizing what would confront them at war's end. If victorious they would have everything to live for; if defeated there would be almost nothing. Such was their euphoria and certainty of victory that they never concerned themselves with the possibility of defeat. If war came, the planters would be fully committed to supporting the Confederacy.

Lastly the Santee Canal contributed to the enslavement of thousands of Africans who worked building the canal and laboring in the cotton fields of Santee Canal country. They toiled with no hope of a better tomorrow, their history and contributions to the canal muted by those who benefited from their labors.

END OF OPERATION

Construction on the Santee Canal proceeded unhindered at the beginning, with progress made on excavation and building infrastructure. Issues, however, that neither Senf nor the Santee Canal Company probably could have expected or planned for were an immediate drain of the finances of the company and a harbinger of things to come. At the forefront were diseases, especially malaria. Although the canal was cut mostly through highland, all manner of wetlands bordered the right-of-way, meaning that ideal breeding sites for mosquitoes were within flying distance of the canal and its workers. Senf reported on June 10, 1796, three years after construction began, that

> every year there was a change of tradesmen and laborers, as engagements could only be made yearly or monthly, owing to sickness. The last year no tradesmen of any ability would engage to remain on the canal during the summer season, when the most work could be done.
>
> From the year 1793 to the beginning of 1800 twenty-four white persons died at the canal from fevers, of which number two were physicians, two assistants, three commissaries, two master carpenters, three master bricklayers and two head overseers. The rest were journeymen tradesmen and overseers. It may easily be conceived that, under such circumstances and changes, it is impossible to affect what might even reasonably be expected.[2]

These references were only for white workers. No numbers were recorded for the enslaved workers who died. Senf, however, gave insight into their plight. Included in his Final Report is a list of deductions from a workforce of seven hundred employed over the course of a year from the beginning of 1793. He estimated that there would be four sick per hundred workers.[3] Obviously sickness of enslaved workers was a drain on the canal's finances. Given the pestilent environment of the canal, there was no relief for the Canal Company or the workers, especially during the warm months when malaria was prevalent. Work quality and schedules suffered because of turnover in the labor force as planters often asked for return of their enslaved people for their own needs, especially during cotton harvest time. The owners' need to have their enslaved people working at home drove up the wages of laborers, overseers, and other employees who worked on the canal by fifty percent.

In January 1796 a great flood ravaged the Lowcountry and Santee Canal country. Philip Porcher Sr. of Oldfield on the Santee was among the unfortunate who met with a total loss of crops that year. The freshet rose so high that it became the standard by which all subsequent inundations were measured. The flood wreaked havoc on the early infrastructure of the canal, costing the company considerable time and funds to repair the damage. But Senf and workers pushed onward, and the Santee Canal became a reality in 1800.

In terms of engineering, the Santee Canal was a technological masterpiece. When there was adequate water in the reservoirs, it operated precisely as Senf had designed, and income rose steadily during the first years of operation. A thousand vessels traveled through the canal in 1814. The most prosperous period of the canal was around 1830, when 720 vessels brought seventy thousand bales of cotton to Charleston. Dr. Henry Ravenel of Pooshee wrote in his "crop notes" on April 20, 1838: "Sent by Deveauxs Boat—14 & 1/2 Bales of Cotton. 9 Stained & 5 & 1/2 of white. 2 of which were from Sea Island Seed. The Sea Island sold to Gourdin & Smith at 35 [cents per pound]."[4] On June 5, 1839, Ravenel wrote: "Sent by McBeths [sic] Boat 3 & 1/2 bales Sea Island Cotton & 15 Bales Stained Santee Cotton."[5] He was just one planter in Santee Canal country that benefited from the canal. His father, René, also sent his cotton from Pooshee down the canal. Countless other planters in Santee Canal country did the same. For a period it was the lifeline for their plantations' success.

Despite the technological success of the canal and the profitable days early on, all would not be well in Santee Canal country. Once the canal opened, a series of events ultimately led to its closing in 1853. René Ravenel recorded in his diary on July 24, 1800, that "[a] great Fall or rain, a higher Fresh in the Swamp that has been seen since last October, carry'd the Bridges on the Road, the Water run'd over the Bank of the Santee Canal in several places and made a breach in the Bank Ten Feet. N. B.—The Santee Canal Bank broke in three places in Wantoot, and carry'd away about 25 or 30 feet on the bank in each place."[6] Repairing breaches in the bank would have been costly, although a workforce was retained by the Canal Company to tend to such matters.

Just four years after the canal opened for traffic, a newspaper article reported that an extraordinary rise of water in the neighboring swamps caused damage to it: "In one part it became necessary, to save a lock and give vent to the torrent, to cut the bank of the canal, and part of the aqueduct which passes under it, between White and Live Oak plantations, was washed away."[7] After the waters subsided, repairs were made, and the canal reopened for traffic.

As early as 1807, there were concerns that the canal would not be financially successful. Secretary of the Treasury Albert Gallatin reported on financial difficulties that would prevail with operation of the canal:

> The want of success in this undertaking, which though completed is very unprofitable, may be ascribed to several causes. The expense, compared with the work, is much greater than might have been expected, and probably, than was necessary. The locks are too small for large boats, which are therefore obliged to pursue the former route down the Santee, and by sea to Charleston; and want of water is alleged as a sufficient reason for the size of the locks. But a canal in that situation cannot in America be profitable, unless the navigation of the main river with which it communicates is rendered safe and permanent; and whenever that of the Santee itself shall have been improved the utility and profits of the canal will be considerably increased.[8]

The problems outlined by Gallatin surfaced repeatedly during the life of the canal and ultimately contributed to its closure. As Gallatin pointed out, if the canal was to succeed, the rivers that fed its traffic had to be kept free of obstructions.[9] When canal mania swept the country after the War of 1812, the Santee Canal's future looked brighter. The state began a program to clear the rivers of obstructions and/or build bypass canals around the rapids. The project, however, had limited success. The rivers quickly became obstructed again, as nature abhors a vacuum. The program was costly, and when other navigation projects became higher priorities, it was shut down. Kapsch states the problem succinctly: "Cleared rivers did not remain cleared. After having spent almost two million dollars on these waterways and related works, the state legislature was in no mood to spend additional funds. Navigation on these rivers conflicted with other uses, such as water-powered mills and fishing."[10]

It took between three and five men to bring a vessel down the Santee River. The owners of the vessels realized that these same men could pull them through the canal and not use the mules and horses provided by the Canal Company, lessening the cost of passage through the canal. The Canal Company did not have to maintain a stable of animals and pasture ground, thus saving funds needed for other operations. The authors found no answer in the archives as to whether the funds saved by not keeping animals offset the loss of revenue significantly.

Owners also began stacking vessels on the return passage, thus paying just one toll for two vessels. The Canal Company never adjusted their tolls to compensate for this loss of revenue. Legal suits against the company, although rare, also drove up costs of operation. Col. Robert McKelvey (1756–1814), a local planter, sued the Santee Canal Company to recover financial dispensation for his eight enslaved people that worked on the canal. McKelvey was awarded seventy-seven pounds seventeen shillings for past wages.[11] Medical expenses for workers, not budgeted for, were costly. All these outlays drove up the cost of the canal considerably beyond initial estimates of operation.

In 1816 the *Camden Gazette* issued an ominous warning to investors of the Santee Canal about an invention: steamboats.

> When enlightened citizens shall fully understand and fairly appreciate the advantages of steam navigation, they will not long deprive themselves of its benefits. The Santee, not less that the Savannah, the Mississippi or the Ohio, is adapted to the use of this noble invention. And on account of the dangers and difficulties of boat navigation around the coast to Charleston from the circumstance of the unfortunate failure of the Santee Canal for the last year, the improvements in this kind of navigation present themselves with pecular [*sic*] interest.[12]

The years 1816, 1818, and 1819 were ones of extreme drought. The droughts were so protracted that two steam engines were employed to pump water from the river into the canal. The attempt was a failure. The company never completely recovered from the financial losses attributed to this three-year closure of the canal and the costly attempts to fill the Summit Canal using steam pumps.

After the end of the War of 1812, cotton production Upstate fueled a demand for easier transportation to Charleston. In December 1818 the General Assembly appropriated funds for internal improvements to the state and created a board of public works to oversee projects. Construction began on a 110-mile state road that would connect Charleston with Columbia. The road was paid for by tolls, but high costs and low income from the tolls made it a failure. The General Assembly halted funding in 1829 and turned over authority for its operation to local commissioners and private interests. Although the road was probably used minimally for shipping cotton to Charleston, any decrease in vessel traffic on the canal would have been detrimental to its finances.[13]

Steamboats eventually eclipsed the usefulness and advantages of canals. They could carry 750 bales of cotton per trip and diverted significant business from the canal. In 1822 the *Southern Patriot* reported on steamboat passage from Granby near Columbia to Charleston: "The steamboat South Carolina arrived this morning from Granby, in the remarkably short passage of four days, and before the manifest of her cargo has been received in this City [Charleston], by the mail. We thus see the facility of this system of navigation, and its benefit to our City realized on every side."[14]

The Savannah River was navigable as far upriver as Hamburg, across from Augusta, Georgia, and by 1823 the steamboat *Hamburg* was operating between Charleston and Hamburg via Beaufort and Savannah, carrying commerce such as cotton and tobacco. Although steamboat traffic took longer and had to brave the vicissitudes and perils of ocean travel, steamboats could carry more cargo faster and did not have the overhead of canals. Steamboats began to cut into traffic on the Santee Canal.

Another natural event plagued the canal. On January 3, 1827, a freeze shut down operation, Thomas Porcher Sr. of Ophir recorded: "It is still very cold. Dr. Ravenel [of Pooshee] wrote me today that there were Nine Boats in sight of the Bridge at Black Oak confined by the Ice, a circumstance he says that has never take place before since the Canal was made. They attempted to break the ice with Poles this morning."[15] Although this was probably a one-time event, a business operating on a small profit margin could not afford work stoppages such as this one.

The success of Santee Canal depended upon free and uninterrupted river traffic in the rivers that fed into it. By 1823 the state no longer was willing to spend funds on clearing rivers that had already been improved. In 1828 the legislature stopped all expenditures on internal river improvements. The rivers above the Santee became less navigable as trees and other debris clogged them and sandbars caused havoc with vessels. This caused the state to look for other means of transportation.

The rise of cotton production in the Upstate checked the growth of grain production and, by giving a local market for the entire output, stopped all shipment of grain to the coast. Shipping cotton instead of grain was advantageous as cotton was far lighter in weight and more precious in value. During periods when the canal was closed or severely limited in access, cotton could be shipped by land, while grain could not have been shipped that way. The loss of revenue from shifting away from grain was significant to the canal's finances.

The development of a railroad system in the state, although not initially fatal to the canal's operation, ultimately contributed to its demise. On December 13, 1827, a legislative committee reported out a bill "to authorize the formation of a Company for construction of Rail Roads or Canals, from the city of Charleston to Columbia and Camden, and to the Savannah River at or near the town of Hamburg."[16] The bill was ratified and became law. By 1830 the Charleston-Hamburg line was in operation. In 1842 the completion of the Branchville and Columbia Railroad left the Santee Canal with traffic only from the Wateree River, from which it enjoyed a fair income until 1846. When the railroad was extended from the Columbia area to Camden in 1848, most of this revenue was lost. Although sending goods by railroad was more expensive, it was quicker and less apt to be disrupted. Canal traffic was ultimately too uncertain to compete with the railroads, and there were no conveniently located railroads to the Santee Canal where goods could be unloaded.

In 1838 the *Charleston Mercury* reported that the Canal Company found it so hard to collect tolls that it prohibited vessels from entering the canal "without either paying the amount of the Canal Toll due upon the trip in cash, or else to bring as security for the payment of the same a written order signed by some responsible person already known in the business transactions of the Canal . . . and against whom a bill may be rendered payable on sight."[17]

The poor state of the Canal Company's financial position in the decade before the Civil War did not allow for repair of normal wear to the infrastructure. The wooden gates of the locks were in advanced states of deterioration and were increasingly unable to withstand the water pressure from a flooded lock. Maintenance of the bridges of the canal, probably unforeseen originally, required funds the Canal Company could not afford. The brick abutments that supported the canal bridges gradually deteriorated from the pressure of the vehicles going over the bridge. Since the Canal Company's charter required keeping communication between land separated by the canal, the bridges had to be replaced or repaired.

By 1840 all the river navigation systems and canals that fed the Santee Canal, except for the Lockhart Canal on the Broad River, were shut down.[18] With no system to send vessels to the canal, there was no way for it to operate. Its imminent demise was a foregone conclusion. To shore up its finances, the Canal Company by 1841 had subdivided its shares. Each three-hundred-dollar share, once worth eight hundred dollars, was subdivided into parcels of twenty-five dollars each. Charles Macbeth owned thirty of the subdivided shares (fig. 8.1). Subdividing shares had no effect on profits of the canal.

In 1852, when it appeared the canal might be closed, local planters signed a petition requesting that the Santee Canal project not be abandoned. The petition read: "CITIZENS OF ST. STEPHENS AND ST. MICHAELS PARISHES,

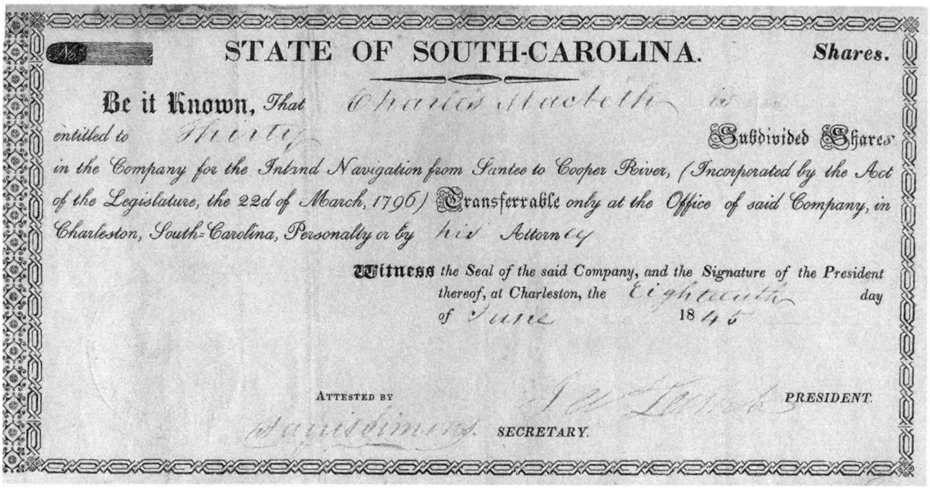

STATE OF SOUTH-CAROLINA. Shares.

Be it Known, That Charles Macbeth is entitled to Thirty Subdivided Shares in the Company for the Inland Navigation from Santee to Cooper River, (Incorporated by the Act of the Legislature, the 22d of March, 1796) Transferrable only at the Office of said Company, in Charleston, South-Carolina, Personally or by his Attorney

Witness the Seal of the said Company, and the Signature of the President thereof, at Charleston, the Eighteenth day of June 1845

ATTESTED BY PRESIDENT.

SECRETARY.

FIGURE 8.1. Charles Macbeth's thirty subdivided shares of the Company for the Inland Navigation from Santee to Cooper River, June 1845. Personal archives of Sarah Cain Spruill, Cheraw, South Carolina.

COUNTER-PETITION ASKING THAT THE COMPANY FOR THE INLAND NAVIGATION FROM SANTEE TO COOPER RIVER NOT BE ALLOWED TO ABANDON THE SANTEE CANAL, BUT IF SO, THAT IT BE TRANSFERRED TO OTHERS WILLING TO KEEP IT OPEN."[19] Nothing came of the request.

Macbeth owned shares in the Canal Company and planned to benefit from the canal's demise. In 1853 he owned Wantoot and Oakfield, through which four miles of the canal passed, including locks 8, 9, and 10. This section of the canal had a reliable source of water from springs. If he could gain control and require tolls, Macbeth saw a possibility of financial gain from local planters who still used this lower section of the canal. He petitioned the General Assembly to grant him the section of the canal between Wantoot and the Cooper River. He said he would maintain the canal "under the same conditions and limitations, and duties to the Public as were imposed upon and invested with the same privileges and rights as were granted to the said Company by the Original Charter."[20] The Committee on Incorporation decided not to grant Macbeth's request. The General Assembly did not want to grant him rights implied in the original charter to the Santee Canal Company, particularly the right to charge tolls. Harris Simons, secretary and treasurer of the Canal Company, placed the following notice in the *Charleston Courier* on June 28, 1853: "Notice is hereby given that the Company for the Inland Navigation from Santee to Cooper River, (commonly known as the Santee Canal Company,) will apply to the Legislature at its next session, for leave to surrender its charter and close its affairs."[21]

On December 12, 1853, one last effort was made to keep the Santee Canal open. A group of citizens was convinced that with proper management and in enterprising hands, the canal "would yet pay a remunerating profit; and we should not be at all surprised if Northern capitalists, in default of home action in the premises, should embark in the enterprise."[22] Nothing came of this petition, either.

The finances of the Santee Canal Company are hard to determine today since many records of the company have not surfaced.[23] By 1853 it was evident that the canal's finances had deteriorated considerably because of its various problems, and the Canal Company petitioned the General Assembly to surrender its charter. The petition pointed out the dire financial status of the company, noting that it had paid out dividends to its subscribers only twice.

The fate of the canal was sealed with this answer from the Committee on Incorporation: "That after a full consideration of the facts addressed before them the several Petitioners, they were satisfied that the said company was annually exhausting the little property left it by its charter and recommended that the prayer of the said company be granted upon certain terms and under terms set forth in a Bill to authorize the sale or Surrender of the Charter of the Company."[24] The Canal Company surrendered its charter to the state in 1853 and went out of business. After the canal officially closed, it was used only for local traffic from Woodboo to its terminus. Springs provided water to operate the locks.

Diaries kept during the war by Henry William Ravenel, Susan Ravenel Jervey, Charlotte St. Julien Ravenel, and Mary Rhodes Henagan did not mention operation of even the lower section of the canal (see Jervey and Ravenel, *Two Diaries*) When Col. Charles B. Fox, who headed the Fifty-Fifth Massachusetts, stopped at Somerset and Mexico on April 7, 1865, his only mention of the canal was en route: "The march was continued until the head of the column arrived within a short distance of Moncks Corner, when it turned to the left, on the south side of the Santee Canal, and moved toward Pinopolis."[25]

As previously mentioned, it does not appear that the canal was a concern to Union forces. If it had been considered strategically important to the war effort, the locks and other remaining infrastructure might have been destroyed. Santee Canal country, however, was not spared the wrath of Union forces as they marched through the countryside.

NINE

Field Survey of the Santee Canal and Environs, 2019–21

During 2019–22 Richard Porcher and friends trekked and boated through the extant sections of the Santee Canal and its environs as part of research for this book. The authors thought it might add to the book's interest if the status of remaining infrastructure on sections of the canal not flooded by the lake were documented for future researchers and for efforts to protect that historic infrastructure. Of particular interest to the authors were the structures and sites that Senf included on his General Plan and Final Report and were associated with the canal's operations from 1800 to 1853. Much of this infrastructure has never been included in historical accounts of the canal. Richard Porcher and friends trekked the Santee Canal from the Santee River to where it enters Lake Moultrie and from the railroad trestle where it crosses the canal near the powerhouse to Biggin Creek. They canoed Biggin Creek from Tide Lock to where Biggin Creek enters the Tailrace Canal. In addition they explored several sites in the general vicinity of the abandoned canal that were important to its history.

They did not traverse the Santee Canal in one continuous hike but made the passage in several treks. Richard Porcher shared the trips with numerous friends. They made what might have been lonely outings into a celebration of shared history. Rather than identifying which friends went on each trek, this is the list of all participants: Rebecca Fanning, Benny Starr, Joshua Robinson, Lloyd Hill, Nolan Williams, John Brubaker, Rick Wilson, Keith Gourdin, Roy Belser, Henry Keer, Drew Ruddy, Jonathan Holland, Angela Halfacre, Tommy Graham, Brent Fortenberry, and coauthors Billy Judd and Elizabeth Connor.

To assist in ground-truthing the passage along the canal from the Guard

Lock on the Santee River to Santee Basin, lidar images were consulted (figs. 9.5 and 9.9).[1] Lidar readily shows elevations in the form of ditches, banks, and other landforms. It was necessary to distinguish landforms from the canal's operational time from the countless ditches and canals that have been constructed in the vicinity of the canal since commercial operation ceased in 1853.

Before the trek down the Santee Canal, two sites of interest in the canal's environs were surveyed: the high bluff along the river where Thomas Walter established his botanical garden and the proposed site of the ferry canal to Cotteaux Lake.

THOMAS WALTER'S GRAVE

The first sign they were approaching the canal entrance on their river trip was the high bluff along the river where Thomas Walter established his botanical garden. Walter died in 1788, and while involved in early canal planning, he would have known nothing of the canal's construction.[2] Walter was the first post-Linnaean author who published a sizable flora of eastern North America that used Linnaeus's system of classification. Walter's *Flora Caroliniana*, published in England in 1788, was a landmark in the botanical history of the United States.

Many botanists who worked in Carolina have made the obligatory trip to Walter's grave on the Santee River.[3] Richard Porcher's great-great-uncle Henry William Ravenel visited the gravesite some sixty-five years after Walter's death and wrote a report on his visit.[4] He reported that little remained of the garden except one Chinese tallow tree. Richard Porcher visited the gravesite numerous times, mostly with his field botany classes from The Citadel. No sign of Walter's garden exists today, and the tallow tree is long gone. It is hard to believe that here was one of the first botanical gardens of America, created and planted with care and skill by the man whose mortal remains lay at one's feet. On his plantation Walter was one of the first to kindle an interest in botanical science in the New World.

Standing by Walter's grave, Richard Porcher reflected on how one botanist, in such a short life (Walter died at age forty-nine), could have accomplished so much scientifically as well as serving in many civic roles.[5] Later, trekking down the canal, they saw ironwood (*Carpinus caroliniana* Walter) along the canal bank, perhaps the offspring of the specimen Walter used to describe the species. Walter's gravesite was restored in 1931 after many years of neglect and today is on private property (figs. 9.1 and E3).

FIGURE 9.1. Thomas Walter's grave, 2019. Photograph by Richard Dwight Porcher Jr.

FERRY CANAL/COTTEAUX LAKE

An act in 1786 to establish "The Company for the Inland Navigation from Santee to Cooper River" empowered the Santee Canal Company to build a ferry canal on the northern side of the Santee River opposite the entrance to the Santee Canal. The ferry canal would have connected the Santee River and Santee Canal with highland on the opposite side of the Santee and Wateree Rivers and a public road leading to the High Hills of the Santee.[6] The ferry would have carried passengers and goods from the High Hills to the Santee Canal. The act gave the company the right to charge sufficient tolls for passages and goods. In his Final Report, Senf wrote:

> The Swamp opposite the mouth of the Canal is five and a half Mile wide, and being intersected with several small creeks and Lagoons, would make it very difficult nay almost impossible to make a Causeway of any strength for the Ferry.... The only practicable and profitable Mode is to dig a Canal from the River to Cotteaux Lake in the summer season, when the River is

low, of forty feet in width and as deep to have allways [*sic*] two or three feet in the Canal in dry seasons. The Ground which is dug to be thrown all to the lower side of the Canal, none of the Creeks which cross the Canal be obstructed, and the course of the Canal be in such a Manner, as shown in the annexed Plan to the General Plan that in freshes the Canal may have a Current to prevent from filing up. The Distance to Cotteaux lake is two and a half Mile—from thence the Lake can be made navigable with a small Expense to the highland which is three miles, where Warehouses may be built, between Nelson's blue House and Norvelles as the Plan shews [*sic*].[7]

In 1794 Senf advertised in the *City Gazette* for proposals to build the ferry canal. Persons who were inclined "to undertake this work by contract, will be pleased to send their proposals to the subscriber in short time, and mention in particular at what time they would engage to have the work accomplished. The plan will be shewn whenever applied for."[8] Senf's advertisement indicated that the plan for the ferry canal as outlined in his Final Report was a serious consideration.

Based on extensive field work, the authors have determined that the ferry canal was never completed or even begun (figs. 9.2 and 5.21). But it was an ingenious and bold plan. The authors first sought a plat with Cotteaux Lake, so it could be located in the field. Theywere unable to find one. The closest thing they found was a lake identified as Coutawxs on the map of the Santee Canal in Drayton's *A View of South Carolina*.[9]

There is a color version of Drayton's map, with no record of who drew it or when, in the South Carolina Historical Society. This map leaves off "Coutawxs," which appears on Drayton's original map, so the authors have added Cotteaux Lake to figure 9.2, since it is believed that evidence will show that the two are the same.

The color map includes the label "Ferry Canal," which is not on Drayton's map. How the maker of the color map knew where to add it is unknown. The 1881 copy of Senf's General Plan shows the ferry canal (fig. 5.21), so perhaps the author of the map had access to that version.

The 1943 Chicora Quadrangle (fig. 9.3) shows Little River flowing toward the Santee River with a widened section that is more than likely Cotteaux Lake. The lake is roughly two and a half miles from the entrance of the Santee Canal and in the general direction indicated on the 1881 General Plan by the direction in which the ferry canal was to run. This body of water was located on an

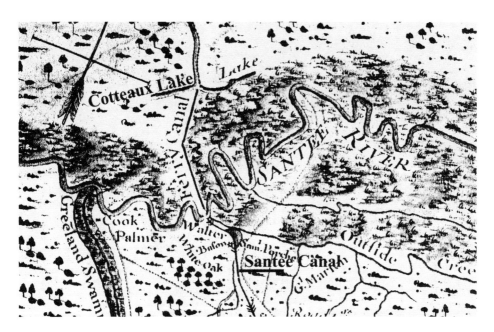

FIGURE 9.2. Ferry Canal through Santee Swamp to Cotteaux Lake. South Carolina Historical Society, Elias Ball Bull Papers (call number 376.00, 2000.181.027), No date or author. The original plat in the South Carolina Historical Society is in color; a section of the original plat is reproduced here in black and white. The original plat labeled the ferry canal. Authors added Cotteaux Lake and Santee Canal.

October 2019 field survey, and it is the same body shown on the 1943 Chicora Quadrangle. It was undoubtedly a lake and is a wider portion of Little River. Based on the location in the field and comparisons of Drayton's map, the color map, and the Chicora Quadrangle, it can be confidently said that the widened body of water is the same as Drayton's Coutawxs Lake, which is Cotteaux Lake. Santee Cooper's Wilson Dam, constructed in 1942, is just a short distance from the western end of the lake, so Cotteaux Lake was not affected.

Senf's plan envisioned making the ferry canal navigable to Cotteaux Lake and then making Cotteaux Lake navigable to the highland three miles away, where "warehouses may be built, between Nelson's Blue House and Norvelles."[10] It is uncertain how Senf planned to make Cotteaux Lake navigable to the highland. Cook's 1773 map (fig. 9.4) shows Nelson and Norvel on the highland across the swamp from Cotteaux Lake. Norvel is undoubtedly the same as Norvelles. These were probably towns or outposts in 1773 and were the ultimate destination of Senf's ferry canal. He planned for wagons to bring goods and passengers to the warehouses at Nelson and Norvelles, after which they would

Field Survey of the Santee Canal and Environs ~ 169

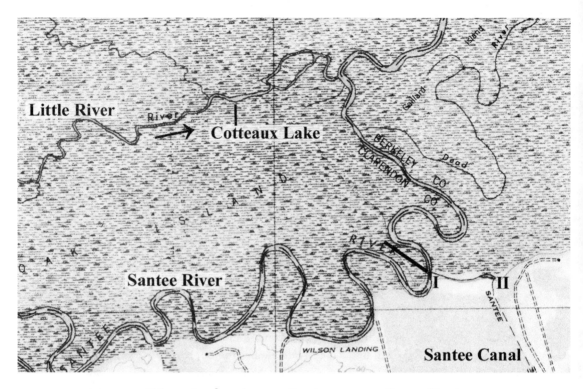

FIGURE 9.3. Chicora Quadrangle, 1943. War Department, Corps of Engineers, US Army, First Edition, Based on the Chicora Quadrangle of 1921. Authors added Cotteaux Lake, Little River, Santee River, Locks I and II, and the location of the ferry canal based on the 1881 General Plan. Senf's proposed ferry canal is represented by the black line across the Santee River from the Guard Lock (I).

be loaded on vessels to transport through Cotteaux Lake and the ferry canal to the Santee River and the Santee Canal's entrance. No trace of these two towns or outposts are known in today's Clarendon County. They lie under the waters of Lake Marion.

A lidar image does not reveal evidence of the ferry canal in the Santee Swamp across from the entrance of the Santee Canal. If the ferry canal had been constructed or even begun, the remains of the canal and earthen bank would still be visible by lidar. It would have been a daunting task to construct the ferry canal to Cotteaux Lake and then make a navigable connection to the highland three miles away at Nelson and Norvel. Senf's ferry canal was never constructed. The only evidence of his grand scheme is what was included on the 1881 copy of his General Plan, as featured in figure 9.2.

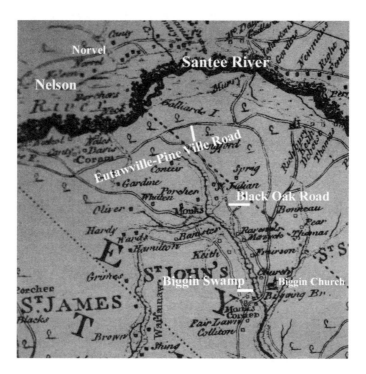

FIGURE 9.4. Section of "A Map of the Province of South Carolina" by James Cook, 1773. South Caroliniana Map Collection (call number Map 1773). Authors added Nelson, Norvel, Eutawville–Pine Ville Road, Santee River, Biggin Church, Biggin Swamp, and Black Oak Road.

SANTEE RIVER TO HIGHWAY 45

The first point of interest along the actual canal is the entrance on the river leading to the Guard Lock, which was originally 150 feet from the river's edge. Erosion cut into the riverbank, and now the ruins of Guard Lock are about 100 feet from the river's edge. Although the river's flow has diminished from the time the canal was constructed because its waters were diverted into Lake Moultrie via the Diversion Canal, the entrance from the river is still visible. No remains of the epis and wing dam were evident.

Porcher Embankment was the next destination. The story of Samuel Porcher of Mexico and Samuel Foxworth, his overseer, has been told often. Foxworth was nineteen years old at the beginning of this remarkable project. Santee River freshets were flooding Porcher's croplands in the river swamp converted to fields. For thirty years Foxworth knew virtually nothing but the embankment. He and a driver, George, oversaw the construction and upkeep of an embankment four miles long, anchored at the Santee Canal and running through the swamp (figs. 9.5 and 9.6). The embankment was wide enough for two horses to walk side by side. The embankment partially enclosed thirteen hundred acres and successfully held back the waters of the Santee freshets, and Porcher's fields again became a land of plenty. George was promised his freedom when the embankment was complete, a promise Porcher kept.[11]

Did the Porcher embankment stand the test of time? In 1840 the *Charleston Courier* reported:

> Major Porcher's Embankment.—We are gratified to learn that this noble monument of agricultural enterprise has suffered so little from the late freshet in the Santee River, as to be readily capable of repair, and indeed to furnish a conclusive test of the practicability of reclaiming river swamp for

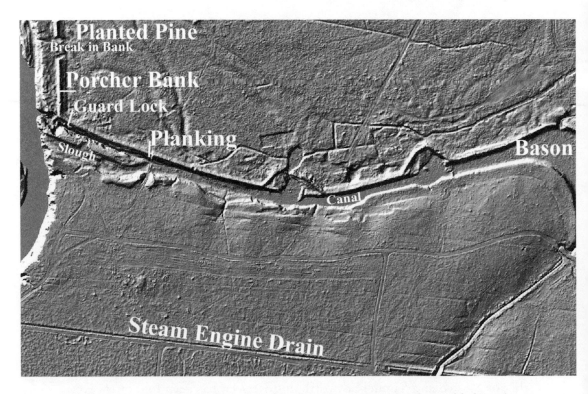

FIGURE 9.5. Lidar image from Guard Lock to Santee Basin. Authors added Porcher embankment, break in Porcher embankment, Santee Basin, slough, Guard Lock, canal, planted pine, drain from the steam engine on the Santee River, and approximate site of planking. Lidar courtesy of Berkeley County GIS Department, Moncks Corner, South Carolina.

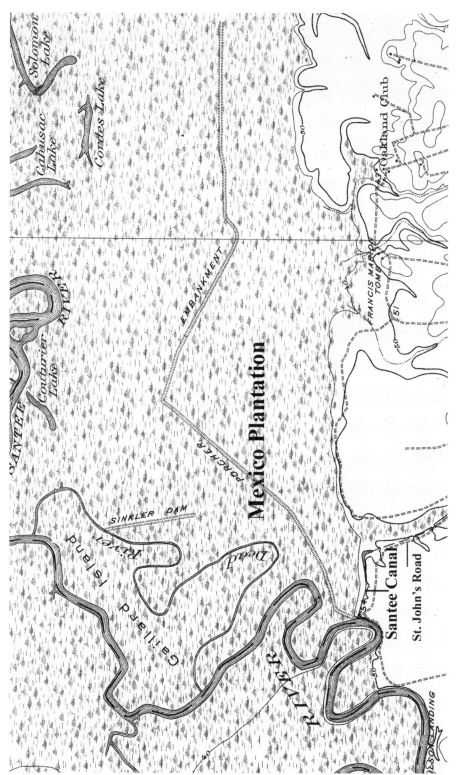

FIGURE 9.6. Porcher embankment. Chicora Quadrangle, edition of 1921, reprinted in 1947. United States Department of the Interior Geological Survey. Authors added Mexico, Santee Canal, and St. John's Road.

the purpose of profitable culture. Major Porcher's embankment is 4 miles in length, and resting on a base from 40 to 50 feet in width, and rising to the average height of 10 feet, and yet there have been but four breaks in the whole line, making an aggregate of only 600 feet destroyed. Thus, although Major Porcher has lost his provision crop by the freshet, yet may he be congratulated on the preservation of his great work, and the undoubted proof now afforded of its stability and permanence.[12]

On the lidar map there appears to be a break in the embankment (fig. 9.5). Nothing in the archives mentions such a break. Richard Porcher and friends walked the embankment to the break, where a stand of loblolly pines had been planted inland and adjacent to the embankment by a timber company. Undoubtedly the company cut the embankment to drain the land where the pines were planted. Mystery solved.

Richard Porcher observed a stand of pawpaws on his first trip to the Santee Canal in 1974. Pawpaw (*Asimina triloba*) is a small tree or large shrub, native to the area, that yields delicious fruits readily consumed by animals. The trees were still growing along the canal bank just past where Porcher embankment joins the canal. There were no fruits. Wild food aficionados seldom see the fruits in the wild because raccoons consume them as soon as they ripen. Perhaps canal workers feasted on them as they paused for lunch.

Guard Lock, just past where Porcher Embankment joins the bank of the canal, was the next point of interest. The walls of the massive lock collapsed inward years ago from erosion of the sand foundation upon which they rested (fig. 9.7). There was no trace of marble facing or means to attach marble facing on the walls.

Looking over the lock's ruins, Richard Porcher was reminded of a day years ago when he led a botany field trip in the area and showed the class the lock's ruins. A student brought to his attention a loose brick with a fingerprint pressed into it. The bricks for the canal's locks were handmade by enslaved workers hired from nearby plantations. Who was he or she? What were they thinking about as they labored all day, with no hope of a better life? Freedom? Hardly! They were surrounded by plantations, and there was nowhere to hide. Richard Porcher has no record of what happened to the brick with the fingerprint. Could another brick with a fingerprint be found, one to photograph for the book? During field work on the canal, another brick with a fingerprint was not found.

Following the canal from Guard Lock, Richard Porcher and friends came

FIGURE 9.7. Guard Lock, 1977. Photograph by Richard Dwight Porcher Jr.

to the remains of the planking on the bed constructed to stop leakage (fig. 7.5). This artifact is discussed in chapter 7. Adjacent to the canal was a shallow slough (fig. 9.5) of unknown function. It ran from the river parallel to the south side of the canal and emptied into the canal. Four stones in sets of two were laid out about fifty yards apart along the slough's edge. The pairs of stones were placed opposite each other on either side of the slough. The stones were similar to stones used in the quoins. Figure 4.2 shows White Oak Landing with a woods road leading from the landing. As stated previously, Senf used the woods road as the path of the canal bed because it would have been free of trees. Senf might have constructed the slough to unload goods brought up the Santee for the canal's construction while he excavated the canal cut along the woods road. Why the two sets of stones were installed and by whom is a mystery that future historians might investigate.

Richard Porcher and friends were next in an oak-hickory forest (fig. 4.3). Oak-hickory forest dominated much of the original route of the canal, but the original growth trees were larger than what grows today. Even trees over a hundred years old, however, are impressive and give a sense of the enormity of the task that faced the workers in cutting the canal through the forest. But clear and cut they did, working their way to Frierson's Lock and beyond. How did

Field Survey of the Santee Canal and Environs ~ 175

they remove the massive stumps of the hardwood trees? Perhaps some type of primitive hoist?

Where was Izardtown? Ralph Izard, who owned White Oak before it was bought by the Canal Company, envisioned a town along the canal. Senf's 1800 General Plan and the White Oak/Big Camp plat (fig. 9.8) show the proposed Izardtown on the south side of the Santee Canal between Guard Lock and White Oak Lock. Nothing found in the archives during research for this book indicates the town was established. A ground search of the proposed town site revealed no physical artifacts, and today's vegetation does not exhibit signs of disturbance associated with an abandoned settlement or town. Without evidence to the contrary from an archaeological study, the authors argue that Izardtown never existed except on the two cited plats. But it was easy to visualize a series of houses situated in a beautiful oak-hickory forest with a clear view of the canal and Santee River.

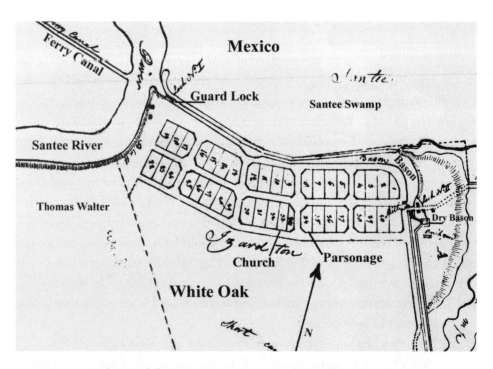

FIGURE 9.8. White Oak/Big Camp, ca. 1800. South Carolina Historical Society, Elias Ball Bull Papers (call number 376.02 (H) 01.08.01, box 22). There is no date or surveyor on the plat. Authors cropped the section with White Oak. Authors added Ferry Canal, Thomas Walter, Santee River, Guard Lock, Santee Swamp, Church, Parsonage, Basin (Santee), White Oak, Mexico, and Dry Basin.

176 ⌣ THE SANTEE CANAL

Approaching White Oak Lock, the canal widened into Santee Basin, which Senf described (figs. 5.8, 9.8, and 9.9): "From this [Turning Basin] to the Santee Bason the Canal is in the Shape of half Moon, 1000 feet long and 245 feet broad in the middle, where a brick overfall discharges all the surplus water above six feet."[13] Riverboats would pass to Santee Basin, unload their cargoes to the smaller canal vessels, and then return to the Santee River for the trip back.

The Santee Basin in October 2019 was dry, but in wet seasons it is full of water and provides vital waterfowl habitat. On our passage a variety of wetland shrubs and swamp trees dominated the basin. There was no sign of the overfall Senf mentioned. The wooden planking may have long deteriorated, and the bricks removed for salvage.

The next point of interest was White Oak Lock (figs. 5.11 and 5.12). The wooden gates of the lock have long deteriorated, as has the bridge over the lock.

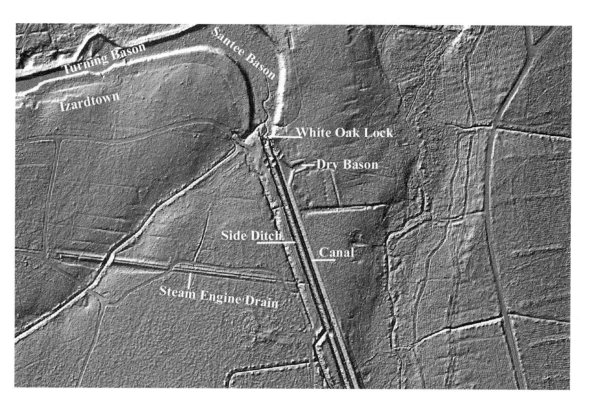

FIGURE 9.9. Lidar map in vicinity of White Oak Lock. Authors added White Oak Lock, dry basin, Izardtown, side ditch, Santee Canal, and drain from the steam engine on the Santee River. Courtesy of Berkeley County GIS Department, Moncks Corner, South Carolina.

Field Survey of the Santee Canal and Environs ~ 177

The lock walls are intact and the sluices that let water into the lock are visible, but the wooden sluice gates (fig. 5.6) have long deteriorated. The openings of the sluices into the lock chamber are intact (fig. 5.11, insert). Three of the quoins that held the lock gates are still present. White Oak Lock was the toll lock, and steps allowed the owner or operator of a vessel to climb from his boat to a tollhouse, where he paid his passage down the canal. After all these years, this artifact of the canal's history was still extant but highly deteriorated (fig. 5.10).

The recesses in the lock's walls that allowed the open gates to lie flush with the wall are still visible (fig. 5.12). The brickwork of the enslaved masons who fashioned the lock of brick, stones, and mortar more than two hundred years ago is a testimony to their skill. The molded angled bricks that defined the lock's entrance are still visible.

In October 2019 Richard Porcher and friends cleared vegetation from the lock. Tree roots tend to damage the walls' integrity as they grow, and vines and shrubs tend to produce carbon dioxide, which reacts with water to produce carbonic acid that weathers the limestone mortar. With continued protection from invading vegetation, the lock will long be a reminder of the craftsmanship that went into the Santee Canal.

On the western side of the Santee end on the lock are the remains of the mill. The brickwork is so disturbed that nothing can be gleaned of its construction. The millpond today is a swamp community along the private road (formerly St. John's Road) that runs along the canal. It was formed by the bank of the Santee Canal, which stopped the natural flow of water in the swamp. The side ditch that leads from the millpond to the mill is still visible (fig. 9.9). The millpond, fed by rainwater and natural drainage, also functioned as a reservoir to supply water for the canal.

Just past White Oak Lock is the dry basin on the eastern side of the canal, where repairs were made to vessels (figs. 5.8 and 5.15). The excavated section in the bank of the canal was plainly visible. No remains of the floodgates that controlled the water into and out of the dry basin were visible.

Past the dry basin was the section of the canal bed Senf elevated over natural grade through a wetland for four hundred yards. The amount of fill and labor required to create this elevated bed must have been enormous. Even today one can still see the bed.

Samuel Porcher established a second settlement at Mexico within sight of the Santee Canal (fig. 4.5) after he abandoned the settlement on the Santee River bluff. His son, William Mazÿck Porcher (1812–1902), inherited Mexico upon Samuel's death in 1851. Henry William Ravenel wrote in his journal on

FIGURE 9.10. Left, William Mazÿck Porcher (1812–1902), date and photographer unknown. Personal archives of Dorothy Pratt-Thomas, Charleston, South Carolina. Right, Mazÿck in Mexico's yard, date and photographer unknown. Photograph from H. E. Ravenel Jr., *Ravenel Records*.

April 20, 1865, that René Ravenel "was then taken along with the army to Mexico where they spent the night at the generals [sic] quarters. The black troops discovered some 6 or 800 bottles wine & became furious. They burnt nearly all the buildings in the yard including the dwelling house—Mazÿck Porcher was captured & carried off with the army."[14] Porcher was later released and spent his remaining days at Mexico living in the overseer's house, which was spared burning. Two photographs exist of Porcher at Mexico, one from when he was a young man and one from late in life (fig. 9.10).

According to the General Plan, Mexico house was located on a bend of the Santee Canal north of Big Camp Lock (fig. 4.5). The house ruins were located in the general area indicated by the plan, a few acres in extent and within sight of the Santee Canal. Forest trees shared the site with a mix of grasses, giving it a parklike appearance, typical of long-abandoned houses in the Lowcountry. Broken and whole handmade bricks abounded throughout the site. A rectangle pit four by ten feet and about four feet deep, perhaps some type of cellar, was found in the center of the site.

The location of the house site gives support to the report that the Porchers watched vessels going through the canal from the porch of their main house. The house site is on private property and is not available to the public without permission.

Field Survey of the Santee Canal and Environs ⁓ 179

Richard Porcher could conjure up an image of his great-uncle Mazÿck sitting on his piazza at Mexico, sipping Madeira in the evenings while watching vessels loaded with cotton passing along the canal at the foot of his lawn and hearing the songs of the boatmen. Mazÿck lived many years after the Santee Canal ceased operation and undoubtedly witnessed its slow deterioration. In the photograph of him standing in Mexico's yard, one might imagine him watching someone fish for Santee bream in the waters of the abandoned canal.

As Richard Porcher trekked the bank of the canal near where Mexico house once stood, he thought maybe he could find the lost treasure of Mexico. Descendants of Porcher's enslaved people claim house servants buried the family's gold and silver before the Yankees arrived. Maybe they buried gold and silver in the canal bed? Family lore states no one returned to retrieve the treasure, so somewhere may lie the hidden Porcher treasure of Mexico.

Senf's General Plan shows the director's house just north of the canal along the Pine Ville–Eutawville Road (today's Highway 45), just across the road from St. Stephen's Basin. The house was associated with the support structures for the canal at Big Camp. A search yielded no remains of the house or any support structures. Three small chinaberry trees were the only evidence that the site had been inhabited. Chinaberry trees were often planted in yards of early Lowcountry houses—especially around enslaved dwellings because the plant was viewed as a fleabane—and almost always indicate past inhabitation. The trees were small but could have been from seeds of trees that died. Perhaps Gertrude Senf intended to use chinaberry as a folk remedy for canal workers.

No sign of the steam engine mount was found southeast of the Big Camp Lock (fig. 7.1). A brick base and elevated pipe like those found at the river were nowhere to be seen. The bricks were probably recycled after the canal closed.

HIGHWAY 45 TO LAKE MOULTRIE

Leaving Big Camp, Richard Porcher and friends crossed Highway 45 and began the trek down White Bridge Road, which follows the canal for three-tenths of a mile. Where Highway 45 crosses the Santee Canal is the bed of the original Pine Ville–Eutawville Road where the bridge (depicted in fig. 5.18) was located. Senf said "next to the bridge is St. Stephen's Bason."[15] The location of St. Stephen's Basin, which is clearly visible, places the old bridge where Highway 45 crosses the canal. Nothing is left of the original bridge. To the east the

Pine Ville–Eutawville Road ran parallel to the Santee River to the King's Highway in Charleston County. Its original route is too obscure to try to explain in this book.

Highway 45 follows the original Pine Ville–Eutawville Road west of where it intersects with Edgewater Road. Edgewater Road is the continuation of the original road and ends at the shoreline of Lake Marion at Harry's Fish Camp. Originally the road ran all the way to Eutawville.

It is easy to see the canal from White Bridge Road, one of the two places where the public can view the canal and not be on private property. The walls of the basin have washed down, so its outline is not clear, but nonetheless we knew we were in the basin. No trace of a brick warehouse was found. Senf wrote that this warehouse was next to the basin.

Richard Porcher and friends next took a detour from the canal to the Glendkamp Cemetery located on land of the Oakland Club toward the end of Sandlapper Lane south of Highway 45 and east of the canal. The cemetery lies in an unkempt wooded thicket, making it hard to see the individual grave markers. A grave marker indicates the burial place of the Reverend Henry Glendkamp (1809–85), determined by the authors to be one of the six children of the past superintendent of the canal, Henry Glindkamp.[16] (The name *Glindkamp* has been spelled differently over time.) No marker for Henry Sr. was found in the cemetery. Lack of a grave marker, however, does not mean he was not buried in the family cemetery, because permanent grave markers were not always used. Henry was married to Jenny Wilson (1770–?), a free woman of color originally from Virginia. Glindkamp descendants live in the Pineville-Russellville area today. Glendkamp stated in his will that he farmed Pine Hill. The farm is also listed on some plats as Glen Camp, obviously a derivation of Glendkamp. Pine Hill was located adjacent to Belle Isle along the Santee Canal opposite the Great Reservoir (figs. 4.4 and E3). Within sight of the Santee Canal, in an unkempt graveyard known to just a few people, perhaps reposes the late superintendent Henry Glindkamp, whose life's work helped shape the future of Santee Canal country.

The six-hundred-foot dam Senf created to hold the water in the Great Reservoir (fig. 9.11) was the next point of interest. Returning to Highway 45, we took the old St. John's Road that runs southwest along the canal to the dam (fig. 5.21). The floodgates Senf employed to control the flow of water from the reservoir into the canal have long vanished (fig. 5.20), replaced by modern culverts. St. John's Road parallels the canal, making for an easy trek and view. During the

Field Survey of the Santee Canal and Environs

FIGURE 9.11. Great Reservoir bank, early 1970s. Reservoir is to the right; Santee Canal is to the left. Photograph by Richard Dwight Porcher Jr.

active life of the canal, the Great Reservoir was treeless; today it is forested with a variety of swamp trees. The dam and St. John's Road are on Oakland Club property; permission must be obtained to visit the dam.

Completion of the field survey of the Great Reservoir necessitated a drive to Black Oak Road. Senf used Black Oak Road as a dam to keep water in the Great Reservoir from draining into Bull Town Bay. Black Oak Road first appears in archival documents on James Cook's 1773 "A Map of the Province of South Carolina" (fig. 9.4). It shows clearly in the 1825 *Mills' Atlas* (see frontispiece). By 1825 the major plantations of Santee Canal country had been established, and the road's route was better defined. Black Oak Road exited Murray Ferry Road (US 52 South of today's Santee Circle) near Tibbekudlaw (today's Tiverton Lawn) and paralleled the Santee Canal for almost its entire route. It passed through Tibbekudlaw, Oakfield, Fair Springs, Woodboo, Wantoot, Pooshee, Chelsea, and Woodlawn, crossed the Santee Canal at Frierson's Lock, and tied into the Pine Ville–Eutawville Road. Black Oak Road north of Lake Moultrie today is Springwood Road (State Road S-8-23) and Thomas Walter Road. Springwood Road begins at Quattlebaum Landing and intersects Whispering Pine Lane (fig. 9.12), where the original Black Oak Road formed the western bank of the Great Reservoir. Springwood Road continues to Highway 45, where it crosses 45 and becomes Thomas Walter Road, which ends at Eadytown at the lake's edge.

FIGURE 9.12. Intersection of Whispering Pine Lane and Springwood Road (State Road S-8-23), 2020. The Great Reservoir (Kirk's Swamp) is to the left. Springwood Road (Black Oak Road) formed the western bank of the reservoir. Photograph by Richard Dwight Porcher Jr.

Today the portion of Black Oak Road south of Lake Moultrie at Santee Circle is State Road S-8-907. Black Oak Road cuts off Powerhouse Road and runs northwest, crossing the dike, where it becomes Boy Scout Lane and ends at the shore of Lake Moultrie. South of Powerhouse Road, it runs through a subdivision, ending at US Highway 52.

With permission from the manager of Quattlebaum Landing at the southern end of Springwood Road, Richard Porcher and friends reached a section of the original Black Oak Road that runs parallel to a modern canal cut for access to the lake. This section was abandoned and never converted into a modern road. One can still see the side ditches that defined the original road and walk the old roadbed. Shrubs and trees grow there but are not dense, so walking is easy. Black Oak Road crosses Bull Town Drain and runs to the lake's edge. During extreme lake drawdowns, one can see the trace of the roadbed to Frierson's Lock, which it crossed on its run south.

Field Survey of the Santee Canal and Environs

Richard Porcher and friends returned to St. John's Road and continued their trek toward Lake Moultrie. The next point of interest was where the Santee Canal intersects Bull Town Drain. The drain is obvious (fig. 7.3). During its active period, its waters that flowed into the Summit Canal were probably controlled by a floodgate. The floodgate has long disappeared, and the drain is blocked off from the Summit Canal. The trek along the Summit Canal ended at the lake's edge. Lake Moultrie flooded the Santee Canal all the way to the Pinopolis powerhouse.

POWERHOUSE TO COUNTY ROAD 343 (DOCK ROAD)

As the General Plan indicates, Senf constructed an access road through Biggin Swamp parallel to the Santee Canal from Hope Lock to the Moncks Corner/Biggin Church Road. This section of the canal is often referred to as Biggin Canal because it runs entirely through Biggin Swamp (fig. 9.13). Biggin Canal and the access road can be reached from an old woods road exiting the parking lot at the end of Reid Hill Road at Hidden Cove Marina. Approximately one-and-a-half miles of the access road exist today on the section of the canal from the woods road to the railroad trestle crossing Biggin Canal near the powerhouse (fig. 9.13). Santee Cooper owns the land adjacent to the canal. Past the trestle the construction of the powerhouse obliterated the canal and Hope Lock. The abandoned woods road and canal toward Highway 52 are blocked by a modern boating canal. The access road along the canal is easy walking, although one must maneuver around patches of shrubs and an occasional tree and one or two cuts in the road holding water during wet seasons. One is immediately surrounded by deep swamp and woods of unbridled beauty and solitude. Hiking toward the trestle, one passes from swamp land to upland forest. Here the workers had to make a deep cut. Senf did not construct a towpath along Biggin Canal, and vessels had to be poled the distance between Hope and Tide Lock. Although there is no infrastructure remaining on this section of the canal, one can understand the work that went into excavating it in a time before machines and enjoy the solitude of the Lowcountry wilderness.

The "new course of Biggin Creek" intended by Senf to connect two severed sections of the creek was represented as "red dotted line" on the General Plan.[17] The new course was to help clear out Tide Lock of sediment. It was to be "30 feet wide at the bottom even with the Bed of the Creek, 48 feet on the Top, and 9 feet deep from the surface of the ground."[18] An excavation of this nature would still be present and would easily show on lidar. A field survey,

FIGURE 9.13. Abandoned access road and Biggin (Santee) Canal, 2023. Photograph by Brent R. Fortenberry.

however, was unable to find the new course, and it does not show on lidar. The authors conclude it was never excavated and existed only on Senf's General Plan.

COUNTY ROAD 343 (DOCK ROAD) TO COOPER RIVER

Dock Road is the original road that ran from Moncks Corner to Biggin Church, appearing on the 1800 General Plan. The Tailrace Canal severed the road to Biggin Church, and today's Dock Road dead-ends at the Tailrace Canal and Gilligan's Restaurant. One of Senf's communication bridges carried the original road across the canal to the church. No trace of this bridge exists. Parking at the end of Dock Road, we made the short walk back down the road to where it crosses the Santee Canal. Construction debris deposited on the east canal bank partly obscured it. Within a hundred feet or so, the original bank of the canal was apparent. Richard Porcher and friends trekked down the east bank of Biggin Canal the two-tenths of a mile to the end of the bank. Biggin Canal was

Field Survey of the Santee Canal and Environs ~ 185

full of water, obviously a result of water flow in Biggin Creek, which has been altered over the years by the Tailrace Canal and other structures.

Parallel with the canal is a side ditch. The ditch was not mentioned in Senf's Final Report to the directors, and it does not show on the General Plan. It follows the bank past Tide Lock, cuts at an angle at the end of the canal bank, and enters Biggin Creek. The side ditch probably carried excess water from adjacent Biggin Swamp past the canal into Biggin Creek, keeping rainwater from overflowing and eroding the bank and flooding the canal with excess water. The authors could not determine whether it was constructed by Senf or the Canal Company after Senf left.

In 1987, under contract with the Santee Cooper Public Service Authority and in cooperation with the South Carolina Department of Parks, Recreation and Tourism, the South Carolina Institute of Archaeology and Anthropology conducted an archaeological survey of Tide Lock and environs.[19] The institute published its results in 1989. Since keeping the site of Tide Lock from the public was paramount, GPS coordinates of the lock were not included in its report. Archaeology was done underwater since the canal could not be drained, although heroic efforts were made to do so. In 2020 Drew Ruddy located and surveyed the lock remains for the authors. The results of the two surveys provided the data for Judd's diagram of the lock (fig. 5.38).

The west bank ends a hundred feet before the east bank. One can see the end of the west bank easily from the east bank. The east bank continues a hundred feet farther down Biggin Creek to where the side ditch enters Biggin Creek.

There is a sign in the water at the junction of Biggin Creek and the beginning of the excavated Biggin Canal that reads "Number 10." The sign was originally in a visitor's brochure published when the Old Santee Canal Park was a county park before Santee Cooper became the owner. According to a brochure, it was site 10 as one came up from the park by boat or on foot and marked the junction of Biggin Creek and the beginning of the excavated canal bed. The trail is not part of the present Old Santee Canal Park and is abandoned. An abandoned footbridge, still passable, crosses the canal upstream from Tide Lock, a holdover from when this section of the Santee Canal was part of the county park trail system.

Senf's General Plan shows a spring draining into Biggin Creek from the highland just past Tide Lock south of Biggin Creek. The thought of finding a flowing spring was exhilarating, since all the springs associated with the canal were flooded by the lake. We followed the run of the spring, and it led to the base of the bluff along Biggin Swamp at the edge of Biggin Creek MTB Trail on Rembert Dennis Boulevard. On inspection we determined that it was not an artesian spring, as explained by figures 5.33 and 5.34. It was a seep and added to water in Biggin Creek. A seep forms when rainwater percolates down into the ground. If the water hits a hardpan it cannot penetrate, it moves laterally above the hardpan. Where the highland slopes as a bluff and intersects a wetland like a swamp and exposes the hardpan, the water will seep out above the exposed hardpan and form a small stream that runs to the mainstream, which is Biggin Creek.

The last section of passage along the Santee Canal began at Old Santee Canal Park. We canoed Biggin Creek from the Canal Park to where the excavated Biggin Canal began. The creation of the Tailrace Canal as part of the Santee Cooper Project obliterated the terminal portion of Biggin Creek, which originally joined with Wadboo Creek (or Fair Forest Swamp by some sources) to form the West Branch of the Cooper River. Stony Landing House today sits on the edge of the Tailrace Canal but is still no less majestic and impressive than when it appeared before construction of the canal. One can still get a sense of what those in vessels experienced as they passed down Biggin Creek on their way to the Cooper River (fig. 6.9). There was no infrastructure of the canal visible on the passage along the creek, and no signs of the methods Senf employed to change the creek's course. Our passage down the Santee Canal from the Santee to the Cooper River was over. A new chapter in the history of the Santee Canal was complete.

OWNERSHIP TODAY OF THE FORMER SANTEE CANAL COMPANY'S LANDS

Most of the Santee Canal today lies under the waters of Lake Moultrie. The following is a summary of the current ownership of the more prominent extant (unflooded) lands that were sold by the Santee Canal Company after it surrendered its charter. We will refrain from identifying the private owners who allowed us to visit the lands so as not to breach their trust. No attempt was made to trace the chronological title changes from the time the Santee Canal Company's charter was surrendered in 1853 to the present ownership of the extant properties.

The general land that was White Oak (figs. 4.2 and E3) was combined with Walter's plantation and is privately owned. A conservation easement was placed on the property in 2022. Located on this private land are the Guard Lock and White Oak Lock, Thomas Walter's grave site, the remains of the steam engine mount on the river and the drain to the canal, the beginning of the Porcher Embankment, the Santee Basin, the dry basin, the section of the canal that was planked with cypress, and about two miles of the canal.

The Oakland Club owns the former lands of Mexico east of the canal except for Mexico Cemetery. A section of the Porcher Embankment in the Santee Swamp is now owned by the Oakland Club as well as the site of Samuel Porcher's first settlement on Mexico on the bluff along the Santee Swamp.

A section of Big Camp was purchased by Mazÿck Porcher and made part of Mexico but is now part of the Oakland Club. The eastern section of Big Camp along Highway 45 is privately owned today by the Gourdin family of Pineville and harbors the remains of Big Camp Lock and the director's house site. All infrastructure of Big Camp has long disappeared.

The Oakland Club also owns Glen Camp (Pine Hill) and where Glendkamp Cemetery is located, which Oakland has pledged to preserve and allow family members to visit.

The Great Reservoir is owned by the Oakland Club. Santee Cooper owns much of Bull Town Bay, where the Cross Generating Plant and fly ash disposal site are located.

The Santee Cooper powerhouse and Pinopolis Dam, the southern edge of Lake Moultrie, lie over Hope and Hope Lock. The route of Biggin Canal from the powerhouse to the remains of Tide Lock at the end of the constructed canal are Santee Cooper property. Santee Cooper owns the highland along Biggin Creek as part of its Old Santee Canal Park.

Epilogue

Richard Dwight Porcher Jr.

As I gazed over the waters of Lake Moultrie from Frierson's Lock during the lake drawdown in 2007, my mind followed the route of the flooded portion of the Santee Canal to Black Oak. I lamented the history that had been lost under the muddy waters of the manmade lake. My mind returned to a day in 1953 when I boated with my father to an island in Lake Moultrie, a section of highland of Northampton that was left unflooded during drawdowns of the lake. The island has vanished because of erosion, but when the lake level drops, a clay bank is exposed that represents the eroded remnant. I was only fourteen at the time and had little knowledge of the history of Middle St. John's or the Santee Canal and the loss my immediate family and extended families had endured when their homes and lands were condemned and flooded. The lake was a paradise where Pinopolis friends and I fished, hunted, boated, and courted, and the shorelines were sites for Native American relic collecting.

As my father and I stood in the open area on the island that was a former field on Northampton, he gazed over the land and said that he remembered his father, Percival, planting the field. Looking over the field, with a heavy heart and sadness and resignation in his voice, he said: "Gone with the breezes; gone with the breezes." This was his allusion to *Gone with the Wind,* where the South was swept desolate by the ravages of the Civil War. St. John's was his Tara, and Santee Cooper was the Civil War. Many times afterward, sitting on the porch of our summerhouse built on the shoreline of Pooshee and gazing over the lake, he would repeat these lines, always with a sense of sadness and resignation. He never resigned to his loss, and it became the defining aspect of his life—albeit a sad and tragic one—and the lives of many others, both Black and white, who lost their St. John's heritage.

Dwight was not the only planter descendant and landowner to carry to their grave the loss of their St. John's heritage to the Santee Cooper lakes. The Cain siblings of Somerset; my Uncle Percy; Henry Lucas and his sister, Florence, of White Hall; the Gourdin brothers of Woodlawn; the Dennis family of Fair Springs; Henry Francis Porcher of Ophir; the Kirks of Mt. Pleasant; the Sinklers of Belvidere and Eutaw all harbored resentment toward Santee Cooper and its backers. J. Russell Williams, co-owner of Hanover, upon hearing the South Carolina Supreme Court's denial of the appeal of three power companies against the Santee Cooper Project, the final obstacle against the project, was heard to say, "I'll never eat a fish that comes out of that damn lake." And according to his family, he never did.

The campaign to create the two lakes (Marion and Moultrie) and establish the South Carolina Public Service Authority (commonly referred to as Santee Cooper) was long, arduous, and bitter, placing legislatures and citizens on different sides. As far back as 1773, South Carolinians envisioned wedding the Santee and Cooper Rivers to transportation throughout the state. The Santee Canal was the first such wedding. The Santee Canal Company surrendered its charter in 1853. Surveys for the canal route revealed that the bed of the Santee River was thirty-five feet higher than the bed of the Cooper. This would come into play in the future.

In 1902 state legislator Benjamin Elliott resurrected the idea of connecting the two rivers for water traffic and introduced a joint resolution into the legislature. He found little support, mainly because of a new steamboat line between Columbia and Georgetown in 1910. The Georgetown Harbor was inferior to Charleston but was preferable to the cost of building another canal or restoring the Santee Canal.

The next attempt to wed the two rivers occurred in 1917 when Charleston mayor John P. Grace, prompted by the Chamber of Commerce, wrote to Colleton senator J. P. Padgett outlining a plan for a new canal; this time the possibility of using waterpower to create electric power was in its infancy. A canal could then have a double use: navigation and hydroelectric power. Nothing came of this venture.

Thomas Clay Williams and his partners in the Columbia Railway and Navigation Company operated steamboats on the Santee from Columbia to

Georgetown. Williams envisioned greater profits for his company if inland water passage could be arranged between Columbia and Charleston, whose port facilities far exceeded that of Georgetown. By this time hydroelectric power was in widespread use in the country. Williams's navigation project evolved into a hydroelectric possibility when New York engineers William S. Murray and Henry Flood became partners. In 1930 the Murray-Flood Company constructed Dreher Shoals Dam, forming Lake Murray, and they envisioned constructing a dam on the Santee River and creating two lakes for navigation and hydroelectric power. The Depression ended their venture for lack of private funding. Nevertheless, the idea of connecting the two rivers would not die.

President Franklin Roosevelt, elected in 1932, expanded the federal government's power to bring relief from the Depression. His Works Progress Administration, established to put citizens to work, directed federal funds to be used for internal improvements across the depressed nation.[1] Hydroelectric plants, which made use of the nation's cheap and abundant water sources, were a main goal of Works Progress Administration. The state alone could not pay for the project, and private funds were nonexistent. Business interests in South Carolina, however, saw the means to bring the moribund Santee and Cooper project back to life: federal funding.

Establishing a state authority to oversee the project was the first official step. Early on, proponents suffered several defeats but were undaunted in the belief the project was in the best interest of the state. They finally persuaded enough legislators to support it. On April 7, 1934, the state legislature passed Act 887 establishing a "corporation completely owned by and to be completely operated for the benefit of the people of South Carolina for the improvement of their health, welfare, and material prosperity."[2] The corporation was the South Carolina Public Service Authority (SCPSA, called Santee Cooper). Santee Cooper could not pledge the credit of the state in any way; federal grants and loans were to be its entire funding. Act 887 gave the state the power to "develop the Santee, Cooper and Congaree rivers for navigation; produce and distribute electric power; reclaim swampy lands; reforest the watersheds of the state's rivers; build canals, dams, and power plants; divert the waters of the Santee; set rates for the electricity it produced; and borrow money and issue bonds."[3] A suit was filed challenging the constitutionally of the act, but on September 10, 1935, the state Supreme Court affirmed that it was constitutional.[4]

The plan of the Santee Cooper Project was simple: construct a dam across the Santee River just above Wilson's Landing, backing up the river to form a one-hundred-thousand-acre lake (named Lake Marion after Gen. Francis

FIGURE E1. Jefferies generating station. Note the angled gates of the lock to withstand the pressure of the lake's waters. Photograph courtesy of Norman Sinkler Walsh, 2007.

Marion). The dam would create a lake thirty-five feet above the level of the Santee River. Spillways in the dam would allow water to be released downriver from the dam in time of heavy rains. A diversion canal would be constructed from Lake Marion to the sixty-thousand-acre St. John's Basin to create Lake Moultrie.[5] Elevated dikes constructed at the southern end of the basin, running from Cross to Eadytown, would confine the waters to form the lake. Since surveys made during the construction of the Santee Canal reveled that the Santee was thirty-five feet higher than the Cooper River, raising the Santee an additional thirty-five feet with Wilson Dam would create a seventy-foot waterhead where Biggin Swamp exited the basin near Pinopolis, the basin's lowest elevation.[6] A seventy-foot waterhead would be adequate to run turbines to create electricity. A hydroelectric generating station (fig. E1) would create electricity from turbines turned by water falling through massive tubes in which the turbines sat.

Water to run the turbines would be jetted into a tailrace canal excavated four miles to the Cooper River, which emptied into Charleston Harbor. Since inland water navigation was touted as one of the reasons for the project, the world's largest single-gate lock would be constructed to lower vessels from the lake into the tailrace canal or raise vessels in the reverse direction (fig. E1).

But not everyone bought into the project during Santee Cooper's tortuous passage through the legislature. One senator expressed concerns that an unrestricted public company would gain control of existing public companies in the state, forcing them out of business. One representative doubted the project's technical and financial practicality and believed the state's timber industry would be disrupted, increasing unemployment. Another representative feared Santee Cooper would become a political machine (which it did and remains). The act reeked of socialism, long anathema to South Carolinians. Other legislatures were sympathetic to environmental concerns raised by owners of game preserves and farmlands and believed the project would be too costly to construct and would not work as presented.

Environmental opposition became a rallying cry for numerous groups and individuals, virtually until flooding began in 1941. Charleston mayor Burnet Maybank (1899–1954), one of the most vocal proponents of the project (perhaps to further his political future), was so taken aback by the opposition to it that he published an enemies list of those opponents.

Environmental concerns were varied. Would the limestone base of the proposed lakes hold water? (So far it has.) Would bird populations, especially migratory, be devastated? Would tourism based on birding be suppressed? Would the Santee Delta suffer irreversible damage as the salt point moved inland, and would Cape Romain be degraded as a wildlife refuge? Would the project destroy the last sizable habitat of the rare ivory-billed woodpecker, causing its extinction?

South Carolina poet laureate Archibald Rutledge joined the opposition, and for his effort he was stripped of his laureate position in the Senate. To its credit, the lower house did not go along with the Senate. Rutledge became one of Maybank's enemies. Even the conservative *News and Courier,* based in Maybank's hometown of Charleston, was against the project. Editor William Ball wrote that politicians backed the project and not engineers or those familiar with the power industry.[7]

Opposition from plantation owners was expected, since it was their lands, heritage, and homes that would be lost to the lakes. Francis Marion Kirk Sr. of Mt. Pleasant in Upper St. John's Parish articulated the position of the planter descendants in opposition to the project. He published a series of articles in the *News and Courier* from 1935 to 1936. Countless families who lost their lands still hold his articles in their archives for their descendants to read. Kirk's articles presented Upper and Middle St. John's as a land of great historical significance to the Lowcountry and South Carolina's past, one that could never be replaced or reproduced. Kirk's family genealogy and heritage ran deep in the Lowcountry and St. John's, as his given names suggested. In his articles he projected a romanticized version of St. John's with stories of Francis Marion played against a background of the area's wild natural beauty. The Santee Swamp was Marion's hideout as he led his Patriots against the British.

Indianfield house, the original home of the Mazÿck family in Middle St. John's, was situated on a high rise and commanded a view of the Santee Canal and fields and forest of St. John's. Each standing home was placed in a natural background to give them added meaning. Towering live oaks graced the plantation yards. Woodboo had numerous artesian springs that once fed its rice fields, a crop that made the planters of Middle and Upper St. John's prosperous in the 1700s. The Rocks was the site of the first successful crop of Santee long-staple cotton that replaced rice and indigo as the main money crop after the Revolution. Kirk pointed out that in the 1930s many plantations were successful; while they were not utilizing the latest technology, the richness of St. John's farmlands yielded productive commercial and domestic crops.

Wide piazzas on all sides amplified Eutaw's architectural symmetry, piazzas being a staple social gathering place. Exquisite slave-made woodcarvings adorned many houses such as White Hall and Somerset. Belvidere was the beautiful manor house owned by the Sinkler family: "Built high from the ground and of frame construction, the house is perfectly preserved. The building has an eastern exposure and commands a beautiful sweep of wide, green lawn."[8] The Sinklers were horse lovers, and some of the finest horses in the South were bred at Eutaw and Belvidere.[9]

Kirk painted slavery in a favorable light, with descriptions of enslaved people's hunting skills when they were guides for the planters, part of a time-honed social order of racial harmony before and after the Civil War. He mentioned the corner cupboard made by enslaved people at Woodboo, extolling their skill. Kirk wrote that the plantation culture produced outstanding physicians like Dr. Francis Peyre Porcher and Edward Porcher, botanists like William Henry Ravenel, and Patriots during the Revolution like Francis Marion, Peter Sinkler, and Peter Gaillard. He even described the life of St. John's in the decade before Santee Cooper, citing family picnics at the Rocks Church and Trinity Church Black Oak (fig. E2).

No matter how eloquently Kirk portrayed St. John's, it would never resonate

FIGURE E2. Trinity Church Black Oak, family picnic, ca. 1935. Courtesy of Patricia Langley Dwight.

with those who supported the project. He was a voice in the wilderness, speaking only for those who shared his love for the region.

The last hope to derail the project was a lawsuit by three utilities, Broad River Power Company, Carolina Power and Light, and the South Carolina Power Company, that claimed the project was a scheme for the government to take control of private power companies; that navigation touted in the project had no relation to hydroelectric (which would prove true since the project never functioned as envisioned for navigation); that the proposed project subjected them to injurious and unfair competition; that the cost of the project would be more than estimated (which would also prove true); that the limestone formation upon which the lakes would rest would not hold water; that they could supply the rural areas to be served by Santee Cooper with electricity; and that the two-hundred-mile operating radius of Santee Cooper would overlap their domain. Even if Sen. Strom Thurmond, Gov. James Byrnes, and Mayor Maybank were convinced the three utilities could and would supply electricity to the rural areas, it would not have mattered to them. The project was a way to raise their public profiles and further their political careers. Santee Cooper was their train that they would ride into the sunset of political grandness.

Epilogue ~ 195

The US Fourth Circuit Court of Appeals denied the utilities suit, and on May 23, 1938, the Supreme Court refused the companies' appeal. With all legal battles finished, in July 1938 a contract was signed with the Harza Engineering Company of Chicago to design and supervise construction of the vast and complex project. The necessary agreements with the Roosevelt government were signed in 1939, whereby 45 percent of the project cost would be an outright grant to the state and 55 percent would be a federally backed loan.

Unlike the Tennessee Valley Authority, Santee Cooper did not hire the workers. Harza Engineering hired the laborers and fed and housed them. The Work Projects Administration oversaw the land clearing. Eleven permanent work camps and eleven portable camps were built, each designed for 275 workers, housing approximately 6,000 workers in all. Ultimately 12,000 workers were employed to complete the project. Malarial control measures were put into place to protect them.

Once the last legal issue had been resolved, the assembly passed the Eminent Domain Act of May 1, 1939 (Section 9111-9125 of the South Carolina 1942 Code of Laws). The act gave Santee Cooper the power to take private property and convert it into public use through condemnation. The act also allowed for the repurchase at the original price of any land by its former owner if the land was not used for the specified purposes outlined in the Santee Cooper charter within five years of implementation. By June 1939 title to 1,100 tracts of land had been obtained (either by condemnation or willingly), totaling 177,000 acres. The entire Santee Cooper Project took only two years, six months, and twenty-six days to complete from the initial clearing of the proposed lake sites to the filling of the lakes, an incredibly short time. Modern machinery, however, made rapid progress possible. On November 12, 1941, the last spillway in the Santee Dam at Lake Marion was closed, and the muddy waters of the "River of the Carolinas" soon created the Santee Cooper lakes (fig. E3).[10] On February 17, 1942, the Unit 2 turbine was activated, and the first electricity was generated. By June all five turbines were running at full operation. Santee Cooper became a reality.

The arrogance of Santee Cooper in their dealings with former landowners did not end with the legal finality of the project and the Eminent Domain Act. Santee Cooper violated the act many times, but only the Cain family had the resources to successfully challenge these abuses.[11] Elizabeth Ravenel (née Lucas) Cain, widow of William Cain Sr., devised Wampee at her death in 1941 to her and William's offspring, William (Willa) Cain Jr., Charles Lucas Cain, Joseph Palmer Cain, and Elizabeth Ravenel Cain. The four siblings owned Wampee when it was condemned by Santee Cooper. The house was situated on a high pine ridge at the northern end of Pinopolis. When the lake came, a thirty-three-acre section of the property where the house stood was left unflooded and jutting into Lake Moultrie. The South Carolina Public Service adopted Wampee as a conference center and political retreat for its supporters and cronies. The four siblings wanted the land returned since it was not being used for purposes specified by the Eminent Domain Act.

Joe Cain waited until after his two brothers returned home after World War II in 1945 to file his case against Santee Cooper jointly with his three siblings. John Cosgrove of Charleston and Rembert C. Dennis of Moncks Corner were the Cains' lawyers. (After Cosgrove's death, Samuel Want of Darlington worked with Dennis.) Cosgrove knew the case would be difficult, since Santee Cooper would fight to protect their investment in the property and also seek to dissuade others from filing similar suits. He also knew that Santee Cooper had powerful allies in the legislature and courts, but the Cains were undaunted in their belief that they had been wronged by Santee Cooper. Cosgrove informed Santee Cooper that the Cains wanted Wampee returned at the same rate for which it was condemned, $18.25 per acre. Santee Cooper refused to resell; subsequently the case was filed in the Berkeley County Court of Common Pleas. Santee Cooper argued that the tract was crucial to its operation; that it was not sufficiently raised above the water line; that it was used for malarial research; and that the peninsula had been used by anti-sabotage patrols during World War II to protect the powerhouse and dam, which had been deemed vital to the war effort. Santee Cooper also had the gall to argue that the act did not extend to the heirs of the original owner, Elizabeth Cain, trying to negate a history of legal inherited property that still holds today. Judge John Grimball ruled in favor of the Cain family on July 3, 1948, rejecting Santee Cooper's arguments and agreeing with the family that Wampee was being used for purposes other than those specified in its charter. Santee Cooper appealed to the South Carolina Supreme Court, which affirmed the lower court's ruling. Since the court did not award legal fees (in this way Santee Cooper did win), the family was financially unable to keep the property, and they sold Wampee back to Santee Cooper for $1,000.00 per acre, considerably more than what they were originally paid. Today Santee Cooper maintains Wampee as a conference center, with the restored (but, unfortunately, painted) Wampee house as a main attraction.

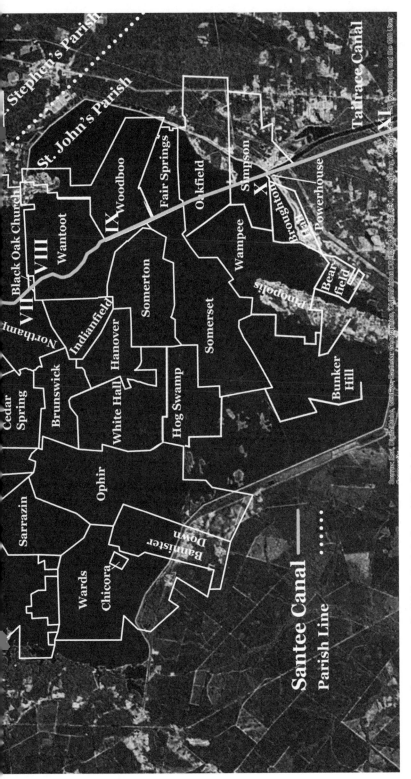

FIGURE E3. Plantations of Middle St. John's and English Santee overlaid on Santee Canal country. The eleven locks of the Santee Canal are labeled I–XI. Authors added contemporary structures: Tailrace Canal, Rediversion Canal, Diversion Canal, Spillway, Santee Dam, Hwy. 45, Pineville, Lake Marion, and Lake Moultrie. Created by Robert Joseph Hauck, Richard Dwight Porcher Jr, Cecelia Naomi Dailey, and Shannon Marie Donohue.

Black residents were also cheated out of valuable property—property that was never flooded by the lake. They did not have the means to contest the unlawful taking of their land, and today others enjoy the benefits that should have come to them. Campbell AME Church was condemned by Santee Cooper to make way for the lake. The church building was torn down and relocated to its present site at 1059 Black Oak Road. Upon relocation the name was changed to Mt. Carmel AME. The site of Campbell AME Church was not flooded, although it lies within the East Dike. A modern home occupies the former church site. Nearby in the woods is the cemetery of Campbell AME Church. When the land was not flooded, Campbell should have had the chance to buy back the land at the condemned price. Campbell could have then resold the land as a residential home site at a much higher price.

Lost in the drama over Santee Cooper and the white landowners were the Black inhabitants of Middle St. John's. Nine hundred Black residents were displaced. Although Black communities suffered the most from removal by the Santee Cooper Project, their voices were lacking as part of Santee Cooper's official record. Descendants of enslaved people, whose labor planted the fields of long-staple cotton and helped build the wealth of the Lowcountry, were totally left out of the history of St. John's Basin. None of the documents produced by Santee Cooper before the clearing of land for the lakes recorded the history of Black settlements established after Emancipation or those who lived in them. Black history was considered unimportant, and its documentation would delay the project. The loss of this history is regrettable—and inexcusable since their history could have been easily documented before flooding. The history of Black settlements was just as important as the history of the plantation houses. It would have taken virtually nothing in terms of time and cost to have collected and preserved anecdotes furnished by African Americans who lived in the Basin before Santee Cooper.

Richard Porcher and Cecile Ann Guerry transcribed interviews with ten Black residents who either lived in the Basin before the lake came or their parents did.[12] They tell a story far different from Santee Cooper's in its haste to start and complete the project. Life in the Black-owned settlements was subsistence life at its barest. There was no electricity. For many there was no work, especially during the Depression. Welfare, Social Security, and food stamps were not available in pre–Santee Cooper St. John's Basin. But as William Canty related, "The land produced all our needs."[13] Canty lived at Coon Hill on a tract of land once owned by Elizabeth Clevland Hardcastle called Raccoon Hill (fig. E3): "We were 'poor' as viewed by Whites, but not necessarily in our view."[14]

The families at Coon Hill were self-sufficient, producing all they needed in their own gardens. Every family had a plot of land and planted a garden, raised their own livestock, fished from Coon Hill ponds, and hunted small game from their backyard woods.[15]

Coon Hill was like numerous other Black-owned settlements established by freed people after Emancipation and scattered throughout the basin before the lake came. Newlands, Hog Swamp, Moorfield, Barrow Hill, and others were home, where Black people had families, churches, and land.

Some of the nine hundred Black residents who were displaced did not own land but lived at a plantation where their ancestors had lived as enslaved people. Northampton, for one, had a large settlement of Black workers who were employed by the owners, northerners Albert M. Barnes and Clarence Dillon, who bought seven thousand acres of land in St. John's for hunting and timber investment. On Northampton Black South Carolinians were provided a home and work.

Black families also suffered the brunt of displacement. Black children were placed in inferior schools around the lake area. Although families were in many cases established in better homes and supplied with farm animals, the lack of adequate education more than offset the successes touted by Santee Cooper.

Each Black settlement had its own family network and support group, and generally those who lived there were related. Displaced families of the settlements were not always able to keep together, and Black residents were separated from their heritage. Rural electricity was touted by Santee Cooper as a main reason for the project, but Black households could not take advantage of it for years. The jobs touted for Black workers never materialized, because industries never located along the shores of the lakes where Black families settled. The unexpected fishing industry that happened with the ecological adaptation of the anadromous rockfish to the landlocked lake was of little value to Black fishermen because few could afford motorized boats.

Santee Cooper also neglected to document Native American history. Countless Native American burial grounds were located in the proposed lakebed. Archaeological surveys of these burial grounds could have added much to the history of the first inhabitants of Santee Canal country. But as with African Americans, documenting their history would have stood in the way of "progress."[16]

One day, as I looked over where the Santee Canal lay under the waters of the lake, I reflected on my many years in the Lowcountry as a field botanist, historian, and environmentalist. Is a man-made lake, an unnatural system, a better use of the land than what farmers, timber companies, environmentalists, tourists, cultural historians, and hunters might do with it? Is Lake Moultrie truly a "wilderness experience," as marketers tout? The land might have been designated a historic district, with tourist attractions. Perhaps a section of the Santee Canal could have been restored, and people could experience going down the canal and through a lock. Agriculture and tourism are current mainstays of the South Carolina economy. Has the lake and rural electricity of Santee Cooper brought enough people to Berkeley County and the Lowcountry to justify changing forever what our ancestors fought for and treasured and replacing it with gaudy development and overpopulation? Those who view southern Berkeley County today might be concerned that northern Berkeley will one day share its fate.

And I thought, perhaps I am fortunate. I am toward the end of my stay on planet Earth, and, hopefully I will not have to witness any more Lake Moultries in what is left of my St. John's home or the Lowcountry. But I am fearful of the world I leave behind for my grandchildren in what is left of Santee Canal country.

SOURCE NOTES

Johann Christian Senf produced three major documents on the Santee Canal: (1) "General Plan of the Canal and Its Environs between Santee and Cooper Rivers in the State of South Carolina"; (2) "Final Report to the Directors of the Santee Canal Company"; and (3) thirty-eight "particular plans." Mabel L. Webber stated that the Final Report, dated November 11, 1800, and the General Plan "have long been in the hands of the late Mr. William Cain of Somerset Plantation, St. John's Berkley [Berkeley], who deposited them through Mr. Henry Dwight with this Society [South Carolina Historical Society] for safe keeping."[1] A copy of Senf's General Plan is included in this book. There is no printer's mark on the General Plan. The authors could not find out where it was printed or determine the identity of the company or printer. Webber transcribed Senf's Final Report and published it in two issues of the *South Carolina Historical and Genealogical Magazine*.

The authors have also been unable to find the "thirty-eight particular plans" that Webber mentions but did not locate. We checked several archives and asked Cain family members that we suspected might have or know where the plans are located but had no luck. No other research on the history of the Santee Canal included any information on the plans. Hopefully someone reading this book will recognize the plans in their archives (if they still exist) and make them available to the public.

Senf's General Plan shows nine damaged areas. When and how the damage occurred is unrecorded. More than likely it happened while in private hands before it was gifted to the Historical Society. No attempt has been made to repair the map. Fortunately, the damaged areas are below the route of the canal, so their relevance is minimal. Likewise, Webber's copy of the Final Report contains numerous "illegible" entries, meaning she could not transcribe the words, so the damage must have occurred before she transcribed the text.[2]

Dr. Charles Drayton's diary from 1799–1805 includes a valuable account of the canal's early history. His sketch on the bridge that crossed what is today's Highway 45 gives valuable information on its construction.[3] William Robert Judd used this sketch to diagram the bridge and accessory structures depicted in figure 5.18.

In 1823 the Committee on Internal Improvements asked Abram Blanding, South Carolina's superintendent of public works, to recommend ways to improve the water supply of the Santee Canal. He responded with a report titled "The Santee Canal" and included it in his annual report to the legislature for 1823. The breadth of his report was impressive for the time period in which he worked, and it provided much information of the history of the Santee Canal that might have been lost.

In 2016 Karen Stokes and Richard Porcher found a previously unpublished manuscript in the archives of the South Carolina Historical Society. This manuscript, dated 1868, featured an intended chapter 2 of Professor Frederick Porcher's "Upper Beat of St. John's Berkeley" that included a section on the Santee Canal. In this article Porcher first wrote about Ralph Izard and Senf's account of the canal's route. Stokes and Richard Porcher published Frederick Porcher's unpublished chapter 2 in 2016.[4]

In 1875 Frederick Porcher wrote "The History of the Santee Canal" and dedicated the handwritten manuscript to the South Carolina Historical Society.[5] Although extensive in content, much of what he wrote was not based on his observations of the canal while it was in operation, so it is suspect in several respects. His determination that Senf chose White Oak for the starting point of the canal at the behest of Ralph Izard is questioned by the present authors (see chapter 4). Still it contains much valuable information on the canal's history. This original history does not contain any plats or maps.

In 1881 the US Army Corps of Engineers was charged with ascertaining if the Santee Canal could be repaired and reopened. The cost of basic structural repair was examined, as were several methods for correcting the lack of water from the reservoirs at the summit during droughts or seasonal dry weather. The army's report concluded that the Santee Canal would be plagued by the same problems it experienced during its years of operation, and no attempt to reopen the canal resulted. But two important documents came from the study. Included with the report was a redrawn version of Senf's General Plan. It was also in color and made minor changes to Senf's original. Fortunately for historians, it was copied from the original Senf 1800 General Plan before it was damaged. Senf's Final Report was also included in the 1881 report. Unlike Senf's Final Report published by Webber, the army's version did not contain the "illegible" notations that Webber included. Evidently the army's copy of the Final Report was made prior to damage. A section of the army's redrawn version of the General Plan was used to depict the flow of water in Senf's reservoir system (fig. 5.21).

Porcher's *History of the Santee Canal* was reproduced in 1903 and published by the South Carolina Historical Society as a pamphlet. Like the 1875 document, the 1903 one did not contain any maps or plats. It did contain an appendix by A. S. Salley Jr.[6]

Charleston surveyor John Palmer Gaillard Sr. (1874–1962) made a copy of Senf's General Plan. His copy must have been made from either the 1881 version or Senf's original (or both), since it does not show the damaged areas. Gaillard made his copy in black and white, evidently making it easier for mass distribution. His copy has his name at the bottom of the document: "Copy by J. P. Gaillard." There is no date with his name, so we do not know when Gaillard made his copy.

In 1950 Santee Cooper published a pamphlet version of Porcher's *History of the Santee Canal* for wide distribution and included a copy of Mouzon's "Map of the Parish of St. Stephen's in Craven County" as well as a copy of J. P. Gaillard's copy of Senf's General Plan.

Robert B. Bennett Jr. and Katherine H. Richardson's *History of the Santee Canal 1785–1939*, written as a background for the development of the Old Santee Canal Park in Moncks Corner, included original diagrams drawn by William Robert Judd, one of the coauthors of this book. Bennett and Richardson give a broad history of the Santee Canal. They found a treasure trove of archival documents, many of them cited in this book and never previously used by historians who wrote on the canal.

Newell and Simmons conducted extensive underwater archaeological work on Tide Lock and Biggin Creek. Their work led to archival material on vessel construction, the construction of lock doors, and the construction of Tide Lock. William Robert Judd based his diagram of this lock partly on their work (fig. 5.38).

The last major published work on the history of the Santee Canal is Kapsch's *Historic Canals and Waterways of South Carolina* (2010). Kapsch pulled together many previously unpublished statistical facts about the canal. In a larger view, his book documents the network of canals and waterways from the 1790s to the 1830s that built the early wealth of South Carolina. His cited sources were invaluable to this book. Kapsch included a copy of the General Plan he attributes to J. P. Gaillard. Clearly, however, it is the Gillmore version of the General Plan. Gaillard's signature does not appear at the bottom, and there are two references to the 1881 report on the document. This may actually be a fourth version of the Senf's General Plan, as there are noticeable differences in the 1881 plan compared to the one housed in the South Carolina Historical Society that the authors of this book consulted.

William Robert Judd, coauthor of *A History of the Santee Canal,* created twenty original diagrams for this book that have never been published in any work before. His comprehensive research in the Santee Canal and other mechanical projects gives him broad experience in mechanical diagrams. He has done extensive field research on the Santee Canal and contributed to Newell and Simmons's study on the Santee Canal Sanctuary project, providing diagrams for their work.

In addition to the major works above, there are numerous contemporary newspaper articles, many cited in this book and documented in the bibliography. These contemporary newspapers cover a wide array of topics, from life along the canal, construction techniques, personnel, to problems with water control.

Countless documents on the canal's history are found in the South Carolina Department of Archives and History, the South Carolina Historical Society, the South Caroliniana Library, and the Charleston County Office of Deeds. Many of these are cited throughout this book.

During field research GPS coordinates were documented for thirty-four sites. These coordinates, mostly on private property, are not given in this book to protect privacy concerns. They will be given to the Berkeley County Museum and Old Santee Canal Park in Moncks Corner for future research. Both organizations will be asked to vet any person requesting the coordinates and inform the requester that permission must be obtained to visit sites on private property. For sites on public property, the locations can easily be gleaned from the many plats and maps included in this book.

NOTES

Introduction

1. Readers may be more familiar with regions of South Carolina such as the Midlands or Midcountry and the Upstate or Upcountry. According to Saberton, "The backcountry is an amorphous expression describing the vast swathe of territory now entered by the British. Though other interpretations are wider or more restrictive, it is used here to refer to the then Districts of Camden and Ninety Six. In the east the outer boundary began at the confluence of the Congaree and Wateree, extended northwards to the North Carolina line, continued westwards along that line to the Cherokee nation, and followed the Georgia line to a point just below Augusta. From there it proceeded in the south to a point on the Saluda midway between the village of Ninety Six and the Broad River before following the Saluda and Congaree eastwards." Saberton, "South Carolina Backcountry in mid 1780."
2. Ramsay, *Ramsay's History of South Carolina,* 1:143.
3. DuBose, *Address Delivered at the Seventeenth Anniversary of the Black Oak Agricultural Society,* 8.
4. The authors established contact with several of the descendants living in the Santee Canal region and have learned a great deal about their families.
5. As early as March 11, 1778, Continental Congress president Laurens (1724–92) wrote to planter-statesman John Lewis Gervais (1741–98) asking Gervais to introduce Senf to General Howe. Laurens wrote, "Capt Senf is a Saxon & speaks a tongue which you have no aversion to." Gervais was of Huguenot descent but was raised in Saxony. Laurens, Chesnutt, and Taylor, *Papers of Henry Laurens,* 16: 541.
6. Moultrie, *Memoirs of the American Revolution,* 205.
7. In 1875 Porcher wrote that Senf "seemed to be governed by an inordinate vanity, which could brook not even the appearance of a rival. Thus, though his judgment approved of Mouzon's line from Greenland Swamp, he deviated from it as much as it was possible for him to do, and instead of using the natural channel of Greenland Swamp, he commenced on a bluff of the river on which the current was perpetually wearing, and which, therefore, had to be protected from injury by artificial breakwaters." Porcher went on to concede that "it was not jealousy of Mouzon which

governed Col. Senf in the choice of a location, but that he was acting in obedience to the will of one of the directors [Ralph Izard], who, possessing a large body of land on the riverbank, hoped to improve its value by running the canal through it." Porcher and Salley, *History of the Santee Canal.* 4.

8. Porcher and Judd, *Market Preparation of Carolina Rice.*
9. The practice of hiring out enslaved workers (male and female) for projects such as canals, bridges, and roads provided much-needed income for planters who were recovering from wartime losses and had not yet shifted into more profitable crops. The disadvantages of these practices included the perpetuation of slavery as a source of a viable workforce, inconsistent treatment of enslaved people by different masters, and commodification of human beings. Martin criticized slave hiring for reframing enslaved people as "individual units of financial return." Martin, *Divided Mastery,* 19.
10. Porcher and Salley, *History of the Santee Canal.*

ONE. *Transportation in Early South Carolina*

1. For more information about internal improvements in South Carolina, consult Raiford, *South Carolina and the Issue of Internal Improvement;* Kohn and Glenn, *Internal Improvement in South Carolina.*
2. Lawson, *New Voyage to Carolina,* 9.
3. Col. David Humphreys (1752–1818) was Washington's aide-de-camp. Washington, *Writings of George Washington,* 114–15.
4. Levine and Moultrie, "Letter from William Moultrie at Charleston to George Washington at Mount Vernon," 118.
5. George Washington, Mount Vernon, to William Moultrie, North Hampton Plantation, 1786, reprinted in the *Charleston News and Courier,* January 20, 1936.
6. Krawczynski, "William Drayton's Journal of a 1784 Tour of the South Carolina Backcountry," 204.
7. Meyer and MacGill, *History of Transportation in the United States before 1860,* 276.
8. DuBose, "Reminiscences of St. Stephen's Parish," 66.
9. Lewis, *Carolina Backcountry Venture,* 369n42.
10. Lewis, *Carolina Backcountry Venture,* 250.
11. Porcher and Salley, *History of the Santee Canal,* 4.
12. The Church Act of 1706 created the parish of St. John's Berkeley. The residents of St. John's Parish unofficially divided it into Upper, Middle, and Lower St. John's, each with its own community center. The settlement in Upper St. John's was Eutawville. In Middle St. John's it was Black Oak. In Lower St. John's there were two settlements, the Barrows and Cordesville.
13. Kirkland and Kennedy, *Historic Camden, Part Two,* 36.

TWO. *Formation of the Santee Canal Company*

1. Wade, "Mount Dearborn," 209.
2. Ely, "'That Due Satisfaction May Be Made,'" 14.
3. *South Carolina Gazette and Public Advertiser*, November 1785. As Charleston was the state capital during this period, the State House was located at the corner of Broad and Meeting Streets. When the decision was made in 1786 to move the capitol to Columbia, a State House was built in Columbia, and the original State House in Charleston was then used as a courthouse.
4. *Charleston Columbian Herald*, no. 117.
5. Cooper and McCord, *Statutes at Large of South Carolina*, 7: 541–43.
6. Statesmen who signed the petition included state Speaker of the House of Representatives John Faucheraud Grimke, former governor John Rutledge, state congressman Edward Rutledge, future US senator Ralph Izard, and other notables.
7. In March 1786 Gov. Moultrie was elected president of the Santee Canal Company (*Charleston Morning Post and Daily Advertiser*, March 25, 1786). For excellent documentation of the Santee Canal Company leadership and venture capitalists throughout the years, consult Bennett and Richardson, *History of the Santee Canal*, 235–49.
8. Levine and Moultrie, "Letter from William Moultrie at Charleston to George Washington at Mount Vernon," 118–19. Throughout the planning James Brindley's name was floated as an experienced engineer capable of designing and building the Santee Canal. Brindley was the namesake nephew of the James Brindley who designed the Bridgewater Canal. "Account of James Brindley."
9. Conger, "South Carolina and the Early Tariffs," 420. Conger reports on this 1807 government document: Gallatin, Latrobe, and Fulton, *Report of the Secretary of the Treasury, on the Subject of Public Roads and Canals*.
10. It is not known whether the company records remained in Charleston or were transported to Columbia when the state capital was moved.
11. As state engineer for South Carolina, Senf was involved in many internal improvement projects during this time.
12. George Washington, Diary, June [1786], Founders Online, National Archives, https://founders.archives.gov/documents/Washington/01-04-02-0003-0006.
13. George Washington, Diary, June 14, 1786]," Founders Online, National Archives, https://founders.archives.gov/documents/Washington/01-04-02-0003-0006-0014. By Great Falls, Washington is referring to the Potomac River. Col. George Gilpin (1740–1813) often visited Mount Vernon, and he served as a pallbearer for Washington's funeral in 1799.
14. [Antoine] Terrasson to Thomas Jefferson, April 29, 1788," Founders Online, National Archives, https://founders.archives.gov/documents/Jefferson/01-13-02-0045. This letter referred to canal plans written in English and French, but the enclosures have

not been found. Interestingly *Bulletin of the Bureau of Rolls and Library of the Department of State*, no. 6 (July 1894), lists this entry on page 453: "Terrasson, ———, 1788, May 7, Paris, Canal of the Santee and Cooper rivers, Series 1, vol. 3, No. 73." The authors found no record of Terrasson serving on the Santee Canal Company board.

15. Thomas Jefferson to Antoine Terrasson, May 7, 1788, Founders Online, National Archives, https://founders.archives.gov/documents/Jefferson/01-13-02-0065. By *douceur* Jefferson means a bribe.
16. *Charleston City Gazette and Daily Advertiser*, February 1, 1792.
17. *Charleston City Gazette,* December 24, 1791.
18. Thomas Pinckney to Edward Rutledge, April 29, 1792, in Schulz, *Papers of the Revolutionary Era Pinckney Statesmen*, https://rotunda.upress.virginia.edu/founders/PNKY-01-01-02-0019-0026.
19. David Ramsay to Thomas Pinckney, May 31, 1792, In Schulz, *Papers of the Revolutionary Era Pinckney Statesmen,* https://rotunda.upress.virginia.edu/founders/PNKY-01-01-02-0019-0036-0001.
20. Charles Cotesworth Pinckney to Thomas Pinckney, July 14, 1792, in Schulz, *Papers of the Revolutionary Era Pinckney Statesmen,* https://rotunda.upress.virginia.edu/founders/PNKY-01-02-02-0001-0005.
21. David Ramsay to Thomas Pinckney, July 14, 1792, in Schulz, *Papers of the Revolutionary Era Pinckney Statesmen,* https://rotunda.upress.virginia.edu/founders/PNKY-01-02-02-0001-0007.
22. The *Star* reported that "Mr. Sheridan presented a Petition from Mr. Clifton, stating that he had invented an Engine, for which he had obtained a patent. It was for the purpose of cutting and clearing away the earth, in making Canals. This engine was worked by ten men, who did the work of one hundred."
23. David Ramsay to Thomas Pinckney, July 1, 1793, In Schulz, *Papers of the Revolutionary Era Pinckney Statesmen,* https://rotunda.upress.virginia.edu/founders/PNKY-01-02-02-0002-0576.
24. Charles Cotesworth Pinckney to Thomas Pinckney, July 17, 1793, in Schulz, *Papers of the Revolutionary Era Pinckney Statesmen,* http://rotunda.upress.virginia.edu/PinckneyHorry/ELP0956.
25. *Charleston City Gazette and Daily Advertiser,* March 26, 1795.
26. In a 1796 letter to the newspaper, Senf expressed hope that "late misfortunes to Charleston" would not be "an impediment to the progress of this very important communication with our upper country." *Charleston City Gazette and Daily Advertiser,* June 22, 1796. See Fehlings, "America's First Limited War."
27. Charles Cotesworth Pinckney to James McHenry, April 19, 1799, in Schulz, *Papers of the Revolutionary Era Pinckney Statesmen,* https://rotunda.upress.virginia.edu/founders/PNKY-01-03-02-0001-0040-0003.
28. David Ramsay to Jedidiah Morse, July 20, 1799, in Brunhouse and Ramsay, "David

Ramsay, 1749–1815," 149–150. According to several accounts, Ramsay used part of his wife's inheritance from her father, Henry Laurens, to buy shares. Ramsay's wife was Martha Laurens Ramsay (1759–1811). Brunhouse and Ramsay, "David Ramsay, 1749–1815."

29. For a thorough discussion of Santee Canal Company share prices, subdivisions, and dividends, consult Bennett and Richardson, *History of the Santee Canal.*
30. *Charleston Courier,* May 19, 1849.
31. *Charleston Courier,* June 28, 1853, 2.
32. South Carolina, *General Assembly Reports,* n.d., no. 2267, South Carolina Department of Archives and History. A memorialist is one who petitions a legislative body.
33. *Charleston Courier,* December 5, 1853.
34. Bennett and Richardson, *History of the Santee Canal,* 96.
35. Ibid., 98.
36. South Carolina, *General Assembly Reports,* n.d., no. 2266, South Carolina Department of Archives and History.
37. South Carolina, *General Assembly Reports,* n.d., no. 2995, South Carolina Department of Archives and History. Despite efforts to surrender the Santee Canal Company charter in 1853, in 1854 the board of directors decided to sell bonds to pay stockholders, paid dividends, and closed the canal during the summer season. In 1855 the Santee Canal Company waffled on charging exorbitant canal tolls. In February 1855 they announced a two-hundred-dollar toll. In March 1855 they rescinded it.
38. *Charleston Courier,* March 30, 1864.
39. US Bureau of Statistics, *Report on the Internal Commerce of the United States,* 262.
40. DuBose, "Reminiscences," 66.

THREE. *Johann Christian Senf*

1. Henry Laurens to John Lewis Gervais, March 11, 1778, in Laurens, Chesnutt, and Taylor, *Papers of Henry Laurens,* 12: 541. Gervais was known to speak English, French, and German, as he was of Huguenot ancestry and born in Hanover, Germany.
2. Johann Christian Senf to Benjamin Guerard, February 4, 1784, *South Carolina Department of Archives and History,* http://www.archivesindex.sc.gov/.
3. North, *Travel Journals of Henrietta Marchant Liston,* 31.
4. Hamlin, *Benjamin Henry Latrobe,* 564.
5. Related to inaccurate transcriptions or indexing, Lesser noted that "four or five documents from or relating to South Carolina's easily identified state engineer of the period, Colonel John Christian Senf, are incorrectly cataloged under Charles, Colonel Senef, or John." Lesser, "Review: Papers of the War Department," 308.
6. Gen. John Stark's sobering account of the captives from Walloomsac was detailed

in a letter to the Council of New-Hampshire dated August 18, 1777: "We recovered two pieces more of their cannon, together with all their baggage, a number of horses, carriages, &c.; killed upward of two hundred of the enemy in the field of battle. The number of wounded is not yet known, as they are scattered about in many places. I have one lieutenant colonel, since dead (Colonel Baum), one major, seven captains, fourteen lieutenants, for ensigns, two cornets, one judge advocate, one baron, two Canadian officers, six sergeants, one aide-de-camp, one Hessian chaplain, three Hessian surgeons, and seven hundred prisoners." Stark and Stark, *Memoir and Official Correspondence of Gen. John Stark,* 128. According to Coburn, the Bennington prisoners, except for the Tory captives, "were forwarded to Massachusetts, under the care of Gen. Fellows." Coburn, *History of the Battle of Bennington,* 46. See also Nadeau, "German Military Surgeon in Rutland, Massachusetts."

7. Helga Doblin, introduction to Wasmus, *Eyewitness Account of the American Revolution and New England Life,* xvii. For more information about Brunswick troops, see Melsheimer, *Journal of the Voyage of the Brunswick Auxiliaries* and Smith, Brunswick Deserter.

8. Wasmus, *Eyewitness Account of the American Revolution and New England Life,* 105–6. Senf's likely title was muster clerk, not master clerk. Muster clerks handled various writing duties related to the regiment such muster, payroll, and correspondence. It is not clear when Senf started working as a draftsman. A map of the Sorel River near Quebec dated 1777 has Senf's signature on it. This indicates that he was drawing maps as early as 1777 despite his official role as muster clerk. "Plan Du Retranchement de Sorel." According to Stone in his translation of Major General von Riedesel's memoirs, maps were sketched "on the spot" by the campaign's engineers. Stone, *Memoirs, Letters and Journals, of Major General Riedesel,* vol. 1, v. See Walker, *Engineers of Independence* for more information about wartime engineers.

9. Jefferson, *Writings of Thomas Jefferson,* 36–37. For more information about Virginia's canal work, consult Perez, "Bonds of Friendship and Mutual Interest."

10. "Thomas Jefferson from Beesly Edgar Joel, March 14 1781, Founders Online, National Archives, https://founders.archives.gov/documents/Jefferson/01-05-02-0189.

11. Dann, *Revolution Remembered,* 182.

12. George Washington to James McHenry, May 13, 1799, Founders Online, National Archives, https://founders.archives.gov/documents/Washington/06-04-02-0052.

13. Porcher and Salley, *History of the Santee Canal,* 2.

14. Ibid., 3.

15. The Glindkamp (Glendkamp/Glencamp) family was intertwined with the families of canal superintendent George B. Artope (1768–1818) and local Pineville and Russellville residents. Henry Glindkamp was named superintendent after Artope's death.

16. Kipping, *Hessian View of America.*

17. Huck, *Soldaten Gegen Nordamerika,* 226.

18. Reuter, *Brunswick Troops in North America,* 78.
19. "1790 United States Federal Census."
20. "United States, New York Land Records, 1630–1975."
21. MacWethy, *Book of Names,* 153.
22. Clinton, Hastings, and Holden, *Public Papers of George Clinton,* 315.
23. "U.S., Dutch Reformed Church Records in Selected States, 1639–1989."
24. New York (State), *Laws of the State of New York,* 703.
25. Johann Christian Senf to George Washington, February 24, 1790, Founders Online, National Archives, https://founders.archives.gov/documents/Washington/05-05-02-0105.
26. See records for the probate court in Fairfield County, available at "South Carolina, U.S., Wills and Probate Records, 1670–1980."
27. Germany's Archive for Family History Research shows Wilhelm Senf and Gottlieb Senff listed as Musterschreiber (master writing clerk, or scribe) for the dragoon regiment. Wilhelm Senf deserted from prison on October 4, 1778, and Gottlieb Senff, listed as five-foot-eight and from Wasungen, deserted on October 20, 1777. *Archiv für Familiengeschichtsforschung* 1 (1997): 107. This latter date was frequently associated with Senf, hence the confusion over whether he was captured at Saratoga or earlier.
28. Irwin and Sylla, *Founding Choices,* 249.
29. C. N. Smith, *German Mercenary Expatriates in the United States and Canada,* nos. 1–2.
30. Froeschle, *German Canadian Yearbook,* 83.
31. Senf was named captain on October 20, 1777, captain engineer in the Continental Army on November 19, 1778, and lieutenant colonel on May 12, 1780. *South Carolina History Magazine,* 86; Johannes Schwalm Historical Association, vol. 4 (1989): 50; Moss, *Roster of South Carolina Patriots in the American Revolution,* 854. Later he was referred to as Colonel Senf, an engineer officer serving Gen. Horatio Gates. Piecuch and Beakes, *Cool Deliberate Courage,* 37.
32. "Henry Laurens to Jacob Christopher Zahn, March 10, 1778," in Laurens and Chesnutt, *Papers of Henry Laurens,* 12: 537. Presumably Senf's "late Master" was Lt. Col. Friedrich Baum (1727–77), who was killed at the Battle of Bennington near Walloomsac, New York. Others perpetuated the myth of Senf's being captured along with Burgoyne. According to an unnamed source cited by Chandler, "The engineer was Col. John Christian Senf, a Hessian, who was captured with Burgoyne, embraced the American cause and was sent to South Carolina." In a footnote to this statement, Chandler wrote that "this statement, contrary to the traditional statement, is derived from a high class contemporary MS. recently discovered by the writer." Chandler, *South in the Building of the Nation,* 55.
33. Henry Laurens to John Lewis Gervais, March 11, 1778, in Laurens and Chesnutt, *Papers of Henry Laurens,* 12: 541.

34. Smith, Gawalt, and Plakas, *Letters of Delegates to Congress,* 393. According to Smith, Gawalt, and Plakas, "Laurens wanted to obtain information on the Saratoga Convention from Capt. John Christian Senf, a former member of General Burgoyne's army, in order to justify Congress' refusal to allow the Convention Army to return to England" (ibid.). Baroness Frederika von Riedesel, wife of Maj. Gen. Friedrich Riedesel, who accompanied him throughout many of his campaigns and later captivity, also commented on the issue of the German regimental flags that were not surrendered as expected at Saratoga and resulted in Burgoyne's troops remaining prisoners of war. When the captives were marched from Massachusetts to Virginia, Baroness von Riedesel noted: "On that occasion, it became incumbent upon me to devise new means of preserving the colours of the German regiments, which we had made the Americans believe we had burned. They did not seem to take this well, though they did not say much about it afterwards. We had, however, only sacrificed the staves, and the colours had been carefully concealed. My husband having told me this secret, while we were preparing for our journey, and desired me to take care of them, I shut myself up in my room with an honest tailor, to make a mattress, into which we introduced them." Gadue, "Aspect of Berufsreise of 'Mrs. General' Freifrau von Riedesel in America," 26.

35. According to Pancake, seven hundred British and German troops were captured at Bennington. Pancake, *1777,* 139. Given the timing of the large capture (summer 1777) and the fact that Bennington, is where Dr. Julius F. Wasmus was taken prisoner, the city (Walloomsac) may be the likelier location for Senf's capture rather than Saratoga, as reported in later accounts of his life. Senf might have been hired after Burgoyne's surrender, but it is unlikely that he was captured at Saratoga. Webler stated: "After the Battle of Bennington, where almost all captives were German troops, the rank and file marched from the battlefield southward to Williamstown [Massachusetts], to Pittsfield, then eastward across the hill towns to Northampton, to Hadley, Palmer, Brookfield, Worcester and Boston. The captive officers, instead of crossing the center of the western counties of the state, were taken from Pittsfield to Great Barrington, then to Westfield, Springfield, Palmer, Brookfield, Worcester and Boston along the Knox Trail. The American military wanted to keep the officers separated from the men so the men could be encouraged to hire out to farmers or desert without admonition or threat from their superiors." Webler, "German (So Called Hessian) Soldiers," 82.

36. Gabriel, *Battle of Bennington,* 18.

37. Ibid., 28.

38. Webler, "German (So Called Hessian) Soldiers," 82.

39. Moultrie, *Memoirs of the American Revolution,* 205.

40. Ibid., 265.

41. Horatio Gates to Thomas Jefferson, September 27, 1780, in Boyd et al., *Papers of Thomas Jefferson,* 3: 668.

42. Marquis de Lafayette to Friedrich von Steuben, May 17, 1781, in Idzerda et al., *Lafayette in the Age of the American Revolution,* 106.
43. Wasmus, *Eyewitness Account of the American Revolution and New England Life,* 235.
44. Morgan's daughters were Nancy, who married Presly Neville, an aide to Gen. Lafayette, and Betsy, who married James Heard. Perhaps the storyteller confused engineer Marquis de Lafayette with engineer Senf.
45. Higginbotham, *Daniel Morgan,* 173.
46. Apparently at one time Gertrude was engaged to statesman John Brown of Virginia (later part of Kentucky), but the reason for not marrying was ascribed to the fact "she could not be happy in Kentucky." Sprague, "Senator John Brown of Kentucky," 114. In 1799 Brown married Margaretta Mason.
47. John Christian Senf to Thomas Jefferson, September 27, 1784, Founders Online, National Archives, https://founders.archives.gov/documents/Jefferson/01-07-02-0326. By *Humphrey*, Senf meant diplomat David Humphreys, who was heading to Europe in 1784 to negotiate treaties. Humphreys, *Life and Times of David Humphreys,* 301. Mr. Dumas was diplomat Charles W. F. Dumas (1721–96).
48. US Department of State, *Diplomatic Correspondence of the United States of America,* 519–20. At the time this letter was written, Dumas served as a translator and secretary for John Adams (1735–1826). The General Demoulin to whom Dumas referred is Jacobus Adrianus du Moulin (1777–1839).
49. By accompanying his esteemed relative Pieter van Berckel to America, Van Hogendorp sought to learn about the new republic, specifically more "about finance and taxes." Van Hogendorp, *College at Princetown,* iv. Upon his return to the Dutch Republic, Van Hogendorp distinguished himself as a statesman.
50. Margaret Armstrong, whose family was friendly with the Van Berckel family, noted: "In New York, Van Berkel gave lots of parties in his house on the corner of William and Wall, and his son and daughter were conspicuous figures in society. Frank Van Berkel was remembered for his gorgeous clothes and the immense size of the horse he drove on a very tall phaeton." Armstrong, *Five Generations,* 39. According to Hill, "[Alexander] Hamilton was not the only official noted for entertainments of this sort, for Van Berckel, the minister from Holland, kept open house at the old Marston mansion on the northwest corner of Wall and William, and here all the members of the diplomatic corps with their wives and families were wined and dined informally and in state." Hill, *Story of a Street,* 461. In Newark, Van Berckel lived on South Broad Street. In 1804 alien resident Gertrude Senf petitioned the state of New Jersey to allow her to own a house and its property in Newark that had been conveyed to her in 1801 in her late father's will. *Acts of the Twenty-Eighth General Assembly of the State of New-Jersey,* Chapter XCVIII (1804), 243–44.
51. "Madame Van Berkel, I believe, never came to this country. I have a pastel portrait of this old lady, with red cheeks and powdered hair, which was given to Margaret

Marshall by Miss Van Berkel when the latter married a Mr. Cenf and went to the West Indies; she never returned as she was lost at sea." Armstrong, *Five Generations,* 39. There is no record of Gertrude or Gertrude's mother being lost at sea. However, after Van Berckel completed his diplomatic service, various members of his family traveled frequently to the East Indies and the West Indies.

52. C. W. F. Dumas to John Adams, March 18, 1785, Founders Online, National Archives, https://founders.archives.gov/documents/Adams/06-16-02-0334.
53. John Adams to C. W. F. Dumas, March 29 [30], 1785, Founders Online, National Archives, https://founders.archives.gov/documents/Adams/06-16-02-0341.
54. John Quincy Adams to Abigail Adams II, July 17–31, 1785, Founders Online, National Archives, https://founders.archives.gov/documents/Adams/04-06-02-0075.
55. Ibid.
56. John Quincy Adams to Abigail Adams II, August 1, 1785, Adams Papers, Massachusetts Historical Society, https://www.masshist.org/publications/adams-papers/index.php/view/ADMS-04-06-02-0079#sn=2.
57. John Adams, Diary, August 1, 1785, Adams Papers, Founders Online, National Archives, https://founders.archives.gov/documents/Adams/03-01-02-0007-0010.
58. J. Q. Adams, *Diary of John Quincy Adams,* vol. 1.
59. Abigail Adams II to John Quincy Adams, September 5, 1785, Adams Papers (Massachusetts Historical Society), https://founders.archives.gov/documents/Adams/04-06-02-0096.
60. Abigail Adams II to John Quincy Adams, October 18, 1785, Founders Online, National Archives, https://founders.archives.gov/documents/Adams/04-06-02-0136.
61. John Quincy Adams to John Adams, September 12, 1795, Founders Online, National Archives, https://founders.archives.gov/documents/Adams/. A witness to the marriage of Gertrude van Berckel and Johann Christian Senf was named Ger. van Polanen, very likely the same person mentioned by Adams in this letter.
62. Holland Society of New York, *Dutch Reformed Church Records in Selected States.* Ger. von Polanen is probably Roger Gerard van Polanen (1757–1833), the person suggested to replace Franco van Berckel. Marg. Kunze was the wife of Dr. John Christopher Kunze (1744–1807), who in 1784 "united the old Dutch Church (Trinity) and the German Lutheran Church (Christ) into the United German Lutheran Churches in the city of New York." Carl F. Schalk, *Source Documents in American Lutheran Hymnody,* 32.
63. *Charleston City Gazette,* July 4, 1792.
64. See *Transactions of the Oneida Historical Society at Utica,* vols. 6–10, 25–26, https://archive.org/details/transactionsoneoouticgoog; and Wallace, *Life of Henry Laurens,* 359, 361, 362, 399.
65. See Nordholt, *Dutch Republic and American Independence.*

66. Passports issued by Thomas Jefferson, 1785–1789 [September 1785], Founders Online, National Archives, https://founders.archives.gov/documents/Jefferson/99-01-02-4240.
67. Clerk's Office, *Book A*, 232, Camden (SC) Court House.
68. Although there are no records of Senf and his wife having children of their own, they served as sponsors for Christian Senf Leuthold (1798–1857), born in Pineville on the Tower Hill Plantation, son of Swiss physician Andrew Leuthold (1760–99) and Catharine Steiger (1764–1840).
69. "Gertrude J. Senf to Thomas Jefferson, September 3, 1806, Founders Online, National Archives, https://founders.archives.gov/documents/Jefferson/99-01-02-4240.
70. Gertrude J. Senf to Thomas Jefferson, September 11, 1806, Founders Online, National Archives, https://founders.archives.gov/documents/Jefferson/99-01-02-4263. The asterisks were in the original transcription of the letter. The assistant sent to Rocky Mount to help Senf in April 1805 was Col. Francis Mentges, native of Deux-Ponts, Zweibruecken, who died at Rocky Mount on September 6, 1805. In a peculiar twist, both Senf's brother and father died at the same location, Rocky Mount, South Carolina, eleven years apart, in August 1788 and June 1799, respectively. Senf himself died at Rocky Mount in 1806.
71. *Charleston Daily Courier,* December 9, 1806.
72. Butler, *Letters of Pierce Butler,* 58. See also Sikes, *Public Life of Pierce Butler.*
73. According to the Account of Sales of the Personal Estate of Colonel Christian Senf, appraised on February 5, 1807, Breithaupt purchased "One Compass No. 2 in a square Box, Two Calibre measures and powder proof, the remainder of Colours and pencils, One Dressing case, Shaving case and apparatus, Silver pen, pencil and Ivory ruler, Lott of Books (viz) Don Quixote in Spanish, French and German Dictionary, Spanish Dictionary, and Italian Grammar and Spanish Geometry." See "Inventories, Appraisements, and Sales, 1801–1844" at "South Carolina, U.S., Wills and Probate Records, 1670–1980."
74. Breithaupt's obituary stated he had resided in South Carolina for thirty-one years. He died of yellow fever on December 4, 1835, followed on December 15 by Gertrude. *Greenville Mountaineer,* December 19, 1835. Breithaupt's good friend Benjamin Yancey (1783–1817), also died at Edgefield after contracting yellow fever in Charleston. According to McCandless, "Between the 1790s and 1850s Charleston hosted numerous epidemics. The victims were primarily white 'strangers': immigrants, travelers, upcountry folk, and children. Few 'natives' of Charleston, black or white, died from the disease." McCandless, "Yellow Fever."
75. Downey, *Planting a Capitalist South,* 123. Some records referred to Breithaupt as Colonel Breithaupt, but his military service is not clear. According to naturalization records, Breithaupt submitted a petition to be naturalized in Fairfield County on November 16, 1807. Holcomb, *South Carolina Naturalizations,* 180.

The Fairfield County seat, Winnsboro, was more than ninety miles from Edgefield. Outside of his strategic marriage to Senf's widow, who was about twenty years his senior, Breithaupt sired several children with other women, including an enslaved woman named Rosetta. His biracial son Freeman Fritz Breithaupt (1800–85); Fritz's wife, Nicy; and their children were sold repeatedly as slaves.

76. As late as 1797, Senf referred to himself as "Colonel of Engineers and one of the Justices of the Quorum of this State." *Records in Clerk's Office*, Camden Court House, Book A, 232. See also Kirkland and Kennedy, *Historic Camden*.

77. Mills, *Statistics of South Carolina*, 53. Grimkeville (named after John Faucheraud Grimké) is near Rocky Mount, SC. Grimkeville was first surveyed in 1792. Ford, "Memories, Traditions and History of Rocky Mount and Vicinity," 6.

78. Ford, "Memories, Traditions and History of Rocky Mount and Vicinity," 9–10. Senf's property may very well be close to the Nitrolee Dam in Great Falls, South Carolina. Chester County (SC) Historical Society, pers. comm. with Elizabeth Connor, February 3, 2021.

79. Eric Spall, "Foreigners in the Highest Trust."

80. Ibid., 351–52.

81. Ibid., 354.

82. Nathanael Greene to John Adams, May 7, 1777, Founders Online, National Archives, https://founders.archives.gov/documents/Adams/06-05-02-0110,

83. Spall, "Foreigners in the Highest Trust," 359.

84. Interestingly, as an officer of foreign birth, Senf would have been required to join the French chapter of the Society of the Cincinnati. For some reason presumably because he was not French, he did not. Hünemörder, *Society of the Cincinnati*.

85. Moore, *Fabric of Liberty*, 5.

FOUR. *Choosing the Santee Canal Route and Land Acquisition*

1. James Cook, "Letter to Mr. Timothy [proposing South Carolina Canals]," *South Carolina Gazette* (Charleston), January 18, 1770.

2. Cook, "Map of the Province of South Carolina."

3. Cook, "Letter to Mr. Timothy."

4. Two men named Henry Mouzon Jr. appear in the literature. They were first cousins. Mouzon the surveyor was from St. Stephen's Parish. Research conducted by Wylma Anne Wates (1928–2015) established that he made the map showing the five possible routes for a canal between the Santee and Cooper Rivers. The authors support Wates's research (http://ncmaps.org/henry-mouzon-jr-one-a-mapmaker-one-a-captain/), posted November 24, 2022, accessed September 18, 2023. Mouzon was the son of Henry Mouzon Sr., grandson of Lewis Mouzon Sr., and brother of Elizabeth (1735–75), who married Peter Sinkler (1725–82).

5. *South Carolina Gazette* (Charleston), November 12, 1785.

6. Besides Moultrie and Rutledge, the directors elected were Judge Burke, Judge

Grimké, Judge Drayton, General Pinckney, General Sumter, General Marion, Commodore Gillon, Major Mitchell, Edward Rutledge, John Huger, Thomas Jones, Thomas Walter, William Doughty, Joseph Atkinson, Henry Laurens Jr., James Sinkler, Theodore Gourdin, Aaron Loocock, and Theodore Gaillard. Dan Bourdeaux was elected treasurer and Stephen Drayton elected secretary. *South Carolina Gazette* (Charleston), November 12, 1785.

7. The text of Moultrie's letter, dated April 7, 1786, is contained in a paper written by Ida L. Levine, in the Elias Ball Bull Papers, South Carolina Historical Society, 376.02 (H) 01.08-01 (Santee Canal).

8. George Washington to William Moultrie, May 25, 1786, Founders Online, National Archives, https://founders.archives.gov/documents/Washington/04-04-02-0078.

9. William Moultrie to George Washington (enclosure), August 7, 1786, Founders Online, National Archives, https://founders.archives.gov/documents/Washington/04-04-02-0187.

10. James Rumsey to George Washington, March 29, 1786, in *The Washington Papers,* 3:613n1.

11. Webber, "Col. Senf's Account of the Santee Canal," 118. The "account" Webber reported on was actually Senf's Final Report to the Santee Canal Company. Webber continued her reporting in "Col. Senf's Account of the Santee Canal (Continued)."

12. James Brindley to George Washington, April 5, 1787, in *The Washington Papers,* 5:124.

13. Webber, "Col. Senf's Account (Continued)," 118.

14. Johann Christian Senf to Gen. Thomas Sumter, January 3, 1790, quoted in Phillips, *History of Transportation in the Eastern Cotton Belt to 1860,* 37–38.

15. Webber, "Col. Senf's Account (Continued)," 125.

16. Ibid., 126.

17. Richard Porcher is familiar with Hell Hole Swamp and knows it is aptly named. Hell Hole was burned during colonial times to keep it open for cattle grazing. In wet seasons, however, it was flooded. Excavating and operating a canal through flooded land would have been a challenge and is one reason why Senf chose an upland route.

18. Webber, "Col. Senf's Account (Continued)," 125.

19. Contour lines on the Chicora Quadrangle topographic map of 1921 (reprinted in 1947), although hard to follow, show an increase in elevation as Greenland Swamp and its small tributaries drain from Bull Town Bay.

20. Webber, "Col. Senf's Account (Continued)," 122.

21. Boyd et al., *Papers of Thomas Jefferson,* 7: 427–28, 462. See also Shackelford, *Thomas Jefferson's Travels in Europe.*

22. Blanding, "Santee Canal," 261.

23. Porcher and Salley, *History of the Santee Canal*, 4.
24. Ibid.
25. Bennett and Richardson, *History of the Santee Canal*, 8. In their appendix F, Bennett and Richardson include a list of stockholders from May 23, 1792, that appeared in the *Charleston Daily Courier*.
26. Senf's General Plan was the map published in 1800.
27. Glen Camp is a derivation of Glindkamp/Glendkamp/Glendcamp/Glencamp. Henry Glindkamp was a German servant who worked for Colonel Senf and then later for General Moultrie. Years later Glindkamp served as canal superintendent. The Ravenel plat (see fig. 4.4) refers to Glendkemp, which the present authors used on the plat. Throughout most of the text, however, we use the original spelling, *Glindkamp*.
28. See also 30-4 Hardcastle, Hardcastle Family History and Genealogy Research Files, South Carolina Historical Society.
29. Bennett and Richardson, *History of the Santee Canal*, 88.
30. Webber, "Col. Senf's Account of the Santee Canal," 10.

FIVE. *Construction of the Santee Canal*

1. The lower section of St. Stephen's Parish was called French Santee, while the section around Pine Ville and the Santee Canal was called English Santee.
2. Quoted in H. E. Ravenel Jr., *Ravenel Records*, 228.
3. DuBose, "Reminiscences of St. Stephen's Parish," 7. For more details about slave hiring in Charleston, consult Greene, Hutchins, and Hutchins, *Slave Badges and the Slave-Hire System in Charleston*.
4. Webber, "Col. Senf's Account (Continued)," 123.
5. Ibid., 116.
6. H. E. Ravenel Jr., *Ravenel Records*, 46, 257. The reports of the confrontation between Ravenel and Senf vary so much in their details that the truth will never be known. But there seems no question that some sort of confrontation occurred and that it was settled without violence.
7. The title of this section comes from Mukerji, *Impossible Engineering*. Mukerji reported that mills, spillways, bridges, intake channels, warehouses, aqueducts, locks, laundries, and small harbors of the Canal du Midi were created based on Roman technology in a chapter titled "New Rome Confronts Old Gaul." The authors of the present work argue that "New Rome" influenced Senf's design of the Santee Canal.

   A summit-level canal is an artificial waterway connecting two distant watersheds separated by an elevated body of land. A summit canal rises through a series of locks as it crosses an elevation and then falls through a series of locks as it runs to the opposite watershed. The Santee Canal rose from the Santee River over a ridge separating the Santee and Cooper Rivers and then descended to the Cooper.

It depended on artificial reservoirs at the highest point of elevation to provide water for the locks.
8. This brief history was derived mostly from Mukerji, *Impossible Engineering*.
9. For more information see Lacoste, *Precis historique du Canal du Languedoc*.
10. Webber, "Col. Senf's Account of the Santee Canal," 9, 10. Although Senf mentioned eight aqueducts in his overview, only seven were built according to his General Plan.
11. Webber, "Col. Senf's Account (Continued)," 116.
12. Frederick Porcher points out that "as the navigation of the Santee required a strong force of hands to take the boats upriver, it was found that they could also draw the boats through the canal nearly as fast as the teams could do it, and these last were abandoned." Porcher and Salley, *History of the Santee Canal*, 6.
13. Ibid., 10.
14. Webber, "Col. Senf's Account (Continued)," 120.
15. Porcher and Salley, *History of the Santee Canal*, 5, 6.
16. Stony, "Memoirs of Frederick Adolphus Porcher," 35.
17. Phillips, *History of Transportation in the Eastern Cotton Belt to 1860*, 39.
18. Bennett and Richardson, *History of the Santee Canal*, 19.
19. Webber, "Col. Senf's Account (Continued)," 118.
20. Webber, "Col. Senf's Account of the Santee Canal," 12.
21. Ibid.
22. Field surveys failed to find any remains of this overfall.
23. Field surveys failed to find any evidence of this small basin, and lidar did not reveal its existence. It may be that the basin was either destroyed to make an outlet from the canal to the Santee River, as some sort of slough leads from the canal to the river (see fig. 9.5), or it was never constructed.
24. "Santee Canal," *Charleston City Gazette and the Daily Advertiser*, April 12, 1800.
25. [Santee Canal Company], *Report of the Board of Directors* (1805), 1–2, South Carolina Historical Society.
26. Webber, "Col. Senf's Account of the Santee Canal," 11.
27. Ibid.
28. Judd, "Report to Santee Canal Park."
29. Quoins are masonry blocks at the corner of a wall. Some are structural, providing strength for a wall made with inferior stone or rubble, while others merely add aesthetic detail to a corner. In lock construction quoins are used to form the structural stones at the angle of the wall into which the gates are hinged. The quoin gives a strong base to hinge the heavy gates. Brickwork alone would not have provided sufficient strength to house the gates.
30. Senf does not mention in his Final Report where the stones for the quoins came from. On examination of the extant quoins, it appears that different types of stone were used. Perhaps in his missing thirty-eight "particulars plans" (see the discussion

of these plans in "Source Notes") Senf mentioned the source of the stone for the quoins.
31. United States, *Report of the Secretary of Treasury*, 29.
32. Crowson, "Santee-Cooper."
33. Webber, "Col. Senf's Account (Continued)," 121.
34. Webber, "Col. Senf's Account of the Santee Canal," 11.
35. *Lidar* stands for "light detection and ranging." It is a remote sensing method that uses light in the form of a pulsed laser to measure ranges (variable distances) to the earth. These light pulses, combined with other data recorded by the airborne system, generate precise, three-dimensional information about the shape of the earth and its surface characteristics.
36. Webber, "Col. Senf's Account of the Santee Canal," 9, 121.
37. Big Camp Lock was not flooded by Lake Moultrie. The lock was bulldozed when a wildlife impoundment was made adjacent to the canal and was virtually destroyed. No photographs survive prior to its destruction.
38. *Charleston City Gazette and the Daily Advertiser*, May 23, 1779.
39. *Pine Ville* and *Pineville* both refer to the same town in St. Stephen's Parish. *Pine Ville* was more commonly used in the 1800s; *Pineville* was a later use. The authors of the present work use *Pine Ville* for the original village from the 1800s until the Civil War; *Pineville* will be used for after the Civil War.
40. Webber, "Col. Senf's Account of the Santee Canal," 12.
41. US Senate, *Letter from the Secretary of War*. The document contained a color version of Senf's 1800 General Plan. The 1881 General Plan does not show the damaged areas that appear on Senf's original plan, so it must have been copied before the damage occurred. A copy of the 1881 plan is housed in the South Carolina Historical Society.
42. Webber, "Col. Senf's Account of the Santee Canal," 13.
43. Black Oak Road today is Springwood Road (State Road S-8-23). One can drive on Springwood Road and view the swamp in the former reservoir at the southeast intersection of Springwood and Whispering Pine Lane (fig. 9.12).
44. Webber, "Col. Senf's Account (Continued)," 118.
45. Kapsch, *Historic Canals and Waterways of South Carolina*, 37.
46. Webber, "Col. Senf's Account (Continued)," 117–18. The authors believe Senf meant the first rather than third reservoir. Water from Bull Town Bay fed the Great Reservoir (the first reservoir), not Greenland Swamp Reservoir.
47. In Senf's General Plan, part of Bull Town Bay is missing because of the damaged areas to the document. The natural drain from Bull Town Bay, however, is clear where the dam D— —D (in red) was built across the natural drain. The small upland drain (C) is no longer visible or extant in the field. The authors used Gillmore's 1881 copy of the General Plan in figure 5.21, which does not have the damaged areas of the map. The dam is clearly visible.

48. More than likely all the locks had counterforts. Underwater archaeology revealed counterforts on Black Oak Lock and Wantoot Lock. For more details about these explorations, see Newell and Simmons, "Santee Canal Sanctuary Part II."
49. Webber, "Col. Senf's Account of the Santee Canal," 14.
50. When Frierson's Lock was exposed in the lake drawdown in 2008, no one thought to examine the inside of the lock's wall to look for the openings, since no one was seriously studying the construction of the locks at that time, especially the side chamber. If the side chamber did not receive water as described in the text, water must have been discharged through the lock's two gates in some manner and flowed to a side chamber next to the gates. The authors found no description of side chambers in the literature on canals. The side chamber may have been original to the Santee Canal.
51. Senf uses the term *overfall* for two different water-control structures. The authors have used *bypass* for the water-control structure that passed water around a lock through a bypass (fig. 5.30). Senf's term is reserved for the water-control structure that passed excess water from the canal under the towpath to the outside of the canal (fig. 5.16).
52. Webber, "Col. Senf's Account of the Santee Canal," 16.
53. Ibid.
54. Ibid., 15.
55. Edmund Ravenel, MD, " Limestone Springs of St. John's Berkeley."
56. Holmes, "ART. XVI.—Notes on the Geology of Charleston," 198.
57. Some sources refer to Hope Lock as Simpson's Lock. Hope Lock was on land owned by William Simpson, so referring to it as Simpson's Lock is certainly appropriate. The authors prefer to go with Senf, who in his General Plan shows the tract of land as Hope, owned by Simpson.
58. Webber, "Col. Senf's Account of the Santee Canal," 19.
59. Ibid.
60. Webber, "Col. Senf's Account (Continued)," 113.
61. Webber, "Col. Senf's Account of the Santee Canal," 19–20.
62. Some of the fossil specimens found at Biggin Swamp during the excavation of the Santee Canal were determined to be *Mammut americanum,* the American mastodon. Drayton's book includes plates describing *Elephas columbi,* now called *Mammuthus columbi,* a North American mammoth that is the state fossil for South Carolina. According to Madden, the Santee Canal findings are the easternmost US examples of *Mammuthus imperator* (imperial mammoth). Madden, "Mammoths of North America." Oliver Perry Hay refers to *E. columbi, M. americanum,* and *E. imperator* specimens. Hay, *Pleistocene of North America,* 156, 162. At the time that the Santee Canal fossils were discovered, the Charleston Library Society (founded in 1748) featured natural history collections that later were transferred to the Charleston Museum (founded in 1773). At first Library Society collections were

located in private homes and then at the Free School on Broad Street. The collections next moved successively to the upper floors of Manigault's warehouse (1765–78), at the statehouse building at the corner of Broad and Meeting Streets (1792), at a bank building at the corner of Church and Broad (1825–1914), and then to its present location on King Street. During the Civil War, the Library Society collections were temporarily stored at the state capitol in Columbia. During the Civil War, Charleston Museum collections were buried on the College of Charleston campus or crated up and stored in a barn located on an Edgefield, South Carolina, plantation rented by museum curator Francis Simmons Holmes (1815–82). Sanders and Anderson, *Natural History Investigations in South Carolina,* 27; Stephens, *Ancient Animals and Other Wondrous Things.* Current Charleston Museum personnel are not aware of any Santee Canal mastodon specimens in their collections but have surmised that these items may have gone to the American Museum of Natural History. That museum's collection includes *E. columbi* teeth (nos. 13707, 13708), but the provenance of these fossils is not known.

63. Webber, "Col. Senf's Account (Continued)," 115.
64. Webber, "Col. Senf's Account of the Santee Canal," 20.
65. Webber, "Col. Senf's Account (Continued)," 113.

SIX. *Grand Opening of the Santee Canal*

1. *Charleston City Gazette,* May 20, 1800. On March 22 Senf had declared the canal open, but it took another two months for the length of it to fill with water.
2. Porcher and Salley, *History of the Santee Canal,* 5. The attendant was Henry Glindkamp (mentioned by Porcher but not by name), whose descendants today live in the Pineville area.
3. *Charleston Times,* May 28, 1800. The authors believe that this Buford was Maj. William Buford (1746–1810), born in Virginia and severely wounded at the Battle of Eutaw Springs in 1781. He lived near Pinckney Court House on the Pacolet River, more than ninety miles north of Granby, South Carolina. Later Buford lived "near [Theodore] Gourdin on the northeast side of the Santee River in Williamsburg district." Richardson, *Genealogical Record with Reminiscences,* 17.
4. On February 23, 1954, Henry Ravenel Dwight Sr. (1873–1961) of Pinopolis donated to the South Carolina Historical Society a photograph of a stone marker that had been placed somewhere on the Santee Canal. The identity of the photographer and the placement of the marker are both unknown. No one in the Dwight family has the marker or knows of its existence. It may have been moved by someone in the Dwight family from the portion of the canal that passed through Middle St. John's before the lake came so it would not be lost. It may have been photographed before it was moved. The photograph shows that the marker was broken into several pieces. The fact that Senf (or whoever) placed a marker dated 1794, six years before the canal was completed, raises any number of questions. We will probably

never know who placed the marker or why, or whether it is still stored somewhere. In the present narrative, the authors place it near where the director's house stood at Big Camp, seemingly a fitting site for it.

5. Robert Marion (1766–1811) was a nephew of Gen. Francis Marion, another early supporter of inland navigation. Burnt Savanna later became part of Belle Isle. Marion also owned Fox Hall, bought by the Santee Canal Company and renamed Big Camp.

6. Some springs made such a roar they could be heard for a distance—hence locals called the gatherings a "harring party," a local pronunciation of the word hearing.

7. According to Sherman Carmichael, these creatures lived in "gullies, streams, springs, waterfalls, sink holes and pools" (*Mysterious South Carolina,* 119). The etymological origin of the word *cymbee* is uncertain. Historian Ras Michael Brown writes that *cymbee* is the local spelling of the Kikongo word *simbi,* since both words match in sound and meaning. Kikongo is a Creole language spoken in the Congo and Angola (M. R. Brown, *African-Atlantic Cultures and the South Carolina Lowcountry,* 112). Nature spirits known as *bisimbi* (plural of *simbi*) took the form of water spirits, and knowledge of this spirit world was probably transferred from West Africa during the Atlantic Passage. See also N. P. Adams, "'Cymbee' Water Spirits of St. John's Berkeley."

8. In 1843 Edmund Ruffin reported this slave account of a cymbee sighting: "After seeing her but a few seconds, she glided into the water & disappeared, as may be presumed in the deep cavern from which the waters of the fountain rush to the surface." Mathew and Ruffin, *Agriculture, Geology, and Society in Antebellum South Carolina,* 166. Henry William Ravenel described the cymbees of Pooshee, near his boyhood home, stating that believers thought that "every spring or fountain of water had a presiding Genius, or guardian spirit, which lived there. They called this thing 'Cymbee.' If anyone disturbed the spring, the Cymbee would be angry. If it was destroyed or much injured from any cause, the Cymbee would leave it, and the waters would dry up. The Cymbees were proportionate in size to the spring." See H. W. Ravenel, "Recollections of Southern Plantation Life," 777. Richard Porcher remembers in his youth the Black men and women that came off the basin telling him to be careful of the cymbees in Tide Hole, an artesian spring, which was a favorite site for Native American relic hunting.

9. Whether rice was grown in 1800 on either Wantoot or Woodboo is unknown. Most inland rice growing ended after the American Revolution. Reading Senf's account of the canal indicates that the fields were in rice or still had the appearance of rice fields.

10. Hanover House is one of two houses saved when Lake Moultrie flooded Middle St. John's Parish in 1942. It stands today at Clemson University. The house at Woodlawn was dismantled and reconstructed at Dover on Winyah Bay in Georgetown County.

11. Keithfield was originally owned by Dr. William Keith Sr., whose family members were close friends with plantation neighbor Elizabeth Clevland Hardcastle. Keithfield was located directly across the Santee Canal from Tibbekudlaw. For more about Hardcastle, see Louise, *Elizabeth Clevland Hardcastle,* and 30-4 Hardcastle, Hardcastle Family History and Genealogy Research Files, South Carolina Historical Society.
12. *Tibbekudlaw* (sometimes referred to as Tippycut Law and similar phonetic spellings) is the Native American name for a hilly part of Wadboo Barony.
13. Kent was formed by Gen. William Moultrie's purchase of lots 11 and 12 (totaling 705 acres) from Wadboo Barony. H. A. M. Smith, "Baronies of South Carolina." 51.
14. Stony Landing was an important location for merchants and plantations to transport their goods during colonial times. Before the Santee Canal, supplies from Charles Town were brought by boat up the West Branch of the Cooper River, unloaded at Stony Landing, and transported westward on the Congaree Road. Conversely plantation goods from St. John's and St. Stephen's were unloaded at Stony Landing for transportation to Charles Town. Although a difficult trip, some goods came from the interior of the state down the Congaree Road to Stony Landing and on to Charles Town.
15. *National Intelligencer and Washington Advertiser* (Washington, DC), September 14, 1801.
16. *Carolina Gazette,* March 18, 1802.
17. *Charleston City Gazette and the Daily Advertiser,* August 4, 1802.
18. Theodore Gourdin was the fourth great-grandfather of Theodore Keith Gourdin of Pineville, who shared his considerable knowledge of the Pineville area with the authors of this book.
19. Charleston Judgment Rolls, 1803, 305A, South Carolina Department of Archives and History, Columbia.
20. H. E. Ravenel Jr., *Ravenel Records,* 231, 251.
21. The term *maroon* refers to a fugitive slave. These fugitives, distinct from runaways, had no intention of returning to the plantation and established self-sufficient hideouts in swamps or other outlying areas, existing independently of local government systems. See Lockley, *Maroon Communities in South Carolina.*
22. The Pineville Police Association Records, South Carolina Historical Society, Charleston South Carolina, #34/301/1-3. The Pineville Police Association appears to have organized to deal with the issue of Joe specifically. Its records run from 1823 to October 1827. There is no formal constitution in the records. Members in 1823 were Theodore Gourdin Sr., Joseph Palmer, James Gaillard, Thomas Gaillard, Thomas Porcher Sr., William Cain, Isaac Porcher, David Gaillard, Henry Ravenel, Philip S. Porcher, John J. Courturier, Samuel DuBose, Edwin Gaillard, William Porcher, Daniel James Ravenel, Peter Gaillard Jr., William DuBose, Daniel Cain, James E. Jerman, Stephen G. Devcaux, Philip Porcher, Theodore S. Gaillard,

Charles C. Porcher, Theodore L. Gourdin, Thomas Porcher Jr., Samuel Cordes, John S. Ravenel, and Isaac M. Dwight.
23. *Camden (SC) Southern Chronicle,* October 8, 1823.
24. *Charleston City Gazette,* May 17, 1824.
25. Porcher and Salley, *History of the Santee Canal,* 9.
26. *Charleston Courier,* November 29, 1833.
27. *Charleston Courier,* June 28, 1834.
28. Porcher and Salley, *History of the Santee Canal,* 8.
29. Mathew and Ruffin, *Agriculture, Geology, and Society in Antebellum South Carolina,* 70.
30. Ibid.
31. Johnson, *Maxcy Gregg's Sporting Journals,* 55–57.
32. H. E. Ravenel Jr., *Ravenel Records,* 253.
33. William Cain Jr. to Mr. Bull, n.d., South Carolina Historical Society, Elias Ball Bull Papers (call number 376.00, box 22, 376.02 (H) 01 08 02). Charles Macbeth (1805–81) served two terms as mayor of Charleston prior to the Civil War.

SEVEN. *Attempts to Solve the Water Deficiency*
1. *Charleston City Gazette,* June 20, 1809.
2. South Carolina, General Assembly Petitions, 1818, 45.
3. The date March 1819 comes from *Miller's Weekly Messenger* (Pendleton, SC), March 31, 1819.
4. Ibid.
5. Porcher and Salley, *History of the Santee Canal,* 11.
6. The engines apparently came from Baltimore. A notice in the *Charleston City Gazette,* July 6, 1816, stated that George B. Artope, the canal superintendent, took the steamer *Ploughboy* to Baltimore to obtain them.
7. Porcher and Judd, *Market Preparation of Carolina Rice,* 231–32.
8. *Southern Patriot* (Charleston, SC), April 17, 1832.
9. Abram Blanding (1776–1869) was born in Massachusetts. He was educated at Rhode Island College (Brown University), where he studied under Dr. Jonathan Maxcy, later the first president of the University of South Carolina. Blanding came to Columbia around 1797 and established himself as a teacher. While teaching he studied law under future governor John Taylor. In 1799 Blanding went to Camden and continued his study of law under Judge Joseph Brevard. He was admitted to the South Carolina bar in 1802. He returned to Columbia in 1819. In the same year, he began the construction on a waterworks in Columbia, which became a profitable investment. He sold the waterworks to the city in 1835. In 1820 he was appointed commissioner of the Board of Public Works. When this board was superseded by the superintendent of public works in 1823, Blanding was appointed to that office. At the end of his tenure as superintendent, he retained his active

interest in improving transportation and bettering commercial conditions in the state. He became the first president of the Commercial Bank in Columbia in 1831. He was active in the development of railroads and was largely influential in the selection of the route for a railroad between Cincinnati and Charleston. Blanding died at Sullivan's Island of yellow fever in 1839 and was buried in the churchyard of the Circular Church in Charleston.

10. Blanding titled his report on the canal simply "The Santee Canal." He served as the superintendent of public works at the time. In 1938 David Kohn, as compiler and editor, and coeditor Bess Glenn published *Internal Improvements in South Carolina, 1817–1828.* This work included a compilation of the reports of the superintendent of public works and numerous pamphlets, newspaper clippings, letters, petitions, and maps. The authors consulted a copy of Kohn and Glenn's publication housed in The Citadel's Daniel Library. It was a rare publication, with only four hundred copies printed. Throughout this facsimile printing, there are handwritten marginalia, presumably written by Kohn and transportation pioneer George L. Champion, who gathered many of these pamphlets. For whatever reason, the words *Santee Canal* were crossed out and *Clarkson's Canal* was substituted. The authors have not seen the Santee Canal referred to as Clarkson's Canal elsewhere, but a William A. Clarkson (1764–1825) was associated with the Santee Canal Company from the very start.

11. Henry Ravenel (1795–1859) was the son of Daniel Ravenel III, Secondus of Wantoot, through which passed the Santee Canal. He posted this notice in the *Southern Patriot* (Charleston, SC), January 19, 1824: "Henry Ravenel, Engineer and Surveyor, keeps his office at his residence, No. 61 Broad-street, next to the City Square." He is the Henry Ravenel credited with figures 4.4 and 7.1.

12. Blanding, "Santee Canal," 258.
13. Ibid., 258–59.
14. Ibid., 260.
15. Ibid., 261.
16. Ibid., 262.
17. Ibid., 263.
18. Ibid.
19. Ibid., 265.
20. Ibid., 268.
21. Bull Town Drain also shows on the 1920 topographical map. The authors used the 1979 map since it shows the relation of the drain to Lake Moultrie (fig. 7.4).
22. Porcher and Salley, *History of the Santee Canal,* 10.
23. Ibid.
24. There is no author given for the article. A. E. Miller's publication of it is in the South Carolina Historical Society in the Santee Canal folder of the Elias Ball Bull Papers (call number 376.02(H)01.08-01).

25. "How to Kill Three Birds with One Stone," *Charleston Courier,* 1852.
26. The Rivers and Harbors Act refers to one of many separate pieces of legislation and appropriations passed by the US Congress since the first such legislation was passed in 1824.
27. US Senate, *Letter from the Secretary of War,* 4.
28. These same letters by Senf were included in Webber's publication of the Final Report in the *South Carolina Historical and Genealogical Magazine* in two 1927 issues and referenced previously. Where Webber indicates missing words by inserting *(torn),* these damages are not mentioned in the 1881 report. Evidently the 1881 report was based on Senf's Final Report before it was damaged. The 1881 report also included a color version of Senf's General Plan. It was based on the General Plan before damage to the map occurred, so it is a complete version of the original plan. Sections of the 1881 General Plan are referenced in this book (e.g., see fig. 5.21).
29. US Senate, *Letter from the Secretary of War,* 4.
30. Ibid.
31. Ibid.
32. Ibid.
33. Ibid., 6.
34. Ibid. The authors were unable to determine the specifics of a centrifugal steam pump. We suggest that it matters not for the discussion in this book. All that matters is that it pumped water from one source to another.
35. Kapsch, *Historic Canals and Waterways of South Carolina,* 143–45, includes a breakdown of all the costs associated with bringing the Santee Canal back into operation, per the army's 1881 report.
36. US Senate, *Letter from the Secretary of War.*

EIGHT. *End of Commercial Operation*
1. For more information about William Loughton Smith, see Rogers, *Evolution of a Federalist.*
2. Webber, "Col. Senf's Account (Continued)," 120.
3. Ibid., 123.
4. Ravenel Family Papers, 1695–1925, South Carolina Historical Society (call number 1171.00, container 12/313/11). The boat to which Ravenel referred was a barge that traveled down the Santee Canal.
5. Ibid.
6. Quoted in H. E. Ravenel Jr., *Ravenel Records,* 231.
7. *South Carolina Gazette,* January 12, 1804.
8. Gallatin, Latrobe, and Fulton, *Report of the Secretary of the Treasury,* 25.
9. Ibid.
10. Kapsch, *Historic Canals and Waterways of South Carolina,* 147.

11. Charleston Judgment Rolls, 1800, 294A, South Carolina Department of Archives and History, Columbia.
12. *Camden (SC) Gazette,* May 2, 1816.
13. Edgar, *South Carolina Encyclopedia,* 925. More than a century later, Interstate 26 essentially retraced the route of the original state road.
14. *Southern Patriot* (Charleston, SC), January 21, 1822.
15. Transcribed copy of "Plantation Book of Thomas Porcher," Laura Heyward Porcher White Family Papers, South Carolina Historical Society (Call # 223.01.01.01).
16. *The Statutes at Large of South Carolina,* December 13, 1827, bill, 1828 revision.
17. *Charleston Mercury,* March 27, 1838.
18. Hollis, "Costly Delusion."
19. South Carolina, General Assembly, House of Representatives, 1852.
20. General Assembly Petitions, 1853, #49, South Carolina Department of History and Archives, Columbia.
21. *Charleston Courier,* June 28, 1853.
22. *Charleston Courier,* December 12, 1853.
23. Bennett and Richardson, *History of the Santee Canal,* and Kapsch, *Historic Canals and Waterways of South Carolina,* address the finances of the Santee Canal Company. The present work provides no additional insights on this subject and cites some of their findings. It is possible that some Santee Canal Company records were lost in Charleston or Columbia in the turmoil of the Civil War.
24. General Assembly Reports, n.d., #2995, (ca. 1853), South Carolina Department of Archives and History.
25. Fox, *Record of the Service of the Fifty-Fifth Regiment,* 69–70.

NINE. *Field Survey of the Santee Canal and Environs*

1. Lidar images were obtained from the Berkeley County GIS Department, Moncks Corner, South Carolina.
2. Even though Walter was not alive during the time of the canal's construction, as early as 1786, he was involved in its early planning as a member of the Santee Canal Company.
3. Coker, "Visit to the Grave of Thomas Walter."
4. H. W. Ravenel, "Coniferae," *Proceedings of the Elliott Society of Natural History,* 2–53
5. In addition to serving as a board member for the Santee Canal Company, Walter was a member of the Continental Association, was deputy paymaster of the state militia, and just before his death had been elected to the General Assembly. For more information on this remarkable scientist's life, consult Maxon, *Thomas Walter, Botanist;* Rembert, *Thomas Walter, Carolina Botanist;* and J. P. Thomas, *Thomas Walter, Botanist.*

6. The High Hills is a long, narrow hilly region in the western part of Sumter County that lies north of the Santee River and east of the Wateree River. The region extends north almost to the Kershaw County line.
7. Webber, "Col. Senf's Account of the Santee Canal," 10.
8. *Charleston City Gazette and Daily Advertiser,* June 23, 1794.
9. Drayton, *View of South Carolina,* 156.
10. Webber, "Col. Senf's Account of the Santee Canal," 10.
11. DuBose, *Address Delivered at the Seventeenth Anniversary of the Black Oak Agricultural Society,* 20.
12. *Charleston Courier,* June 13, 1840.
13. Webber, "Col. Senf's Account (Continued)," 123.
14. Childs, *Private Journal of Henry William Ravenel,* 227. The authors question the number eight hundred for the bottles of wine. We suspect there is an error somewhere in transcribing the original journal. Eight hundred bottles seem excessive, even for a planter in the 1800s.
15. Webber, "Col. Senf's Account of the Santee Canal," 12.
16. Other children of Henry Glindkamp and Jenny Wilson included Isaac (1799–1855), Christiana (1802–?), Nancy/Nanny (1805–?), Mary (1805–?), and Harriett V. (1816–95). Harriett V. Glendcamp had several children with George P. Artope (1803–88), son of George B. Artope (1768–1818), another Santee Canal superintendent.
17. Webber, "Col. Senf's Account (Continued)," 115. The new course is represented by a solid red line on the General Plan, which perhaps the mapmaker substituted for the dotted line Senf drew on the corresponding plat.
18. Ibid.
19. Newell and Simmons, "Santee Canal Sanctuary Part II."

Epilogue

1. By 1939 the Works Progress Administration was renamed the Work Projects Administration.
2. South Carolina, General Assembly, Act no. 887, April 7, 1934.
3. Ibid.
4. U.S. State Supreme Court of South Carolina, 181 S.E. 481, September 10, 1935.
5. Middle St. John's came to be called the St. John's Basin sometime in the 1900s after the land was flooded by Lake Moultrie. *Basin* is a romantic term used by the planter descendants to refer to their lost lands and heritage. The basin was a shallow depression, probably a limestone karst formation. The dike made it possible to flood the basin to create Lake Moultrie (fig. E3).
6. A waterhead is the height difference between the point at which water enters a hydro system and where it leaves.

7. *Charleston News and Courier,* October 6, 1940.
8. Francis Marion Kirk, "Belvidere will sink again if Santee crosses Berkeley, *Charleston News and Courier,* October 13, 1935.
9. Fishburne, *Belvidere.*
10. The plat in figure E3 is not specific to a particular time. Plantations such as Walter and White Oak were incorporated into other lands after the canal ceased operations in 1853 and lost their identity. At the same time, plantations such as Pooshee, Wantoot, and Woodboo retained their boundaries virtually intact from the time the canal was finished until the coming of Lake Moultrie in 1942. Rather the plat was created to show the plantations and lands that were in existence in various periods of the canal's history. Their role and time period in the history of the canal are covered in the text. Mexico, which played a dominant role in the canal's history, changed its boundary so often it is impossible to define a boundary. The general area of Mexico will just be identified with the plantation name. The boundary of Fox Hall could not be delineated. Fox Hall became Big Camp after it was purchased by the Canal Company (see text). Burnt Savanna was incorporated into Belle Isle, and its eastern boundary could not be determined. Major landmarks of today are included for the reader's orientation. The aerial photograph of Santee Canal country came from Esri, DigitalGlobe, GeoEye, Earthstar Geographics, CNES/Airbus DS, USDA, USGS, AEX, Getmapping, Aerogrid, IGN, IGP, swisstopo, and the GIS User Community.
11. The case of the Cain family versus Santee Cooper was taken from Spruill, "Creating the Santee-Cooper Electric Cooperative." Spruill is the granddaughter of William Cain Jr., one of the four Cain siblings who brought the suit against Santee Cooper.
12. The authors, during research for this book, made no investigations of the plight of Black inhabitants in Santee Cooper country with the coming of the two lakes. This was beyond the scope of the history of the Santee Canal. Porcher and Guerry, however, during research for a privately published book titled *Our Lost Heritage: A Cultural History of the Middle Beat of Old St. John's Parish, Berkeley County, South Carolina: 1700–1942,* conducted interviews with Black residents of Middle St. John's. Material in this book is taken from these interviews. We do not have material from Black inhabitants of Upper St. John's. We understand that Black settlements like those in Middle St. John's were not prevalent in the section of Upper St. John's flooded by Lake Marion.
13. Mr. William Canty, interview by Cecile Ann Guerry and Richard Dwight Porcher Jr., August 30, 2011, and December 21, 2011, St. Stephen, South Carolina.
14. Ibid.
15. Ibid.

16. Fortunately, numerous people collected Native American artifacts along the exposed shoreline of the two lakes and donated them to various historical organizations. In most cases the sites where they were collected were not recorded except as "Lake Moultrie" or "Lake Marion." Though not a substitute for archaeological surveys, the artifacts record an eleven-thousand-year inhabitation of Native Americans in Santee Canal country.

Source Notes

1. William Cain Sr. (1874–1926) owned Somerset. The authors could not find out how Cain came into possession of the documents. Henry Ravenel Dwight Sr. (1873–1961) of Pinopolis, whom Webber also mentions, married Elizabeth Macbeth Cain, sister to Cain. If the Cain family had the document, Dwight could have obtained the documents from Elizabeth or another sibling.
2. Senf's 1800 General Plan is housed in South Carolina Historical Society maps/plats collection at the College of Charleston Libraries, 32-105-01.
3. Charles Drayton, diary, 1791-1798. Drayton Hall, National Trust for Historic Preservation, Charleston, https://lcdl.library.cofc.edu/lcdl/catalog/lcdl:27759.
4. Stokes and Porcher, "Newly Discovered Chapter."
5. Porcher's original handwritten "The History of the Santee Canal" is housed in the South Carolina Historical Society, Porcher Family Papers, call number 1082.00.
6. A 1903 edition of *The History of the Santee Canal* is located in the Special Collections, College of Charleston Libraries, F277.S28 P6.

BIBLIOGRAPHY

ARCHIVAL SOURCES

Archival Collections

CHARLESTON, SOUTH CAROLINA

Charleston Library Society
    Album "Northampton Hunting Trip, 1921"
Charleston Museum
Charleston Office of Deeds
    McCrady Plats
College of Charleston, Special Collections
    Frederick A. Porcher, "History of St. John's Parish"
    Samuel Lord Hyde Papers, 1901–1939
Drayton Hall
    Dr. Charles Drayton Diary
Gibbes Museum of Art
South Carolina Historical Society
    Black Oak Agricultural Society Minutes, 1842–1844
    Elias Ball Bull Papers, ca. 1940–1993
    Gaillard Family Papers 1758–1901
    Gaillard Plat Collection, 1835–1989
    Hardcastle Family History and Genealogy Research Files
    Laura Heyward Porcher White Family Papers
    Pineville Police Association Records
    Porcher Family Papers
    Ravenel Family Papers, 1695–1925

CHERAW, SOUTH CAROLINA

Archives of Sarah Cain Spruill

COLUMBIA, SOUTH CAROLINA

South Carolina Department of Archives and History

Charleston Judgment Rolls
General Assembly Petitions, no. 49, 1853
General Assembly Reports, n.d.
South Caroliniana Library, University of South Carolina
Edward L. Green Collection
South Caroliniana Map Collection

GEORGETOWN, SOUTH CAROLINA

Georgetown County Library, Digital Collection

MONCKS CORNER, SOUTH CAROLINA

Berkeley County GIS Department
Berkeley County Register of Deeds Office
Santee Cooper Public Service Authority

MOUNT PLEASANT, SOUTH CAROLINA

Personal archives of Richard Dwight Porcher Jr.

PINEVILLE, SOUTH CAROLINA

Personal archives of Theodore Keith Gourdin

UNIVERSITY OF NORTH CAROLINA AT CHAPEL HILL

Southern Historical Collection, Louis Round Wilson Special Collections

UNIVERSITY OF VIRGINIA

Washington Papers

WASHINGTON, DC

Historic American Buildings Survey, Prints and Photographic Division, Library of Congress, Washington. DC.

Maps and Plats

Cook, James. "A Map of the Province of South Carolina: With All the Rivers, Creek, Bay, Inlets, Islands, Inland Navigation, Sounding, Time of High Water on the Sea Coast, Roads, Marshes, Ferrys, Bridges, Swamps, Parishes, Churches, Towns, Townships, County Parish Districts, and Provincial Lines (Facsimile)." London, England, published according to an Act of Parliament, July 7, 1773. South Caroliniana Map Collection, map 1773. Courtesy of the Map Collection of the Thomas Cooper Library, University of South Carolina, Columbia, South Carolina.

Ferry Canal, n.d. or author. South Carolina Historical Society, Elias Ball Bull Papers, call number 376.00 (2000.181.027).

Gaillard, J. Palmer. "Map of Woodboo and Fair-Spring Plantations, Situate in St. John's Parish, Berkeley County, SC," by J. O. Palmer, March 22, 1806; "A Plan Exhibiting the Shape, Marks, Buttings, and Boundaries of the Woodboo Plantation, Situate in St. John's Parish, Berkeley County and Charleston District, Belonging to Stephen Mazyck," by J. O. Palmer, March 22, 1806. Two plats copied onto one, January 1929. Gaillard's combined plat is located in the South Carolina Historical Society, Gaillard Plat Collection, 1835–1989 (bulk 1900–1980, call number 575.00, G-147).

Mills, Robert. "Charleston District, South Carolina, Surveyed by Charles Vignoles and Henry Ravenel, 1820, Improved for Robert Mills' Atlas, 1825." N. p.: Engraved by H.S. Tanner & Associates, 1825

Mouzon, Henry, Jr. "A Map of the Parish of St. Stephen, in Craven County, Establishing a View of the Several Places Practicable for Making a Navigable Canal between Santee and Cooper Rivers." ca. 1785. Ascribed to Mouzon by the South Caroliniana Library. One version of this map is reproduced in Porcher and Salley, History of the Santee Canal, and in US Senate, Letter from the Secretary of War. The map is hand-dated 1775 in Porcher and Salley's history, but the date may have been added later. The South Caroliniana Library assigns the date 1785 to its copy, which is similar but not identical to Porcher's. Mouzon advertised the map for five pounds in the January 7, 1773, edition of the *South Carolina Gazette*. This date of 1773 appears to be the first date recorded for the map.

Purcell, Joseph. "This plan exhibits the shape and form of the lands in dispute between Ralph Izard, esq, Pentife [Plaintiff] and James Sinkler esq. defendant, with the adjacent tracts From a survey taken in December 1706 in obeden [obedience] to Rule of Court." There is no date on the plat. From other text on it, a date of 1772 seems an appropriate approximate date. Elias Ball Bull Papers, South Carolina Historical Society (call number 0376.00, box 22, 376.02 (H) 01.08.01).

Ravenel, Henry. "The above plan represents several Tracts of Land in Saint John's and Saint Stephen's Parish belonging to the Santee Canal Company and containing together Eighteen Hundred and eighty (1880) Acres," surveyed April 1822. Georgetown County Digital Library/Georgetown County Library (digital collection, 02-1822-04), Georgetown, South Carolina.

———. "Plan Exhibiting the Shape, Size and Situation of 12 Tracts of Land Owned by the Santee Canal Company containing 5,684 1/2 Acres." 1825. Original owned by T. Keith Gourdin, Pineville, South Carolina; copy in personal archives of Richard Dwight Porcher Jr.

———. White Oak owned by Samuel Porcher, 1822, St. Stephen's Parish. Georgetown County Library (digital collection, Real Estates Indentures Collection, #02-1822-04), Georgetown, South Carolina.

St. John's Parish, Berkeley County, ca. 1750. In Terry, "'Champaign Country.'"

Senf, Christian. "General Plan of the Canal and Its Environs between Santee and Cooper Rivers in the State of South Carolina. Commenced in the Year 1793 and

Finished in the Year 1800, by Christian Senf Colonel Engineer and Director in Chief of the Canal." South Carolina Historical Society, Charleston.

US Army War Department Corps of Engineers. Chicora Quadrangle Grid Zone "B." 1943, based on the Chicora Quadrangle of 1921

US Department of the Interior Geological Survey. Chicora Quadrangle. 1921, reprinted 1947. US Department of the Interior Geological Survey, War Department, Corps of Engineers, US Army. South Carolina, Chicora Quadrangle. 1921; reprinted, 1947.

———. South Carolina, Chicora Quadrangle. 1979.

US Senate, Ex. Doc. no. 60, 46th Cong., 3d sess., February 28, 1881, *Letter from the Secretary of War Transmitting a Communication from the Chief of Engineers of February 25, and Accompanying a Report from Lieut. Col. Q. A. Gillmore, Corps of Engineers.*

Wiare, Isaac G. "A Plan of Wantoot, Somerton and Hogswamp Plantations," 1795. Copied by J. Palmer Gaillard, 1915. Courtesy of the South Carolina Historical Society, Gaillard Plat Collection, 1835–1989 (bulk 1900–1980, call number 375.00, G-785).

White Oak/Big Camp. Ca.. 1800. South Carolina Historical Society, Elias Ball Bull Papers (call number 376.02 (H) 01.08.01, box 22); no date or surveyor on the plat.

Newspapers and Magazines

Camden (SC) Gazette
Charleston City Gazette and the Daily Advertiser
Charleston Courier
Charleston Mercury
Charleston News and Courier
Charleston Times
Harper's New Monthly Magazine
Miller's Weekly Messenger (Pendleton, SC)
National Intelligencer and Washington Advertiser (Washington, DC)
South Carolina Gazette (Charleston)
Southern Chronicle (Camden, SC)
Southern Patriot (Charleston)

Published Sources

"Account of James Brindley, a Self-Instructed Genius, and Introducer of the Mode of Still Water Navigation." *Belfast Monthly Magazine* 13, no. 72 (1814): 34–38. http://www.jstor.org/stable/30075344.

Acts of the Twenty-Eighth General Assembly of the State of New-Jersey, Chapter XCVIII (1804), Trenton: Printed by Wilson & Blackwell, 243–44.

Adams, John Quincy. *Diary of John Quincy Adams*. Vol. 1. Boston: Massachusetts Historical Society. https://www.masshist.org/publications/adams-papers.

Adams, Natalie P. "The 'Cymbee' Water Spirits of St. John's Berkeley." *African Diaspora Archaeology Newsletter* 10, no. 2 (2007): 1–12. https://scholarworks.umass.edu.

Armstrong, Margaret. *Five Generations: Life and Letters of an American Family 1750–1900*. New York: Harper, 1930.

Barnhill, Edward Stanley. *The Cains of Somerset*. N.p.: Privately published, 1981.

Bates, Susan Baldwin, and Harriott Cheves Leland. *French Santee: A Huguenot Settlement in Colonial South Carolina*. Baltimore: Otter Bay Books, 2015.

Bennett, Robert B., Jr., and Katherine H. Richardson. *History of the Santee Canal: 1785–1939*. N.p.: Heritage Preservation Associates, Inc., n.d.

Blanding, Abram. "The Santee Canal." In *Report of the Superintendent of Public Works, to the Legislature of South Carolina for the Year 1823*, 257–67. Columbia: Printed by D. & J. M. Faust, 1823.

Boyd, Julian P., et al., eds. *The Papers of Thomas Jefferson*. 46 vols. Princeton, NJ: Princeton University Press, 1953.

Bragg, C. L. *Crescent Moon over Carolina: William Moultrie and American Liberty*. Columbia: University of South Carolina Press, 2013.

Brown, Michael Ras. *African-Atlantic Cultures and the South Carolina Lowcountry*. Cambridge: Cambridge University Press, 2012.

Brunhouse, Robert L., and David Ramsay. "David Ramsay, 1749–1815: Selections from His Writings." *Transactions of the American Philosophical Society* 55, no. 4 (1965): 1–250. https://doi.org/10.2307/1005920.

Butler, Pierce. *The Letters of Pierce Butler, 1790–1794: Nation Building and Enterprise in the New American Republic*. Columbia: University of South Carolina Press, 2007.

Carmichael, Sherman. *Mysterious South Carolina*. Charleston, SC: Arcadia, 2019.

Carney, Judith, and Richard Porcher. "Geographies of the Past: Rice, Slaves and Technological Transfer in South Carolina." *Southeastern Geographer* 33, no. 2 (1993): 127–47.

Catesby, Mark. *The Natural History of Carolina, Florida and the Bahama Islands: Containing the Figures of Birds, Beasts, Fishes, Serpents, Insects, and Plants*. 2 vols. London: Marsh, 1754.

Chandler, Julian Alvin Carroll, ed. *The South in the Building of the Nation: History of the States*. Vol. 3. Richmond: Southern Historical Publication Society, 1909.

Chapman, John Abney. *History of Edgefield County: From the Earliest Settlements to 1897; Biographical and Anecdotical, with Sketches of the Seminole War, Nullification, Secession, Reconstruction, Churches and Literature, with Rolls of All the Companies from Edgefield in the War of Secession, War with Mexico and with the Seminole Indians*. Newberry, SC: Aull, 1897.

Chappell, Burford S. *The Chappell Family in Early South Carolina*. Columbia, SC: Bryan, 1972.

Childs, Arney Robinson, ed. *The Private Journal of Henry William Ravenel, 1859–1887*. Columbia: University of South Carolina Press, 1947.

Clinton, George, Hugh Hastings, and James Austin Holden. *Public Papers of George Clinton, First Governor of New York, 1777–1795, 1801–1804.* Vol. 5. Albany: State of New York, 1911.

Coburn, Frank Warren. *A History of the Battle of Bennington, Vermont.* Bennington, VT: Livingston, 1912.

Coker, William C. "A Visit to the Grave of Thomas Walter." *Journal of Elisha Mitchell Scientific Society* 26 (April 1910): 31–42.

Conger, John L. "South Carolina and the Early Tariffs." *Mississippi Valley Historical Review* 5, no. 4 (March 1919): 415–33.

Cooper, Thomas, and David J. McCord, eds. *The Statutes at Large of South Carolina.* Vol. 7. Columbia, SC: Johnston, 1836–41.

Crowson, E. T. "The Santee-Cooper: A Pioneer Effort In South Carolina Canaling." *South Carolina Magazine,* August 1971, 6–20.

Dann, John C., ed. *The Revolution Remembered: Eyewitness Accounts of the War for Independence.* Chicago: University of Chicago Press, 1980.

Doar, David. *A Sketch of the Agricultural Society of St. James, Santee, South Carolina: And an Address on the Traditions and Reminiscences of the Parish, Delivered Before Society on 4th of July, 1907.* McClellanville, SC: Archibald Rutledge Academy, 1978.

Downey, Tom. *Planting a Capitalist South: Masters, Merchants, and Manufacturers in the Southern Interior, 1790–1860.* Baton Rouge: Louisiana State University Press, 2006.

Drayton, John. *A View of South-Carolina, as Respects Her Natural and Civil Concerns.* Charleston, SC: Young, 1802.

DuBose, Samuel. *Address Delivered at the Seventeenth Anniversary of the Black Oak Agricultural Society.* Charleston, SC: Miller, 1858.

———. "Reminiscences of St. Stephen's Parish." In *A Contribution to the History of the Huguenots of South Carolina,* 35-86. New York: Putnam, 1887.

Edgar, Walter B. *History of Santee Cooper, 1934–1984.* Columbia, SC: Bryan, 1984.

———. *South Carolina: A History.* Columbia: University of South Carolina Press, 1998.

———. *South Carolina Encyclopedia.* Columbia: University of South Carolina Press, 2006.

Ely, James W., Jr. "'That Due Satisfaction May Be Made': The Fifth Amendment and the Origin of the Compensation Principle." *American Journal of Legal History* 36, no. 1 (January 1992): 1–18.

Fehlings, Gregory E. "America's First Limited War." *Naval War College Review* 53, no. 3 (2000): 101–43. http://www.jstor.org/stable/44638334.

Fishburne, Anne Sinkler. *Belvidere: A Plantation Memory.* Columbia: University of South Carolina, 1949.

Ford, L. M. "Memories, Traditions and History of Rocky Mount and Vicinity." Chester County (South Carolina) Historical Society, unpublished manuscript, n.d.

Fox, Charles Barnard. *Record of the Service of the Fifty-fifth Regiment of Massachusetts Volunteer Infantry,* no. 1. Cambridge, MA: Wilson and Son, 1868.

Froeschle, Hartmut, ed. *German Canadian Yearbook: Deutschkanadisches Jahrbuch.* Vol. 2. Toronto: University of Toronto Press, 1975.

Gabriel, Michael P. *The Battle of Bennington: Soldiers and Civilians.* Charleston, SC: History Press, 2012.

Gadue, Michael R. "An Aspect of Berufsreise of 'Mrs. General' Freifrau von Riedesel in America." *Hessians: Journal of the Johannes Schwalm Historical Association* 21 (2018): 22–34.

Gallatin, Albert, Benjamin Henry Latrobe, and Robert Fulton. *Report of the Secretary of the Treasury, on the Subject of Public Roads and Canals: Made in Pursuance of a Resolution of Senate, of March 2d, 1807.* Washington, DC: R. C. Weightman, 1808. Reprint, New York: Augustus M. Kelly, 1968.

Gates, Horatio. "Letter from Horatio Gates to Thomas Jefferson, September 27, 1780." In *The Papers of Thomas Jefferson, Volume 3: 18 June 1779–30 September 1780,* 668–69. Princeton, NJ: Princeton University Press, 1951.

Greene, Harlan, Harry S. Hutchins Jr., and Brian E. Hutchins. *Slave Badges and the Slave-Hire System in Charleston, South Carolina, 1783–1865.* Jefferson, NC: McFarland, 2008.

Hamlin, Talbot. *Benjamin Henry Latrobe.* New York: Oxford University Press, 1955.

Hay, Oliver P. *The Pleistocene of North America and Its Vertebrated Animals from the States East of the Mississippi River and from the Canadian Provinces East of Longitude 95 Degrees.* Vol. 322. Washington, DC: Carnegie Institution of Washington, 1923.

Higginbotham, Don. *Daniel Morgan: Revolutionary Rifleman.* Chapel Hill: University of North Carolina, 1979.

Hill, Frederick Trevor. *The Story of a Street: A Narrative History of Wall Street from 1644 to 1908, V. Wall Street as the Centre of Fashion.* Reprinted in *Harper's Magazine* 117, no. 699 (1908): 455–63.

Holcomb, Brent H. *South Carolina Naturalizations 1783–1850.* Baltimore: Clearfield, 1985.

Holland Society of New York, New York City Lutheran. *Dutch Reformed Church Records in Selected States, 1639–1989.* Vol. 3, book 87. Provo, UT: Ancestry.com Operations, Inc., 2014.

Hollis, Daniel W. "Costly Delusion: Inland Navigation in the South Carolina Piedmont." in *The Proceedings of the South Carolina Historical Association,* edited Jack S. Mullins, 29–43. Columbia: South Carolina Historical Association, 1968. http://hdl.handle.net/10827/23290.

Holmes, Francis Simmons. "ART. XVI.-Notes on the Geology of Charleston, SC." *American Journal of Science and Arts (1820–1879)* 7, no. 20 (1849): 187–201.

———. *Post-Pleiocene Fossils of South-Carolina.* Charleston, SC: Russell & Jones, 1860.

Hood, Margaret K., and Margit S. Benton, comp. *Berkeley County Cemetery Inscriptions.* Charleston: Charleston Chapter, South Carolina Genealogical Society, 1985.

Huck, Stephan. *Soldaten Gegen Nordamerika.* Berlin: Oldenbourg Wissenschaftsverlag, 2015.

Hünemörder, Markus. *The Society of the Cincinnati: Conspiracy and Distrust in Early America.* New York: Berghahn, 2006.

Humphreys, Frank Landon. *Life and Times of David Humphreys: Soldier-Statesman-Poet, "Belov'd of Washington."* New York: Putnam, 1917.

Idzerda, Stanley J., Robert Rhodes Crout, Carol Godschall, and Leslie Wharton, eds. *Lafayette in the Age of the American Revolution: Selected Letters and Papers, 1776–1790; January 4, 1782–December 29, 1785.* Ithaca, NY: Cornell University Press, 2018.

Irwin, Douglas A., and Richard Sylla, eds. *Founding Choices: American Economic Policy in the 1790s.* Chicago: University of Chicago Press, 2011.

Jefferson, Thomas. *The Writings of Thomas Jefferson: 1781–1784.* New York: Putnam's, 1894.

Jervey, Susan B., and Charlotte St. J. Ravenel, *Two Diaries, From Middle St. John's, Berkeley, South Carolina, February–May, 1865: Journals Kept by Miss Susan R. Jervey and Miss Charlotte St. J. Ravenel, at Northampton and Pooshee Plantations, also Reminiscences of Mrs. (Waring) Henagan, with Two Contemporary Reports from Federal Officials* N.p.: Privately published by the St. John's Hunting Club, 1921.

Johnson, Douglas. *The Mysterious Carolina Bays.* New York: Columbia University Press, 1942.

Johnson, Suzanne Parfitt, ed. *Maxcy Gregg's Sporting Journals 1842–1858.* Columbia, SC: Shortwell, 2019.

Judd, William R. "Report to Santee Canal Park, April 10, 1988." Unpublished document in possession of Richard Dwight Porcher Jr.

Kapsch, Robert J. *Historic Canals and Waterways of South Carolina.* Columbia: University of South Carolina Press, 2010.

Kipping, Ernest. *The Hessian View of America, 1776–1783.* Monmouth Beach, NJ: Freneau, 1971.

Kirkland, Thomas J., and Robert MacMillan Kennedy. *Historic Camden: Colonial and Revolutionary.* Columbia, SC: State Company, 1905.

———. *Historic Camden, Part Two: Nineteenth Century.* Camden, SC: Kershaw County Historical Society, 1905.

Kohn, David, and Bess Glenn, eds. *Internal Improvement in South Carolina, 1817–1828.* Washington, DC: Privately printed, 1938.

Krawczynski, Keith. "William Drayton's Journal of a 1784 Tour of the South Carolina Backcountry." *South Carolina Historical Magazine* 97, no. 3 (1996): 182–205.

Lacoste, Louis. *Precis historique du Canal du Languedoc.* Paris: L'Imprimerie De Fain, 1810.

Laurens, Henry. *The Papers of Henry Laurens.* Vols. 1–4. Columbia: University of South Carolina Press, 1974.

Laurens, Henry, David R. Chesnutt, and C. James Taylor. *Papers of Henry Laurens.* Vols. 12 and 16. Columbia: University of South Carolina Press, 2000, 2003.

Lawson, John. *A New Voyage to Carolina.* Edited with an introduction and notes by Hugh Talmage Lefler. Chapel Hill: University of North Carolina Press, 1967.

Le Blond, Guillaume. *The Military Engineer; or, A Treatise on the Attack and Defence of All Kinds of Fortified Places.* London: Nourse, 1759.

Lesser, Charles. "Review: Papers of the War Department, 1784–1800." *Journal of American History* 98, no. 1 (2011): 307–8.

Levine, Ida L., and William Moultrie. "A Letter from William Moultrie at Charleston to George Washington at Mount Vernon April 7, 1786." *South Carolina Historical Magazine* 83, no. 2 (1982): 116–20.

Lewis, Kenneth E. *The Carolina Backcountry Venture: Tradition, Capital, and Circumstance in the Development of Camden and the Wateree Valley, 1740–1810.* Columbia: University of South Carolina Press, 2017.

Lockley, Timothy James, ed. *Maroon Communities in South Carolina: A Documentary Record.* Columbia: University of South Carolina Press, 2009.

Louise, E. *Elizabeth Clevland Hardcastle, 1741–1808: A Lady of Color in the South Carolina Low Country.* Columbia, SC: Phoenix, 2001.

MacWethy, Lou D. *The Book of Names, Especially Relating to the Early Palatines and the First Settlers in the Mohawk Valley.* Baltimore: Genealogical Publishing, 2010.

Madden, Cary Thomas. "Mammoths of North America." PhD diss., University of Colorado at Boulder, 1981.

Martin, Jonathan D. *Divided Mastery: Slave Hiring in the American South.* Cambridge, MA: Harvard University Press, 2004.

Mathew, William M., and Edmund Ruffin. *Agriculture, Geology, and Society in Antebellum South Carolina: The Private Diary of Edmund Ruffin, 1843.* Athens: University of Georgia Press, 1992.

Maxon, William R. *Thomas Walter, Botanist.* Washington, DC: Smithsonian Institution, 1936.

McCandless, Peter. "Yellow Fever." In *The South Carolina Encyclopedia.* Columbia: Institute for Southern Studies, University of South Carolina, 2019. https://www.scencyclopedia.org/sce/entries/yellow-fever/.

Melsheimer, F. V. *Journal of the Voyage of the Brunswick Auxiliaries from Wolfenbuettel to Quebec.* N.p.: Leopold Classic Library, n.d. https://archive.org/details/journalofvoyageooomelsuoft

Meyer, Balthasar Henry, and Caroline Elizabeth MacGill. *History of Transportation in the United States before 1860.* Vol. 3. Washington, DC: Carnegie Institution of Washington, 1917.

Miller, Daniel A. *Sir Joseph Yorke and Anglo-Dutch Relations 1774–1780*. The Hague: Mouton, 1970.

Mills, Robert. *Statistics of South Carolina: Including a View of Its Natural, Civil, and Military History, General and Particular*. Charleston, SC: Hurlbut & Lloyd, 1826.

Moore, Alexander. *The Fabric of Liberty: The Society of the Cincinnati of the State of South Carolina*. Charleston, SC: Home House, 2012.

Moss, Bobby Gilmer. *Roster of South Carolina Patriots in the American Revolution*. Baltimore: Genealogical Publishing, 1983.

Moultrie, William. *Memoirs of the American Revolution, As Far as it Related to the States of North and South Carolina and Georgia*. Vol. 1. New York: Longworth, 1802.

Mukerji, Chandra. *Impossible Engineering: Technology and Territoriality on the Canal du Midi*. Princeton, NJ: Princeton University Press, 2009.

Nadeau, Gabriel. "A German Military Surgeon in Rutland, Massachusetts, during the Revolution: Julius Friedrich Wasmus." *Bulletin of the History of Medicine* 18, no. 3 (1945): 243–300.

New York (State). *Laws of the State of New York Passed at the Sessions of the Legislature*. Vol. 1. New York State Legislature, 1886.

Newell, Mark M. "Buried Treasure." *American Heritage of Invention and Technology* 7, no. 3 (1992): 35–41.

Newell, Mark M., and Joe J. Simmons III. "The Santee Canal Sanctuary, Part II: Preliminary Archaeological Investigation of a Portion of the Old Santee Canal and Biggin Creek, Berkeley County, South Carolina." The Underwater Antiquities Management Program, South Carolina Institute of Archaeology and Anthropology, University of South Carolina, September 1989, https://scholarcommons.sc.edu/mrd_pubs/8/.

Nordholt, Jan Willem Schulte. *The Dutch Republic and American Independence*. Chapel Hill: University of North Carolina, 1982.

North, Louise V. *The Travel Journals of Henrietta Marchant Liston: North America and Lower Canada, 1796–1800*. Lanham, MD: Lexington Books, 2014.

Pancake, John S. *1777: The Year of the Hangman*. University: University of Alabama Press, 1977.

Perez, L. Jeffrey. "Bonds of Friendship and Mutual Interest: Virginia's Waterways Improvement Companies, 1784–1828." PhD diss., William and Mary, 2000.

Phillips, Ulrich Bonnell. *A History of Transportation in the Eastern Cotton Belt to 1860*. New York: Columbia University Press, 1908.

Piecuch, Jim, and John Beakes. *Cool Deliberate Courage: John Eager Howard in the American Revolution*. Charleston, SC: Nautical and Aviation Publishing, 2009.

"Charles Cotesworth Pinckney to Thomas Pinckney, 14 July 1792." In *The Papers of the Revolutionary Era Pinckney Statesmen Digital Edition*. Charlottesville: University of Virginia Press, 2016. https://rotunda.upress.virginia.edu.

Porcher, Frederick A. "Memoirs," *The South Carolina Historical and Genealogical Magazine* 44, no. 2 (April 1943): 65–80.

———. "*Upper Beat of St. John's Berkeley.*" Transactions of the Huguenot Society of South Carolina 13 (1906): 31–78.

Porcher, Frederick A., and Alexander Samuel Salley. *The History of the Santee Canal: Dedicated to the South Carolina Historical Society, 1875.* Charleston: South Carolina Historical Society, 1903.

Porcher, Richard D., Jr., Robert Joseph Hauck, and Cecile Ann Guerry. *Our Lost Heritage: A Cultural History of the Middle Beat of Old St. John's Parish, Berkeley County, South Carolina: 1700-1942.* Charleston, SC: Nelson Printing, 2022.

Porcher, Richard D., Jr., and William Judd. *The Market Preparation of Carolina Rice.* Columbia: University of South Carolina Press, 2014.

Porcher, Richard Dwight, and Sarah Fick. *The Story of Sea Island Cotton.* Charleston, SC: Wyrick, 2005.

Raiford, Norman Gasque. "South Carolina and the Issue of Internal Improvement, 1775–1860." PhD diss., University of Virginia, 1974.

Ramsay, David. *Ramsay's History of South Carolina, from Its First Settlement in 1670 to the Year 1808.* 2 vols. Newberry, SC: Duffie, 1858.

Ravenel, Beatrice St. Julien. *Architects of Charleston.* Columbia: University of South Carolina Press, 1992.

Ravenel, Edmund. "The Limestone Springs of St. John's Berkeley, and Their Probable Availability for Increasing the Quantity of Fresh Water in Cooper River," *Proceedings of the Elliott Society of Natural History,* September 1860, 28–32.

Ravenel, Edmund, F. E. Melsheimer, and Edward Hallowell. "Meeting for Business, October 29, 1844; Description of Some New Species of Fossil Organic Remains, from the Eocene of South Carolina; Descriptions of New Species of Coleoptera of the United States; Description of New Species of Reptiles from Africa." *Proceedings of the Academy of Natural Sciences of Philadelphia* 2, no. 5 (1844): 96–126.

Ravenel, Henry Edmund, Jr. *Ravenel Records: A History and Genealogy of the Huguenot Family of Ravenel, of South Carolina; with Some Incidental Account of the Parish of St. Johns Berkeley, Which Was Their Principal Location.* Atlanta: Franklin, 1898.

Ravenel, Henry William. "Recollections of Southern Plantation Life." *Yale Review,* Summer 1936, 748–77.

———. "Coniferae." *Proceedings of the Elliott Society of Natural History* 1 (1856): 52–53.

"Record of the Service of the Fifty-fifth Regiment of Massachusetts Volunteer Infantry." Printed for the Regimental Association, Cambridge Press of John Wilson & son, July 1868.

Rembert, David. *Thomas Walter, Carolina Botanist.* Columbia: South Carolina Museum Commission, 1980.

Reuter, Claus. *Brunswick Troops in North America, 1776–1783: Index of All Soldiers Who Remained in North America.* Bowie, MD: Heritage Books, 1999.

Richardson, Elizabeth Buford. *A Genealogical Record with Reminiscences, of the Richardson and Buford Families.* Edited, annotated, and indexed by Judith Reesor Hutchinson, Columbia, SC: State Commercial Printing, 1960.

Rogers, George C. *Evolution of a Federalist: William Loughton Smith of Charleston (1758–1812).* Columbia: University of South Carolina Press, 1962.

Saberton, Ian. "The South Carolina Backcountry in Mid 1780." *Journal of the American Revolution,* May 24, 2017. https://allthingsliberty.com/2017/05/south-carolina-backcountry-mid-1780/.

Sanders, Albert E., and William Dewey Anderson. *Natural History Investigations in South Carolina: From Colonial Times to the Present.* Columbia: University of South Carolina Press, 1999.

[Santee Canal Company]. *Report of the Board of Directors.* 1805. South Carolina Historical Society.

Schalk, Carl F. *Source Documents in American Lutheran Hymnody.* St. Louis, MO: Concordia, 1996.

Schulz, Constance B. "Eliza Lucas Pinckney and Harriott Pinckney Horry: A South Carolina Revolutionary-Era Mother and Daughter." *South Carolina Women: Their Lives and Times* 1 (2009): 79–108.

Schulz, Constance B., ed. *The Papers of the Revolutionary Era Pinckney Statesmen Digital Edition.* Charlottesville: University of Virginia Press, 2016. https://rotunda.upress.virginia.edu/founders/default.xqy?keys=PNKY-print&mode=TOC.

Senf, Johann Christian. "Plan Du Retranchement de Sorel." Hessisches Staatsarchiv Marburg, Karte WHK 28_44. http://www.vhghessen.de

"1790 United States Federal Census." Online database. https://www.ancestry.com/search/collections/5058/ (accessed August 22, 2023).

Shackelford, George Green. *Thomas Jefferson's Travels in Europe, 1784–1789: A Synthesis of His Travel Accounts and Correspondence as Well as Those of Some of His Contemporaries.* Baltimore: Johns Hopkins University Press, 1995.

Sikes, Lewright B. *The Public Life of Pierce Butler.* Washington, DC: University Press of America, 1979.

Smith, Clifford Neal. *Brunswick Deserter-Immigrants of the American Revolution.* Thomson, IL: Heritage House, 1973.

———. *German Mercenary Expatriates in the United States and Canada.* Baltimore, MD: Genealogical Publishing Company, 2006.

Smith, Henry A. M. "The Baronies of South Carolina: IV. Wadboo Barony." *South Carolina Historical and Genealogical Magazine* 12, no. 2 (April 1911): 43–52.

Smith, Paul Hubert, Gerard W. Gawalt, and Rosemary Plakas. *Letters of Delegates to Congress, 1774–1789, Vol. 10, June 1, 1778–September 30, 1778.* Washington, DC: Library of Congress, 1983.

South Carolina. *General Assembly Reports,* 1818, #45. South Carolina Department of Archives and History.

———. *General Assembly Reports,* 1853, #49. South Carolina Department of Archives and History.

———. *General Assembly Reports,* n.d., #2266. South Carolina Department of Archives and History.

———. *General Assembly Reports,* n.d., #2267, South Carolina Department of Archives and History.

———. *General Assembly Reports,* n.d., #2995, South Carolina Department of Archives and History.

"South Carolina, U.S., Wills and Probate Records, 1670–1980." Online database. https://www.ancestry.com/search/collections/9080/ (accessed August 22, 2023).

Spall, Eric. "Foreigners in the Highest Trust: American Perceptions of European Mercenary Officers in the Continental Army." *Early American Studies* 12, no. 2 (2014): 338–65.

Sprague, Stuart Seely. "Senator John Brown of Kentucky, 1757–1837: A Political Biography." MA thesis, New York University, 1972.

Spruill, Sarah P. "Creating the Santee-Cooper Electric Cooperative, 1934–1941." MA thesis, South Carolina Honor College, 1997.

Stark, Caleb, and John Stark. *Memoir and Official Correspondence of Gen. John Stark: With Notices of Several Other Officers of the Revolution.* N.p.: Hansebooks GmbH, 2017.

Stephens, Lester D. *Ancient Animals and Other Wondrous Things: The Story of Francis Simmons Holmes, Paleontologist and Curator of the Charleston Museum.* Charleston, SC: Charleston Museum, 1988.

Stokes, Karen D., and Richard Dwight Porcher. "A Newly Discovered Chapter of Frederick A. Porcher's 'Upper Beat of St. John's, Berkeley.'" *South Carolina Historical Magazine* 117, no. 3 (July 2016): 205–55.

Stone, William Leete, ed. *Memoirs, Letters and Journals, of Major General Riedesel, during his Residence in America.* Vols. 1–2. New York: Arno, 1969.

Stony, Samuel Gaillard, ed. "Memoirs of Frederick Adolphus Porcher." *South Carolina Historical and Genealogical Magazine* 44, no. 2 (April 1943): 65–80.

———. "Memoirs of Frederick Adolphus Porcher." *South Carolina Historical and Genealogical Magazine* 45, no. 4 (1944): 200–16.

Terrasson, Antoine. "To Thomas Jefferson from Terrasson, 29 April 1788." Founders Online, National Archives. https://founders.archives.gov/documents/Jefferson/01-13-02-0045.

Terry, George David. "'Champaign Country': A Social History of an Eighteenth Century Lowcountry Parish in South Carolina, St. Johns Berkeley County." PhD dissertation, University of South Carolina, 1981.

Thomas, John Peyre, Jr. *Thomas Walter, Botanist.* Columbia: Historical Commission of South Carolina, 1946.

United States. Bureau of Statistics. Treasury Department. *Report on the Internal Commerce of the United States.* 1886.

———. Department of State. *The Diplomatic Correspondence of the United States of America: from the Signing of the Definitive Treaty of Peace, 10th September 1783, to the Adoption of the Constitution, March 4, 1789.* Washington, DC: Blair & Rives, 1837.

"United States, New York Land Records, 1630–1975." FamilySearch database. November 16, 1789. Montgomery, New York.

United States. *Report of the Secretary of Treasury, on the Subject of Public Roads and Canals; Made in Pursuance of a Resolution of Senate, March 2nd, 1807.* Washington, DC: Davis, 1816.

United States. Senate. Ex. Doc. No. 60, Letter from the Secretary of War Transmitting a Communication from the Chief of Engineers of February 25, and Accompanying a Report from Lieut. Col. Q. A. Gillmore, Corps of Engineers, upon Survey for the Reopening of the Santee Canal, South Carolina, etc., 46th Congress, 3d session, February 28, 1881.

———. War Department. *Report of the Chief of Engineers, U. S. Army,* Appendix J, April 15, 1880.

"U.S., Dutch Reformed Church Records in Selected States, 1639–1989." Online database. https://www.ancestry.com/search/collections/6961/ (accessed August 22, 2023).

Van Hogendorp, Gijsbert Karel. *The College at Princetown: May 1784 by Gijsbert Karel Van Hogendorp, with an Introduction by Howard C. Rice.* Princeton, NJ: Princeton University Library, 1949.

Wade, Arthur P. "Mount Dearborn: The National Armory at Rocky Mount, South Carolina, 1802–1829." *South Carolina Historical Magazine,* 81, no. 3 (July 1980): 207–31.

Walker, Paul K. *Engineers of Independence: A Documentary History of the Army Engineers in the American Revolution.* Honolulu: University Press of the Pacific, 2002.

Wallace, David Duncan. *The Life of Henry Laurens: With a Sketch of the Life of Lieutenant-Colonel John Laurens.* New York: Putnam, 1915.

Walter, Thomas. *Flora Caroliniana.* London: Fraser, 1788.

Washington, George. *The Writings of George Washington, Being His Correspondence, Addresses, Messages and Other Papers, official and Private, Selected and Published from the Original MSS.; with a Life of the Author, Notes and Illustrations,* vol. 9. Boston: American Stationers' Company, John B. Russell, 1834.

Wasmus, J. F. *An Eyewitness Account of the American Revolution and New England Life: The Journal of J. F. Wasmus, German Company Surgeon, 1776–1783.* Translated by Helga Doblin. Edited by Mary C. Lynn. New York: Greenwood, 1990.

Webber, Mabel L. "Col. Senf's Account of the Santee Canal." *South Carolina Historical and Genealogical Magazine* 28, no. 1 (1927): 8–21.

———. "Col. Senf's Account of the Santee Canal (Continued)." *South Carolina Historical and Genealogical Magazine* 28, no. 2 (1927): 112–31.

Webler, Robert M. "German (So Called Hessian) Soldiers Who Remained in Massachusetts and Neighboring States, Particularly after the Battles of Bennington and Saratoga." *Hessians: Journal of the Johannes Schwalm Historical Association* 9 (2006): 82–88.

Wilson, Robert. *Half-Forgotten By-Ways of the Old South*. Columbia, SC: State Company, 1928.

ABOUT THE AUTHORS

ELIZABETH CONNOR, MLS, MEd is professor emerita of general education at The Citadel, the Military College of South Carolina. Prior to joining The Citadel, Connor worked as an academic medical librarian in Maryland, Saudi Arabia, Connecticut, South Carolina, and the Commonwealth of Dominica. She has published numerous peer-reviewed articles, chapters, and books on a variety of library subjects, including evidence-based practice, building design, reference services, instructional services, and Web 2.0 technologies.

RICHARD DWIGHT PORCHER JR. is from Pinopolis, Berkeley County, South Carolina, and now lives in Mt. Pleasant. He graduated from Berkeley High School in 1957 and the College of Charleston with a BS in biology (1962) and received his PhD from the University of South Carolina (1974), where he studied field botany under the noted field botanist, Dr. Wade T. Batson. He began a thirty-three-year tenure as a biology professor at The Citadel in 1970 and retired as professor emeritus in 2003 from The Citadel. He is past adjunct full professor, department of biological sciences, Clemson University, where he established the Wade T. Batson Endowment in Field Botany to assist students in the study of the state's flora and plant ecology. Porcher has published many books, including *A Guide to the Wildflowers of South Carolina, revised and updated edition* (USC Press, 2022). In 2019, Porcher was awarded the Order of the Palmetto, the State of South Carolina's highest civilian honor.

WILLIAM ROBERT JUDD, a self-taught draftsman–artist, archaeologist, and historian, is retired from the US Space and Naval Warfare Systems Command and lives with his family on James Island, South Carolina. Judd has contributed numerous mechanical drawings and working models or rice machinery to various museums and historical documents. Judd freely gives his time to share his knowledge of Lowcountry history.

Porcher and Judd coauthored *The Market Preparation of Carolina Rice* (USC Press, 2014), with Judd providing the original drawings of rice culture machinery.

INDEX

Adams, Abigail, 11, 29, 32, 33–34
Adams, John, 29, 31, 32, 34, 41
Adams, John Quincy, 29, 32, 34
Artesian springs, 89, 105, 107, 108, 121, 187, 194, 225n8
Artope, George B., xiii, 212n15, 227n6, 231n16
Artope, George P., 227n6, 231n16

Ball, William, 193
Barnes, Albert M., 201
Barrow Hill, 201
Barrows, 208n12
Battle of Bemis Heights, 27
Battle of Bennington, xi, 21, 28, 211–12n6, 213n32, 214n35, 214n36
Battle of Eutaw Springs, 121, 125, 224n3
Battle of Saratoga, 27–28, 213, 214n34, 214n35
Battle of Walloomsac. See Battle of Bennington
Baum, Friedrich, 28, 211–12n6, 213n32
Belle Isle, 181, 225n5, 232n10
Belser, Roy, 165
Belvidere, 190, 194.
Bemis Heights (NY). See Battle of Bemis Heights
Bennington (VT). See Battle of Bennington.
Big Camp, xii, 39, 50, 54, 57, 74, 75, 84, 85 111, 118–19, 137, 176, 180, 188, 224–25n4, 224–25n5, 232n10; Big Camp Lock (III), 77, 84, 85, 89, 91, 97, 118, 119, 137, 141, 179, 180, 188, 222n37; Big Spring. See Mazÿck's Spring
Biggin Basin, xii, 68, 107–108, 110, 127; Biggin Canal, xii, 110, 111, 112, 115, 133, 185, 186, 187, 188; Biggin Church, 133, 171, 185; Biggin Creek, xv, 67, 68, 94, 95, 97, 105, 110, 111, 112, 114, 115, 124, 127, 128, 133, 134, 151, 152, 165, 184, 186, 187, 205, 223n62; Biggin Road, 110, 184; Biggin Swamp, 51, 43, 46, 93, 94, 95, 107, 112, 120–21, 127, 142, 171, 184, 186, 192, 223n62
Black Oak, 11, 123, 124, 133, 134, 155, 161, 189; Black Oak Basin, 68; Black Oak Church. See Trinity Church Black Oak; Black Oak Lock (VII), xiii, xiv, 68, 69, 85, 100, 102–105, 122, 129, 130–32, 134, 142, 149–50, 223n48; Black Oak Road, 44, 89, 95, 96, 134, 147, 171, 182, 183, 200, 208n12, 222n43
Black settlements, 6, 200–1, 232n12, 232n13
Blanding, Abram, xiii, 140–45, 150, 154, 227–28n9, 227–28n10
Boy Scout Lane, 183
Braunschweiger Jaeger, 22, 24, 26. See also Brunswick Dragoons
Breithaupt, Christian Friedrich, xiii, 38–39, 217–18n73, 217–18n74, 217–18n75. See also van Berckel, Geertruid (Gertrude) Jacoba

253

Breithaupt, Freeman Fritz, 217–18n75
Brevard, Joseph, 227n9
Bridgewater Canal 46, 209n8
Brindley, James, xi, 46, 209n8, 219n12
Broad River, 5, 19, 116, 119, 162, 207n1;
  Broad River Power Company, 195
Broad Street (Charleston, SC), 224, 228n11
Brown, John, 215n46
Brubaker, John, 165
Brunswick Dragoons, 4, 20, 26, 28, 212n7
Buford, William, xii, 116–29, 224n3
Bull, Elias, 135
Bull Town Bay, 48, 58–59, 89, 91–94, 140, 146–47, 182, 188, 219n19, 222n46, 222n47; Bull Town Drain xiii, xv, 144–47, 183, 184, 228n21
Burgoyne, John, 119, 225n5, 232n10
Burnt Savanna, 119, 225n5, 232n10
Butler, Pierce, 2, 38
Byrnes, James, 195

Cain, Elizabeth Macbeth, 233n1
Cain, Elizabeth Ravenel Lucas, 196–97
Cain, Charles Lucas, 197
Cain, Daniel, 226
Cain, Joseph Palmer, 156, 197
Cain, William, 156
Cain, William, Jr., 135, 197, 227n33, 232n11
Cain, William, Sr., 196–97, 203, 226, 233n1
Campbell AME Church, 200
Canal de Briare, 49, 63–64
Canal du Midi, xi, 49, 63, 64–65, 220n7
Candy, Jeremiah, 54, 55. See also Fox Hall
Canty, William, 200, 232n13
Cape Romain, 193
Carolina Power and Light, 195
Catawba Canal Company, 39, 40
Catawba River (NC, SC), 10, 19, 26. See also Wateree River

Cemeteries and burial grounds, 6, 39, 40, 166–67, 181, 188, 200, 201
Chapman, Alvan, 134–35
Charleston Library Society, 110, 223–24n62
Charleston Museum, 110, 223–24n62
Chelsea, 98, 182
Chelsea House, 121
Clarkson, William A., 228n10
Clarkson's Canal, 228n10
Clemson University, 225n10
Clinton, George, 24
College of Charleston, 224n62
Columbia Railway and Navigation Company, 190
Committee on Internal Improvements, 140, 203–4
Company for Opening the Inland Navigation Between the Santee and Cooper Rivers. See Santee Canal Company
Congaree River, 1, 9, 10, 16, 45, 116n14, 130, 191, 207n1
Continental Association, 230n5
Cook, James, xi, 43, 169, 171, 182
Coon Hill, 200–1
Cooper River, xi, xiv, 1, 8, 9, 12–15, 18, 21, 43–44, 45, 46, 49, 203, 218, 220n7, 226n14
Cordesville (SC), 108n12
Cosgrove, John, 197
Cotteaux Lake, 166–70
Cotton, long-staple, xii, 60, 61, 123, 124, 155, 194, 200
County Road 343. See Dock Road
Cross Generating Plant / Station, 89, 94, 146–47, 188
Cymbees, 124, 225n7, 225n8

Davies, William, 22
De Bethune, Maximilien, 63

Dennis, Rembert C., 197. *See also* Rembert Dennis Boulevard.
Diversion Canal, 89, 146–47, 171, 199
Dearborn, Henry, 36
Dock Road (County Road 343), 184, 185
Dover, 225n10
Drayton, Charles, xii, xiii, 2, 87
Drayton, Jacob, 130
Drayton, John, 110, 111
Drayton, Stephen, 219
Drayton, William, 9
Dreher Shoals Dam, 191
Dry Basin, 76, 83, 110, 176, 177, 178, 188
Dry dock. *See* Dry Basin
Du Bois, Geertruid Margaretha, 31, 215–16n51
DuBose, Samuel, 1, 9–10, 60, 226n22
DuBose, William Porcher, 156, 226n22
Dumas, Charles W. F., 30–32, 215n47, 215n48
Du Motier, Gilbert. *See* Marquis de Lafayette
Du Moulin, Jacobus Adrianus, 215n48
Dwight, Henry Ravenel, Sr., 224n4, 225, 233n1
Dwight, Isaac, 226–27n22

Eadytown, 119, 146–47, 155, 182, 192
Edel, Francis, 129–30
Edgefield (SC), xiii, xiv, 38, 39, 217–18n74, 217–18n75, 224n62
Edgewater Road, 181
Edwards, Edward, 120
Elliott, Benjamin, xiv, 190
Eminent Domain, xv, 6, 12, 196–97
Eutaw, 190, 194. *See also* Sinkler Family.
Eutaw Springs. *See* Battle of Eutaw Springs.
Eutawville, 57, 107, 181, 208n12. *See also* Pine Ville / Eutawville Road

Fair Forest Creek (Wadboo Creek), 43; Fair Forest Swamp, 43, 44, 127, 187
Fairlawn, 127
Fanning, Rebecca, 165
Fergus, James, 22
Ferry Canal, 5, 92, 112, 166, 167–70
Flint's Lock (V), 98, 102, 120, 141
Ford, George R., 130
Fortenberry, Brent, 165
Fossils, xii, 5, 110, 111, 223–24n62
Fountain Head (Woodlawn), 120, 182, 190, 225n10
Fox, Charles B., 164
Fox Hall, 54, 55–56, 58, 225n5, 232n10. *See also* Big Camp
Foxworth, Samuel, 171–72
Fraser, Charles, xiii, 107–9
Free School, 224
Frierson's, 55, 59; Frierson's Lock (IV), xv, 54, 59, 89, 92–93, 95–98, 118, 120, 140, 141–42, 175, 182, 183, 189, 223n50; Frierson's Swamp. *See* Biggin Swamp

Gaillard, John Palmer, Sr., 204
Gaillard, Peter, 194
Gallatin, Albert, 13, 159
Gates, Horatio, 27, 28, 213n31
German regimental colors, 27–28, 214n34
Gervais, John Lewis, 2, 20, 27, 207n5, 211n1
Gibbes, Andrew, xiv, 69–70
Gillmore, Quincy Adams, 89, 92–93, 94, 144–45, 151, 205, 222n47
Gillon, Alexander, 30, 219
Gilpin, George, 14, 20n13
Glebe Land, 127
Glen Camp, 58, 181, 188, 220n27
Glendkamp. *See* Glen Camp
Glendkamp Cemetery, 188, 197
Glindkamp, Christiana, 231n16

Glendcamp, Harriett V., 212n15, 231n16
Glendkamp, Henry, Jr. (1809–85), 181, 231
Glindkamp, Henry, Sr. (1768–1814), xiii, 58, 181, 220. *See also* Wilson, Jenny.
Glindkamp, Isaac, 231n16
Glindkamp, Mary, 231n16
Glindkamp, Nancy/Nanny, 231n16
Gourdin, Theodore, II, 130
Gourdin, Theodore, 156
Gourdin, Theodore Keith, 165, 226n18
Grace, John P., 6, 190
Graham, Tommy, 165
Granby (SC), xiii, 10, 130, 161, 224n3
Great Falls (Potomac River), xii, 14, 209
Great Falls (SC), xiii, 39, 218
Great Reservoir, 58, 62, 69, 89, 90, 91, 92–93, 94, 120, 151, 181–82, 183, 188, 222n46
Greene, Nathanael, 29, 41
Greenland Swamp, xii, 43, 44–46, 47, 48–49, 51, 53, 89, 91–94, 140, 141, 207–8n7, 219n19, 222n46
Gregg, Maxcy, xiv, 133–34
Grimball, John, 197
Grimke, John Faucheraud, 38, 209n6, 218n77, 218–19n6
Grimkeville (SC), 39, 218n77
Guard Lock (I), 67, 76, 77, 80, 107, 116, 117, 147, 148–50, 152, 153, 167, 171–72, 174–75, 176, 187
Guerard, Benjamin, 20, 30, 49
Guerry, Cecile Ann, 200, 232n12, 232n13

Halfacre, Angela, 165
Halls Community, 146–47
Hamilton, Alexander, 2, 215n50
Hanover, 125, 126, 127, 190; Hanover House, 125, 126–27, 225n10
Hardcastle, Elizabeth Clevland, 55, 58, 200, 220n28, 226n11

Harrison, Benjamin, 22
Heard, James, 215n44
Hell Hole Swamp, 43, 48, 219n17
Henagan, Mary Rhodes, 164
Hepworth, 98; Hepworth Lock (VI), 98, 100, 102, 121, 142
Hidden Cove Marina, 184
High Hills, 9, 167, 231n6
Highway 52. *See* U. S. Highway-52
Highway 45. *See* Pine Ville Eutawville Road
Hill, Lloyd, 165
Hog Swamp, 125, 201
Holland, Jonathan, 165
Holmes, Francis Simmons, 105–6, 224n62
Hope, 188, 223n57; Hope Lock (X), 184, 188, 223n57
Howe, Robert, 2, 207n5
Huger Creek, 43, 44
Humphreys, David, 8, 30, 208n3, 215n47

Indianfield, 108; Indianfield House, 194
Indigo production, 1, 2, 10, 16, 60, 123, 155, 194
Izard, Alice DeLancey, 29
Izard, Ralph, 2, 29, 50, 52–53, 54, 55, 62, 176, 204, 207–8n7, 209n6
Izardtown, 5, 76, 80, 108, 176, 177

Jay, John, 29
Jay, Sarah, 29
Jefferies Generating Station, 192
Jervey, Susan Ravenel, 164
Jefferson, Thomas, xi, 2, 13, 14, 22, 28, 29–30, 31, 34–38, 49, 209–10n14, 210n15, 215n47
Joel, Beesly Edgar, 22
Johnston, Charles, 62, 127

Kerr, Henry, 165

Keith, William Sr., 226n11
Keithfield, 110, 127, 226n11
Kent, 127, 226n13
King's Highway, 181
Kirk, Francis Marion Sr., 193–95
Kirk's Reservoir, 91, 92, 94, 95, 120, 134, 140, 147–48; Kirk's Swamp, 89, 91–92, 95, 120, 183
Klock's Second Regiment, 3, 24
Knox, Henry, 41

Lafayette, Marquis de. *See* Marquis de Lafayette
Languedoc Canal. *See* Canal du Midi
Latrobe, Benjamin Henry, 21, 23
Laurens, Henry, Jr., 218–19n6
Laurens, Henry, Sr., 1, 2, 4, 20, 27, 28, 34, 207n5, 210–11n28, 211n1, 214n34
Laurens, Martha, 210–11n28
Lawson, John, 8
Layton, Peter, xiv
L'Enfant, Pierre, 26
LeQueux, Benjamin, xiii, 139
LeQueux, Sims, xiii
Leuthold, Andrew, 217n68
Leuthold, Christian Senf, 217n68
Library Society. *See* Charleston Library Society
Limestone, 48, 107, 110, 111, 114, 133, 178, 193, 195, 231n5
Liston, Henrietta Marchant, xii, 20–21
Live Oak Plantation, 158
Lloyd, John, 45
Lockhart Canal, 162
Loocock, Aaron, 2, 218–19
Louisville, Cincinnati and Charleston Railroad, xiv
Lucas, Florence, 190
Lucas, Henry, 190
Lynah, James, 54, 58
Lynah's Tract, 54, 55, 58

Macbeth, Charles, 135, 162, 163, 227n33
Macbeth Family, 134
Macomb, Alexander, 36
Mahler, Eulalia, 21
Major Porcher's Embankment, 171–74, 188
Malaria, xiv, 61, 157, 196, 197
Mammoth specimens. *See* Fossils
Manigault's warehouse, 223–24n62
Marion, Francis, 4, 194, 218–19n6, 225n5
Marion, Robert, 225n5. *See also* Fox Hall
Marl, 105, 107, 133
Marquis de Lafayette, 28, 40, 215n44
Mason, Margaretta, 215n46
Mastodon specimens. *See* Fossils
Maybank, Burnet, 193, 195
Mayrant, Robert Pringle, 133
Maxcy, Jonathan, 227
Mazÿck, Stephen, II, 105, 106, 127
Mazÿck's Spring (Big Spring), 46, 47, 62, 105, 106, 127
McHenry, James, 17
McKelvey, Robert ,160
Mentges, Francis, xiii, 3, 36, 217n70
Mexico, 50, 55, 57, 74, 118, 133, 138–39, 164, 171, 173, 176, 178–79, 180, 188, 232n10; Mexico Cemetery, 188
Mifflin, Thomas, 30–31
Mills, Robert, ii, 39
Mohawk River (NY), 26
Moncks Corner, 155, 164, 185, 197, 205, 206
Moore, Thomas, 21
Moorfield, 201
Moreland, Susannah, 55
Morgan, Betsy, 29, 215n44
Morgan, Daniel, 29, 215n44
Morgan, Nancy, 29, 215n44
Morse, Jedidiah, 17

INDEX ～ 257

Moultrie, William, xi, xii, 2, 4, 9, 13, 24, 28, 41, 45, 46, 115, 123, 209n7, 209n8, 218n6, 219n7, 220n27, 226n13
Mt. Carmel AME Church, 200
Mount Vintage (SC), xiii, xiv
Mouzon, Elizabeth, 218
Mouzon, Henry, Jr. (1741–1807), xi, 3, 17, 43, 44, 47–49, 51, 121, 142, 205, 207–8n7, 218n4, 237
Mouzon, Henry, Sr., 218n4
Mouzon, Lewis, Sr., 218n4
Murray Ferry Road (U. S. 52 South), 182. See also U. S. Highway-52
Murray-Flood Company, 191
Murray, William S., 191
M'Whorter, J. G., 38
Myers, Bob, 133

Native American: artifacts, 189, 225n8, 233n16; burial grounds, 201; place-names, 127, 226n12; Sent's servant, xi, 3, 35; Wantoot fortifications against, 125
Naval stores, 1, 10, 122
Nelson's Blue House, 168, 169; Nelson's Ferry, 9, 130
Neville, Presley, 215
Newlands, 201
Nitrolee Dam, 218
Northampton, xii, 24, 115, 123, 134, 189, 201
Norvel, 168–70, 171

Oakfield, 62, 127, 163, 182
Oakland Club, 181, 182, 188
Old Santee Canal Park, 6, 186, 187, 188, 205, 206
Oldfield, 158
Oneyda, Onach Kampae, xi, 3, 35
Ophir, 161, 206
Outside Creek, 50, 65, 75

Pacolet River, 5, 45, 224n3
Padgett, J. P., 190
Peyre, Isabella Sarah, 156
Pierce's Old Field, 58
Pinckney, Charles, 2, 16, 17, 28
Pinckney, Thomas, 15–16
Pinckney's Courthouse, 5; Pinckney's Ferry, 21
Pine Hill, 58, 181, 188
Pine Ville / Pineville (SC), ix, xiv, 4, 54, 74, 95, 155, 181, 188, 199, 212n15, 217n68, 220n1, 222n39, 224n2, 226n18
Pine Ville-Eutawville Road (Highway 45), 44, 85, 87, 88, 119, 171, 180–82, 188, 203
Pineville Police Association, 131, 226–27n22
Pinopolis (SC), 135, 155, 164, 184, 189, 192, 197, 224n4, 233n1; Pinopolis Dam, 188
Pitch. See Naval stores
Poinsett, Joel, 38
Pooshee, 55, 60, 104, 122, 130, 131–32, 158, 161, 182, 189; Pooshee Spring (Ravenel's Spring), 142
Porcher, Edward, 156, 194
Porcher, Francis Peyre, 156, 194
Porcher, Frederick Adolphus, xiv, 3, 10, 23, 51, 52–53, 70, 74, 111, 132, 133, 149–50, 156, 204, 221n12
Porcher, Philip, Sr., 158, 226
Porcher, Richard Dwight, Sr., 104, 189
Porcher, Samuel, 2, 55, 57, 59, 62, 74, 118, 133, 139, 171–72, 178–79, 188
Porcher, Thomas, Jr., 227
Porcher, Thomas, Sr., 161, 226
Porcher, William Mazÿck, 55, 178–79, 180, 188
Porcher's Embankment. See Major Porcher's Embankment
Post, James C., 151

Potter, Edward E., 152
Powerhouse Road, 183
Prinz Ludwig Dragoons, xi, 26
Pug mill, 84–85, 86, 119
Pulaski, Casimir, 40

Quattlebaum Landing, 147, 182, 183
Quinby Creek, 43

Raccoon Hill, 200–201
Railroads, xiii, xiv, 5, 9, 10, 18, 19, 40, 114, 154, 155, 161–62, 184, 190–91, 227–28n9
Ramsay, David, 1, 15–16, 17, 85, 210–11n28
Ramsay, Martha Laurens, 210–11n28. *See also* Laurens, Henry
Ravenel, Charlotte St. Julien, 164
Ravenel, Daniel III Secondus, 2, 62, 105, 121, 124, 126, 127, 228n11
Ravenel, Henry, Jr., 125–26
Ravenel, Henry, Sr., xiii, 54, 56, 76, 137, 138, 140, 226, 228n11
Ravenel, René, 55, 60, 122–23, 130, 131, 158, 179
Ravenel, Henry William, 156, 164, 166, 178–79, 225n8
Ravenel, William Henry, 134, 194
Ravenel's Spring. *See* Pooshee Spring
Ray, Peter, 59, 98
Rehoboth United Methodist Church, 134
Reid Hill Road, 184
Rembert Dennis Boulevard, 187
Rice: cultivation, 2, 7, 10, 61, 62, 105, 106, 107, 124, 125, 127, 151, 194, 225n9; mills, 62, 105, 125, 126, 137; production, 1, 2, 60, 105, 123, 126, 140, 150, 155, 194
Richardson, Carlisle, 58
Richardson, James B., 54, 55
Riquet, Pierre-Paul, 63, 64–65

River Loire, 63
River Seine, 63
Rivers and Harbors Act (1880), 151, 229n26
Robinson, Joshua, 165
Rocks Church, 194
Rocky Mount (SC), xii, xiii, 3, 39, 40, 217n70, 218n77, 218n78
Roosevelt, Franklin D., xv, 191, 196
Ruddy, Drew, ix, 3, 165, 186
Ruffin, Edmund, 125n8, 133
Rumsey, James, 219n10
Russell, Nathaniel, xii, 2
Russellville (SC), ix, 181, 212n15
Rutledge, Archibald, 193
Rutledge, Edward, 2, 15, 38, 209n6, 218–19n6
Rutledge, John, 2, 4, 16–17, 45, 209n6, 218–19n6

St. John's: Basin, 105, 124, 192, 200, 231n5; Hunting Club, ix, 52, 132; Militia, 123; Road, 57, 92–93, 95–97, 173, 178, 181–82, 184
St. Julien Family, 123
St. Julien, Paul, 125
St. Michael's Parish, 162–63
St. Stephen's: Basin, 57, 68, 88, 89, 119, 180–81; Parish, 2, 11, 44, 69, 76, 107, 162–63, 205, 218n4, 220n1, 222n39, 226n14, 232n13.
Saluda River, 10, 45, 207 n1
Santee Basin, 68, 76, 77, 110, 117, 148, 149, 166, 172, 177, 188
Santee Canal: aqueducts; 66, 67, 68, 88, 89, 95–97, 98, 100–101, 105, 121, 124, 125, 151, 158, 221n10; brick kilns, 57, 84–85, 119; director's house, 39, 57, 74, 180, 188, 224–25n4; dry basins, 68, 76, 83, 110, 176, 177, 178, 188; lock-keepers, 59, 77, 103, 104, 108, 118, 119;

INDEX ~ 259

Santee Canal (*continued*)
  marble facing, 82, 174; planking, 76, 111, 147–50, 172, 175, 177; quoins 79, 80–82, 175, 178, 221n29, 221–22n30; steam engines, xiii, 76, 136–41, 160, 172, 177, 180, 187–88; steam pumps, 141, 143–44, 152, 153, 229n34; stone marker, xii, 119, 120, 224n4; superintendent house, 74; tollhouse, 59, 77, 78, 117, 178; towpaths, 68, 84, 85, 117, 118, 151, 184, 223n51; turning basins, 68, 105, 143, 177; water mills, 63, 78; wickets, 72–73, 80–81, 97, 112
Santee Canal Company, xiv, 12–19
Santee Cooper, ix, xv, 4, 6, 68, 114, 154, 169, 184, 186, 187, 188, 189, 190–202
Santee Delta, 7
Saratoga battle. *See* Battle of Saratoga
Saratoga (VA) house, 29
Savannah River (GA, SC), 23, 161, 162
Saylor, Samuel S., xiii, 131–32
Scheinking, Benjamin, 50
Senf, Johann Christian, xi, xii, xiii, 2, 3, 4–5, 11, 13–14, 20–41, 45–53, 91–94, 95–97, 213n31. *See also* Senf, Lukas (Lucas); Vach, Johann Georg; van Berckel, Geertruid (Gertrude) Jacoba
Senf, Lukas (Lucas), xi, xii, 3, 21, 24, 27
Sheinking. *See* Scheinking, Benjamin
Shells, 74, 85, 107
Shultz, Henry, 39
Simons, Harris, 18, 163
Simpson, William, 59, 127, 223n57. *See also* Hope
Simpson's Lock. *See* Hope Lock (X)
Sinkler, James, 218–19n6
Sinkler, Margaret, 54, 55
Sinkler, Peter, 194, 218n4. *See also* Mouzon, Elizabeth

Slave hiring, 4, 5, 60, 118, 123, 155, 174, 208n9, 220n3
Sloan, Samuel, 130
Smith, R. Press, xiv
Smith, William Loughton, 156, 229n1
Society of the Cincinnati, 41, 218n84
Somerset, 127, 164, 190, 194, 203, 233n1
Somerton, 125, 127; Somerton Canal, 62
South Carolina Canal and Rail Road Company, xiii, xiv
South Carolina Department of Parks, Recreation and Tourism, 186
South Carolina Institute of Archaeology and Anthropology, xv, 186
South Carolina Power Company. 195
South Carolina Public Service Authority (SCPSA). *See* Santee Cooper
South Carolina Railroad Company, xiv
Springwood Road, 146–47, 182, 183, 222n43
Spruill, Sarah Cain, 232n11, 235
Stark, John, 211–12n6
Starr, Benny, 165
State Road 22 (Great Falls, SC), 39
State Road S-8-23. *See* Springwood Road, Black Oak Road
State Road S-8-708. *See* Viper Road
State Road S-8-907, 183. *See also* Black Oak Road
Steam engines. *See* Santee Canal steam engines
Steam pumps. *See* Santee Canal steam pumps
Steamboats, xiii, 5, 10, 18, 66, 114, 143, 154, 155, 156, 160–61, 190–91
Steiger, Catharine, 217n68
Stony Landing, 10, 43, 67, 85, 114, 127, 226n14; Stony Landing House, 187
Summerton. *See* Somerton
Sumter, Thomas, 2, 4, 47, 218–19

Susquehanna Company, 46

Tailrace Canal, 112, 114, 165, 185, 186, 187, 192, 193, 199
Tar. *See* Naval stores
Tar kilns, 122
Taylor, John, 227n9
Tennessee Valley Authority, 196
Terrasson, Antoine, 14, 209–10n14
Thomas Walter Road, 182
Thurmond, Strom, 195
Tibbekudlaw, 110, 127, 182, 226n11, 226n12
Tide Lock (XI), 67–69, 70, 80, 110–13, 115, 127, 133, 135, 152, 165, 184, 186, 188, 205
Timothy, Peter, 43
Tippycut Law. *See* Tibbekudlaw
Tiverton Lawn, 182. *See also* Tibbekudlaw
Tower Hill Plantation, 217n68
Trinity Church Black Oak, 194
Turpentine. *See* Naval stores

U. S. Highway-52, 182, 183, 184

Vach, Johann Georg, xii, 2–3, 24
Vache, Delia, 24
Van Berckel, Engelbert Francois, 34
Van Berckel, Franco Petrus, 33, 34, 216n62
Van Berckel, Geertruid (Gertrude) Jacoba (Joan), xii, xiii, xiv, 2, 14, 29, 31–38, 118–19, 180, 215n46, 215n50, 215–16n51, 216n61, 217n74. *See also* Breithaupt, Christian Friedrich; du Bois, Geertruid Margaretha; Senf, Johann Christian
Van Berckel, Pieter, xii, 29, 31, 32, 33, 215n49, 215n50

Van Hogendorp, Gijsbert Karel, 31, 215n49
Vaucluse mill (SC), 39
Viper Road, 94, 146–47
Von Riedesel, Frederika, 214n34
Von Riedesel, Friedrich, 4, 212n8, 214n34
Von Steuben, Friedrich, 28, 40, 41

Wadboo Creek (Fair Forest Swamp), 43, 44, 127, 187
Walloomsac (NY). *See* Battle of Bennington
Walter, Thomas, 50, 116, 166–67, 176, 187–88, 218–19n6, 230n2, 230n5, 232n10. *See also* Thomas Walter Road
Wampee, 196–97
Want, Samuel, 197
Wantoot, 105, 124–25, 126, 133, 142, 158, 163, 182, 225n9, 232n10; Wantoot Lock (VIII), 100, 103, 105, 124–25, 129, 149–50, 152, 153, 223n48
Warneck, Frederick, 22
Washington, George, xi, xii, 2, 8, 9, 13–14, 23, 24–26, 41, 46, 209n13
Washington, Martha, 29
Wasmus, Julius Frederick, 21–22, 28–29, 212n8, 214n35
Watboo Creek. *See* Wadboo Creek
Water spirits. *See* Cymbees
Wateree River, 1, 9, 10, 45, 130, 162, 167, 207n1, 231n6
Wates, Wylma Anne, 218n4
Whispering Pine Lane, 182, 183, 222n43
White Bridge Road, 89, 180, 181
White Oak, xiii, 49, 50, 51, 52–53, 54, 55–57, 76, 187, 204, 232n10; White Oak Landing, 48, 50, 53, 75; White Oak Lock (Toll Lock) (II), 4, 68, 69, 76–82, 91, 95, 98, 117, 137
Whitney, Eli, 8, 37

INDEX ～ 261

Williams, J. Russell, 190
Williams, Nolan, 165
Williams, Thomas Clay, 190–91
Wilson Dam, 169, 192
Wilson, Jenny, 181, 231n16. *See also* Glindkamp, Henry Sr.
Wilson, Richard (Rick) LeNoble, ix, 165
Wilson's Landing, 191
Woodboo, 62, 105–107, 142, 164, 182, 194, 225n9, 232; Woodboo Lock (IX), 105, 107, 127, 152–53

Woodlawn. *See* Fountain Head
Work Projects Administration, 196, 231n1
Works Progress Administration, xv, 191, 231n1

Yancey, Benjamin, 217n74
Yellow fever, 217n74, 227–28n9
Young, Henry, 22

Zahn, Jacob Christopher, 27